THE
CHIC
SHOPPER'S
GUIDE TO
PARIS

THE
CHIC
SHOPPER'S
GUIDE TO
P·A·R·I·S

Maribeth Ricour de Bourgies

St. Martin's Press
New York

To Mom, Dad, and Steph

THE CHIC SHOPPER'S GUIDE TO PARIS. Copyright © 1990 by Maribeth Ricour de Bourgies. All rights reserved. Printed in the United States of America. No part of this book may be used or reproduced in any manner whatsoever without written permission except in the case of brief quotations embodied in critical articles or reviews. For information, address St. Martin's Press, 175 Fifth Avenue, New York, N.Y. 10010.

Production Editor: David Stanford Burr

Design by Richard Oriolo

Library of Congress Cataloging-in-Publication Data

Ricour de Bourgies, Maribeth.
        The chic shopper's guide to Paris / Maribeth Ricour
de Bourgies.
                p.   cm.
        ISBN 0-312-04575-1
        1.   Shopping—France—Paris—Guide-books.   2.
Paris (France)—Description—1975—Guide-books.   I.
Title.
TX337.F82P378   1991
380.1'45'0002544361—dc20   90-19221
                                                                    CIP

First Edition: March 1991

10 9 8 7 6 5 4 3 2 1

Contents

THE ESSENTIALS

THE PROMENADES

More Shopping

Acknowledgments

The idea of writing a shopping guide first came to me in 1987, just before my *Chic Promenade* shopping service got off the ground. A somewhat overwhelming idea became reality thanks to the perseverance and know-how of my agent, Sam Summerlin. Out of a warm friendship grew a close working relationship and soon we found ourselves striving toward similar goals. Thanks, Sam, for having believed in me. Thank you also to my good friend, Michèle Brothers. I'm glad that you decided to introduce Sam to me on that blustery night in Les Halles. Thank you also, Michèle, for having been so supportive of me during the writing of this book and also for spurring me to chuckle about my many French-isms and "Maribeth-isms" in the manuscript when I needed to laugh the most.

I'm very grateful to my editor, Michael Sagalyn, for also having believed so intently in this book and for challenging me every step of the way. It wasn't always easy communicating with so many thousands of miles between us, but his thoroughness provided me with great insight when it came to fine-tuning the final product. I know that many other people at St. Martin's have worked hard to make this book a success; thank you to Ed Stackler for his efficiency and good humor, to Maureen Baron for her much-appreciated advice, and to the various copy editors—whom I'm sure I drove crazy with my endless series of addresses, cross references, and additions.

In Paris, I thank Mark Hunter for having been influential in converting me into a writer, practically overnight. I would also like to thank Jean-Louis Dumas-Hermès for having written such an eulogistic introduction. I can't think of a more appropriate person, nor boutique, for embodying the spirit of this book. *Merci* to Bertrand de Courcy, also from Hermès, for having been so enthusiastic and supportive of this proejct. I'm also grateful to Charles Mackey, from Simmons College (my alma mater) for his influence on me throughout the years, and also for having been so speedy with certain mind-boggling translations.

With each boutique tour I conducted, and with each client I encountered, I learned just a little bit more about the expectations and needs of foreigners shopping in the French capital. Thank you to all of my past *Chic Promenade* clients; you were all very generous in sharing yourselves and your impressions with me, and I thought of many of you when writing this book.

None of this would have been possible without the support, encouragement, and love from my family. Thank you to my parents, Mary Ellen and Frank Clemente, and to my five brothers: Frank, Bob, Dave, Phil, and Paul. Not only have you so tenderly cheered me on throughout the years, but you also gave me the biggest gift of all when I decided to create my own life in France at the early age of twenty-four; one of trust.

Last, but certainly not least, I thank my husband, Stéphane, for helping me to grow and blossom in my life in France. Thank you for having been there when I could no longer write a page, thank you for our many boutique visits, and thank you for having put up with all of those long nights and frozen dinners!

Introduction

Maribeth Ricour de Bourgies's great worth is that first and foremost she knows how to look at shopping in Paris. She is a good guide because she observes well.

She has surveyed the main street of the village of Paris which is the Faubourg–Saint-Honoré; avenue Montaigne, that dazzling thoroughfare; Marais lanes with their historical charisma; the sidewalks of the Left Bank imbued with their special culture.

Her value lies in an affectionate curiosity, a desire to learn, an ability to discover "l'essentiel" that is hidden behind boutique exteriors.

Let yourself be guided by her counsel. You are in good hands!

—JEAN-LOUIS DUMAS-HERMÈS
President of HERMÈS
and the Comité Colbert

A New Discovery
Around Every Corner

My love for shopping in Paris was born out of a desire to discover boutiques full of charm, authenticity, and a uniqueness that is intrinsically French. I'll never forget the tingling feeling that warmed me when I stumbled upon a centuries-old Left Bank antique shop at the tender age of 16, the day I crossed the threshold to a great Paris couture house, or the cold grey Sunday afternoon when I made my first trip to the flea markets. Each time I made a new discovery, I realized that it was nothing quite like the places that I knew back home in America.

The idea of a boutique is inherently French and, even more so, Parisian. In the U.S. I became accustomed to shopping in large, impersonal shopping malls and neon-lit department stores; in Paris I relish the idea of entering a boutique that is quaint, enticingly decorated, and, most of all, with a soul of its own. I am continuously enchanted by the ambiance created within each boutique, whether the setting is an old 17th-century townhouse in the Marais or a new, glittery showplace on the rue du Faubourg–Saint-Honoré. There's no doubt that the French have a flair for embellishing their goods, and even better, it's rare to find the same carefully selected assortment of merchandise in more than a handful of stores throughout town.

When I first started my CHIC PROMENADE boutique excursions in 1987, I became firmly committed to sharing the same joys of Paris shopping with visitors to the capital, whether ardent boutique hounds or wide-eyed tourists. Little did I know at the time that I would learn as much from them as they from me; shoppers have such different tastes and desires that I still find myself constantly revising my little black book in order to best meet their needs. Inevitably when I toss out a shop's address, someone asks me for the same sort of boutique a few days later. I no longer throw out addresses because I know that someday someone will ask me for exactly what I thought they never would!

This book is the fruit of more than three years of shopping in Paris with discriminating Americans, Canadians, and sometimes a few Europeans. I haven't been able to include every address that is of potential interest to visitors to the capital, but as you will see, I've covered a good many of them. Like with my own clients, I've approached this book with one fundamental idea—that shopping should be an exciting experience in Paris. There's no sense pressing your nose up against the wrong shop-windows when you could be enjoying boutiques that would greatly enhance the thrill of your purchase. Shopping in a store that feels and looks quite like nothing else that you've ever seen at home will make your purchase seem all the more special. I've seen too many visitors stray off to the duty-frees in the touristy parts of town, to indicate to you boutiques that aren't worth going out of your way for. There are boutiques out there for everyone's tastes—now it's up to you to let me help you find them.

Follow me through the streets of Paris's most noteworthy shopping districts and maybe you'll just never turn back!

How to Use
This Shopping Guide

The book is divided into three main parts: "The Essentials," "The Promenades," and "More Shopping." "The Essentials" provides you with an introduction to the Paris shopping scene and useful information that you need when shopping in the City of Lights.

"The Promenades" section makes up the beefiest part of the book and is designed to walk you through the most shop-worthy streets in the most important shopping districts of Paris. Within each area (Right Bank, Left Bank, The Marais, etc.), I have suggested one, two, or three shopping itineraries for you to use as guidelines on your own boutique excursions. I recommend that you read over the boutique descriptions listed for each district and mark them off; then you will know which streets tempt you the most. At the beginning of each promenade (just after the introduction to the shopping district), I have included a short paragraph which explains the general flow of the suggested itinerary. You probably will want to use these indications purely as a general guideline, without feeling restrained to stick to the promenade every inch of the way.

These directions are followed by a list of the streets (or passages) that make up the promenade. This list should prove particularly helpful for zeroing in on the streets (or areas) that interest you the most. For example, if your main priority is to see Paris's luxurious table arts stores you may want to skip most of the fashion boutiques in the Promenade Saint-Honoré and head directly to rue Royale where many of these types of elegant boutiques are located. Another example of this sort of pre-selection would be for you to focus on the rue de Grenelle/rue des Saints-Pères section of the Left Bank (Promenade South of the Boulevard) if you primarily want to shop for women's shoes.

As you weave in and out of these streets you will notice that the order of the boutique descriptions does not always coincide with the actual order of their appearance on the street. This is particularly true when there is a large discrepancy between the even and the odd numbers on a street. For example, although the Louis Féraud boutique at no. 88 rue du Faubourg–Saint-Honoré is listed towards the beginning of the St.-Honoré promenade, it is actually located much further down the street (in the direction of the promenade) beyond the Christian Lacroix boutique at no. 73.

Some of the promenades are much longer than others; the Left Bank promenade, south of the bd Saint-Germain, for example, would take at least a week to investigate thoroughly. The promenade through the passages, however, can easily be explored in an afternoon. Either all or parts of these walking shopping tours have been tried and tested on my own clients as well as on the various American women's organizations here in Paris. They've thoroughly enjoyed them, and I think that you will, too.

The idea of these promenades is to approach Paris shopping in a logical manner (it's overwhelming enough in itself), so that you don't have to be dashing in 10 different directions to find gift ideas for yourself and for those back home. Whether you are on foot, traveling by Métro, cabbing it, or riding in your own chauffeur-driven limo, these promenades should prove invaluable in locating your favorite shop-filled streets of the French capital!

The third part of the book, "More Shopping," lists boutiques, stores, and markets under specific sections that are, for the most part, located outside of the promenades. All of these addresses are listed in alphabetical order, according to *arrondissements* (the 20 districts that make up Paris, see p. 27). A few of these listings, however, are situated on the periphery of the promenades, so it's up to you to decide if you want to incorporate a boutique from the third section of the book into one of the promenades.

A certain amount of information is provided (when possible) for each listing mentioned in this book: the name of the establishment, the address (written the French way), the telephone number, the closest subway stop (in case you choose a different starting point for the promenades), and the establishment's opening and closing hours. If the store hours are listed below two or three different addresses for the same boutique, the hours are the same at each branch. For the stores that have many different addresses in Paris, I have only listed a few of them.

If you still haven't found the sort of shops, tearooms or cafés that you are looking for after having studied "The Promenades" and "More Shopping," try referring to the "Quick Reference" index that classifies the establishments according to type. With all of this information in hand, you should have no problem finding your way around in the world's greatest shopping capital, *Paree!*

THE
≈
ESSENTIALS

When to Go

Deciding when to go to Paris depends largely on what you want out of the city in terms of shopping, tourism, and, of course, weather. I consider the spring and fall to be good times to visit the French capital. The weather is grey to great; the selections in the boutiques are still full and fresh; and the overall ambiance of the city is pleasant because it is not overrun by tourists. If you come in May, choose your dates carefully because most of the stores are closed on the three different holidays during that month. During July, August, and September you have to battle with crowds of visitors at the museums and monuments, but it can be a good time for shopping because the boutiques aren't as crowded, and in July and August you can get in on the sales; September offers the first glimpse of the new season's fashions. If you don't mind bleak, drizzly weather and little sunshine, January is an excellent time to go to Paris because the sales are fabulous. Christmas in Paris is a disappointment for most Americans, except those looking to get away from the hustle-bustle commercialization of the holidays in the U.S. It's up to you to choose!

What to Buy

The types of goods that are worth buying in Paris are not only those that represent the best buys but also those that offer a better selection than what is available in the U.S. There's no doubt that your money won't go as far as it did in '84 when the dollar was up to 10 francs, but there still are a few bargains to be had in France and you don't have to wear yourself out trying to find them.

Whenever my clients seem dismayed about the high prices throughout much of Paris, I encourage them to be more selective with their shopping and to do what the French do—buy less but buy better quality.

Antiques. Whether you buy at the flea markets, at the auctions, or from a Paris antique dealer, the selection and value of antiques in France is unbeatable. Although most of the dealers are reputable, if you plan on making a major purchase, know what you're buying (Is it an authentic period piece or is it a reproduction?) and the cost to ship it home (See p. 267 for useful information about antiquing in Paris).

Arts of the Table. Some of the best buys in Paris include Limoges china, Baccarat crystal, and goods from many other leading table-arts manufacturers. (See Paradise Street description p. 277 for details.) Other stores such as Laure Japy, Marie-Pierre Boitard, and Peter specialize in their own refined table accessories that are little known to Americans. Earthenware or *faïence* from Gien, Malicorne, and Segries also offers savings and selection that you won't find stateside, and many of the individual pieces sold in these shops make handsome gifts to bring back home. France, like many of the other European countries, is known for its fine-quality house linens. Martine Nourrisat's (at Diners en Ville p. 160) and Gérard Danton's tablecloths are sure to be a hit at your next dinner party. Antique house linens also represent good value and fine-quality craftsmanship. And last but not least, it's just fun to shop in Paris's tabletop shops because the French set their tables with such elegance and flair!

Children's Clothing. Although children's fashions tend to cost more in France than in the U.S., the quality and craftsmanship is superior. If you're looking for something special, Paris offers a realm of beautiful children's-clothing boutiques specializing in timeless styles. Clothing from Bonpoint, Petit Faune, La Châtelaine, and Tartine et Chocolat may be expensive, but it still is less costly than in the U.S.

Costume Jewelry. Here is the world's leader in high-style costume jewelry. The sphere of creativity among Paris's costume-jewelry designers ranges from Chanel chic to mod Migeon. (See p. 93) The choice and quality is excellent, and not all of the fashions have broken through stateside.

Designer Fashions. The key to buying designer fashions in Paris is to know what you're buying and to do your homework before you leave the U.S.. Keep track of how much your favorite designer fashions cost at home and find out if those fashions are actually made in France or if they have been manufactured with licensing agreements. (These styles in the U.S. are often different and usually less expensive than those of a better quality sold in France.) Savings on true big-name–designer "boutique" collections run about 10–20% (25–35% with tax refund); however, often U.S. sale prices on the same merchandise make it more interesting to buy at home.

Keep in mind that there are a lot of scintillating designer fashions in Paris that are not yet widely known in the U.S. Boutiques such as Lolita Lempicka, Odile Lançon, Paule Ka, Junko Shimada, Emmanuelle Khanh, and Popy Moreni offer selection and value that is not shown outside of Paris. Familiarize yourself with more of the Paris fashion scene (as well as addresses for restaurants and entertainment) by skimming French magazines such as *Elle*, *Marie Claire*, *Vogue*, *Dépêche Mode*, *Figaro Madame* (part of the *Figaro* newspaper on Saturdays) and the saucy trend-spotting American magazine of Paris, *Passion*. Other English-speaking publications include the recently launched magazine, *Boulevard*, the weekly newspaper, *The European*, and of course, *The International Herald Tribune*. (Don't miss Suzy Menkes's fashion reports during the collections.)

Food Items, Fine Wines, and Spirits. The selection of gourmet-food items, fine wines, and spirits in Paris is astounding, providing endless gift ideas in a variety of price ranges. If you want to pick up a few gifts in the $5 bracket, you'll soon find out that there is not much to buy in Paris for such little money—except for maybe a jar of fine-quality jam, mustard, or herbs from Provence—all welcome additions to any self-respecting person's pantry. More prestigious items include *foie gras*, truffles, or a cocoa-brown box of chocolates from La Maison du Chocolat.

As far as wine and spirits are concerned, it almost seems a crime not to take advantage of your customs allowance and to bring back a fine bottle of Château Margaux that will last you an evening or a superb vintage of Armagnac that will last you a year!

Lingerie. Shopping for lingerie in Paris is like looking for a diamond at Tiffany's; the selection and quality are dazzling. From custom-mades to cute and sexy ready-to-wear, Paris offers lingerie for every woman's taste. I can't think of a better investment than an exquisite silk negligé from Sabbia Rosa, whose quality and style are unmatchable stateside.

Perfumes and Cosmetics. The savings potential on French perfumes, beauty products, and cosmetics is similar to those of designer fashions—once again, it's best to know what you're dealing with and what the price equivalent is back home. Not all French products bear the made-in-France label; many of them, such as Lancôme, are made by U.S. subsidiaries. As a general rule, if you (or your friend or the friend of your cousin) have a favorite French beauty product that you want to pick up in France, write down its U.S. price before you go shopping abroad so that you can compare it with those offered in Paris. Don't automatically assume that you will save on French perfumes or cosmetics just because you buy them in Paris.

I often suggest that my clients buy Annick Gouthal, Creed, or P. de Nicolaï fragrances. Not only are their prices fair (up to 40% less than in the U.S. for Annick Goutal), but they also have an exclusive side that prevents them from being sold in duty-free shops around the world. If you are, however, more interested in big-name shopping, your best bet is Catherine's (p. 88) where savings run about 40%.

Women's Accessories. Usually when one of my clients expresses the desire to achieve a more Frenchified look, I steer her more toward women's accessories than clothing. Not only are French fashions much more astronomically priced than American clothing, but accessorizing is the secret of creating a look that is intrinsically French. French women live off of a limited wardrobe of basic black dresses, jeans, and cream silk blouses, but they may change their look 50 times over with the addition of up-to-the-minute accessories. The selection of accessories (bags, belts, shoes, scarves, gloves, and the already talked about costume jewelry) is not only limitless, but it also gives you a good run for your money. Finely crafted leather shoes and bags don't cost any more than their U.S. equivalents, and are priced about 20% less than their French counterparts in the U.S.

A Few Words About Prices

I've tried to establish throughout the book certain guidelines regarding how expensive or inexpensive the boutiques actually are, and in particular, how pricey they are in relation to each other (See "Quick Reference" p. 318). Keep in mind that these indicators are generalizations. They do not mean that all of the articles within a given boutique are expensive—nor do they mean that all are inexpensive either. For example, the couture houses are very expensive, but this should not deter price-conscious shoppers from taking a peak inside because, although these boutiques sell suits in the $2,000 range, you can also walk away with a magnificent silk scarf without spending more than $200.

Once you've skimmed over "Quick Reference" you will also realize that shopping on the Right Bank (Promenade Golden Triangle, Promenade Saint-Honoré) is considerably more upmarket than in areas such as the Left Bank, the Place des Victoires and Les Halles, and the Marais. Boutiques within the Passages, the Bastille and the Sixteenth tend to be even more moderately priced.

Exchange Rates

It's important to have a good sense of the exchange rate before you start spending oodles of money on your trip abroad. This of course becomes a bit more tricky if you're traveling to a half a dozen different countries within a three-week period. The rate that you receive in most banks is slightly lower than the one announced in the newspapers or on the local news. When you use a credit card, you will pay the exchange rate of the day in which the credit-card company processes your transaction—not the rate of the day of your actual purchase. This means that if the dollar goes up in the interim, you will pay less than you anticipated; if it goes down, you will pay more. Minor fluctuations only have much impact on major purchases.

The exchange rate used in the boutique descriptions throughout this book is 5.15 francs to the dollar. In simple terms, if you want to find out how much something costs in France, divide 5.15 into the amount of French francs (written Fr); i.e., something selling for 350 francs is worth $67. If you don't have a calculator handy, you may want to round off to the nearest franc.

Cashing In

The best exchange rates are offered by major banks. A slightly higher rate is given for travelers checks. For large sums of money, it's best to avoid exchanging money at the various exchange places around town or in the lobby of your hotel. Banks usually open at 9 A.M. Some banks close for lunch and most close for the day at 4:30 P.M.; few are open on Saturdays. The following banks practice unbankerly hours:

Crédit Commercial de France (CCF)
115 av des Champs-Elysées, 8e;
tel.: 40.70.70.40;   Métro: George V
open Monday–Saturday 9 A.M.–8 P.M.

Société Financière de Change Lincoln
11 rue Lincoln, 8e,   tel.: 42.25.22.57;
Métro: George V
open daily from April 1st–Sept. 30th 10 A.M.–11 P.M.;
open daily from October 1st–March 31st 10 A.M.–
9 P.M.

Automatic exchange machine:

Banque Régionale d'Escompte et de Dépôt
66 av des Champs-Elysées, 8e;   tel.: 42.89.10.99;
Métro: Franklin-Roosevelt

Other reputable money exchanges:

American Express
11 rue Scribe, 9e;   *tel.: 47.77.77.07;*   *Métro: Opéra*
open Monday–Saturday 9 A.M.*–5:30* P.M.

If you are a cardholder, you may cash personal checks here or draw on your card for cash advances. You may also receive mail and messages addressed to you in care of AmEx.

Chèquepoint
150 av des Champs-Elysées, 8e;   *tel.: 49.53.02.51;*
Métro: Etoile
open 24 hours daily

Chèquepoint
131-133 rue St.-Martin, 4e;   *tel.: 40.29.08.01;*
Métro: Rambuteau (across from the Pompidou Center)
open daily 8:30 A.M.*–10:30* P.M.

If you're down to your last 50 francs and you've reached your maximum credit limit on all three of your major credit cards, you can have cash wired to you at CCF, 115-117 av. des Champs-Elysées. Just give this address to your bank at home, and within 48 hours you should be able to replenish your reserves. Call CCF at 40.70.77.17 to see if your funds have arrived. This system saved me a number of times during my college days in Paris—thanks, Dad.

Automatic Banking Machines

Cash advances may be obtained with foreign credit cards from many of the automatic banking machines in Paris—it all depends on what type of a machine you are using and what sort of credit card you have. If you plan to use your credit card abroad for obtaining cash (in that country's currency), I suggest you find out before you leave the U.S. where you may locate ABMs in the cities that you will be visiting.

Payment

Most of the boutiques in Paris honor one or several different credit cards. The most widely accepted card, however, is VISA. If you plan on doing some antiquing, whether in shops or at the flea markets, you should make doubly sure to bring a fair amount of cash with you. Not only will many of the dealers (especially at the flea markets) refuse credit cards, but cash gives you more leverage in bargaining down the prices.

Even if you're not antiquing, it's always a good idea to have some cash with you. You may easily use French checks or French traveler's checks—don't pay in American dollars or traveler's checks unless you don't care about losing out on the exchange.

For lost or stolen credit cards call:

American Express, tel.: 47.77.72.00
VISA, tel.: 42.77.11.90
Diners Club, tel.: 47.62.75.75

Tax Refunds

The key word to savings in France is *détaxe*, which loosely refers to making a purchase without being charged for the tax. The tax amount, which is included in nearly all of the prices listed in France, is often called T.V.A. or V.A.T. and ranges from 5.5 to 25%. (Important: most stores give a tax refund of 13%.) Nonresidents are entitled to this tax refund if their total purchases in one boutique add up to at least 1,200 Fr or about $240. Certain luxury-goods stores require a minimum purchase of 1,800 Fr. There is no *détaxe* on antiques that are 100 years old or more.

There's no doubt that your greatest savings occur when you take advantage of the *détaxe*, and it's worth it to shop in several well-chosen boutiques in order to achieve the minimum balance required in each establishment than to pick up a lot of odds and ends in 15 different Paris shops. Keep in mind that if your total purchases fall just a couple of hundred francs shy of the 1,200-Fr marker, throwing in another little something is like getting it for free. Also, if you are shopping with friends, you may group your purchases together on one tax form in order to benefit from the *détaxe*. This does not mean that one person has to pay for everyone else's purchases; it does mean, however, that only one person will directly benefit from the tax refund. (She can then treat the rest of you to tea once you're back home in the States.)

It's all very simple and most of the boutiques will make it as effortless as possible. Here's how it goes:

- Once you have reached your minimum balance of 1,200 Fr, it's best to pay with a credit card so that you don't have to worry about cashing your tax-refund check in francs back in the States. (Banks charge hefty commissions on foreign checks.)
- There are two different ways of handling your refund on a credit card: crediting you for the tax amount or never charging you for it in the first place. The latter is the most common method; instead of charging you the full amount and then later crediting you for the tax amount, most boutiques write up two sales slips: one with the purchase amount not including tax, the other with the tax amount. Once you have processed your papers correctly, the boutique will then tear up the sales slip with the tax amount and you will only be charged the taxfree price.
- At the moment of your purchase, the salesperson will help you fill out the tax forms. (It's important to have your passport or just your passport number with you at this time.) The salesperson will put the forms in a stamped envelope that bears the address of the boutique.
- Show these papers along with your plane ticket and passport to the customs officer at the airport, the train station, the port, or (if in a car) the border the day of your departure from France. Do this before you check your luggage or have your purchases with you in a carry-on; chances are slim that you will be required to show your goods, but if you are asked where they are, you should at least have your bags with you. He or she will stamp your tax forms and show you which one to mail back to the boutique (the mailbox is right at the customs counter); you keep the green slip for yourself.
- Once the boutique receives your tax form, the sales slip with the tax amount will be torn up, or in some instances your account will be credited. If you don't go through the paperwork, you will of course be charged for the tax.
- If you have paid with cash, check, or traveler's checks, either you will receive your V.A.T. check in the mail

(this takes two to three months) or you may arrange to pick it up at the boutique the next time you are in Paris (or have a friend do this for you).

Facing the Music: U.S. Customs and Duties

Unfortunately I have to reserve my best customs hints for my own clients. It's not that I don't want to share them with you, but if I do, I might be banished from my own country. (France is swell, but I do like to go home every once in a while.) My best advice is to be well informed yourself and to use your own good judgment. Going through customs can be a breeze or it can be a living nightmare—it all depends on who you are up against and how you play the game. It's risky business, and if you try to smuggle in a suitcase full of Hermès scarves, you may be able to sail right through or you may get stuck paying duty *and* a penalty. In any event, whatever route you decide to take, dress appropriately; if you go wheeling through with a whole set of matching Gucci bags, you can be sure that you will be stopped. Here's what you should know before you go (or at least before you come back):

- Articles totaling $400 or less may be entered free of duty as long as you have not benefited from this exemption within the past 30 days; this includes items purchased in the duty-free shops, gifts, and—believe it or not—any repairs or alterations made to any of your belongings while you were away.
- Each individual family member, including infants and children, is entitled to the $400 exemption; joint declarations may be made for all members.
- You pay a flat rate of 10% duty on the next $1,000 worth of goods that exceeds the $400 allowance. In other words, if your total purchases amount to $1,400, you pay $100 duty.
- If you have acquired more than $1,400 worth of merchandise abroad, duty is calculated separately for each additional item. Duty fees vary considerably and can be as low as 5% on perfumes and as high as 25.5% on wool sweaters.
- Duty-free items include antiques at least 100 years old (with certificate of authenticity), books, bona fide artwork, and diamonds.

- You may bring home some fresh, creamy pastries, but meats (canned pâté is OK), fruits, vegetables, and unpasteurized cheese are forbidden. Real ivory and tortoise shell are also off-limits.

- You are only entitled to one carton of cigarettes and one liter of wine or spirits (although duty on wine and spirits is less than $1 per liter once over the $1,400 limit—10% otherwise).

- If the customs officer really wants to come down on you, he or she may ask you to pay duty on possessions that you might have acquired on your previous trip to Europe. In order to avoid such a fiasco, you may want to register susceptible goods (or carry proof of U.S. purchase) before you leave home.

As a last reminder, be cooperative and courteous to the customs officer and your life will be made a lot easier.

For more information about U.S. customs and duties, call the U.S. embassy in Paris at 42.96.12.02 or write for a free and detailed brochure:

U.S. Customs Service
P.O. Box 7407
Washington, D.C. 20044
tel.: (202) 566-8195

Store Hours

Although all of the store hours have been indicated for each boutique, keep in mind that the French are rather inconsistent about set hours in general. You will also notice that each one varies as much as the next, reinforcing the notion that you should always check the store hours before you set out purposely with one particular boutique in mind. I've rarely done a tour with my clients without encountering at least one sign on a store window saying "be back in five minutes." Of course five minutes is never five minutes, so be prepared to do a certain amount of waiting when you're out on your shopping promenade. (Maybe this is why cafés thrive so much in Paris.) The same rule applies to holidays, birthdays, and impromptu days off; it's not unusual for a French person to spontaneously decide to close for the rest of the day. Only a handful of boutiques close for the whole month of August, however some do close for part of the month, particularly those around the place des Victoires and the Bastille. If there is a boutique that you really want to see during a holiday week (such as Easter, winter break, or Assumption Day on August 15), I suggest you call ahead to see if the boutique is open.

Sales

Sales or *soldes* don't take place nearly as often in France as in the U.S., but in January and July, prices are marked down 20–45%. This is when the savings on designer fashions are the most interesting, and if you're willing to push and shove with the Parisians, you can come up with some real bargains. Most stores give tax refunds at this time, but not all take credit cards as payment.

The major department stores also have sales during a week in March and October, (called "les 3 J" at Galeries Lafayette and "les 7 Jours en Or" at Printemps) but the biggest event during these months is the week-long sale at Hermès, conducted on the third floor of this prestigious store. Parisians wait in line for hours in anticipation of snatching up a few Hermès scarves and other exclusive goods at 50% off. Most sales are announced in the *Figaro* newspaper the week of the sale.

Store Returns

If you haven't already, you will soon find out that the French aren't as flexible as Americans, thus making it extremely difficult to make exchanges in most boutiques. If you hesitate about what you are buying, tell the salesperson that you have some reservation and want to show it to your husband or friend back at the hotel. If what you bought doesn't work out—and if you are charming and clever enough (and even speak the language)—you may be able to return the merchandise the next day for a store credit.

If ever you experience a horror story with a certain boutique, such as you paid a small fortune for a handbag that was claimed to be all leather and made by hand, and you later discover that it's in fact vinyl and machine-stitched, you may want to file a consumer complaint. Of course you would first want to try to come to some kind of agreement with the boutique, but if this gets you nowhere, send a letter (in French or English) to the following address. Be sure to include all necessary information such as a copy of your receipt, the name and address of the shop, and an explanation of your complaint. Note: don't rely too much on this bureau for settling complaints about antiques or artwork *unless* you have received a certificate of authenticity stating the exact nature of the piece.

Direction Départementale de la Concurrence, de la Consommation, et de la Répression des Fraudes
8 rue Froissart, 75153 Paris 15003; tel.: 40.27.16.00

Shipping

Shipping purchases home has become increasingly less difficult in France since the mid-1980s. Your best bet is to let the boutiques handle shipping for you; now even the smaller boutiques are ready and willing to do the necessary job. It's up to you to choose how you want your purchase to be mailed home. Federal Express is the fastest (only about a week), the most reliable (it assures door-to-door delivery), and of course the most expensive. Surface mail costs almost half the price of Federal Express but takes from two to three months. It's always wise to insure your purchase and, if it is of particular value, take a picture of it before it leaves the shop (in case any damage occurs on its voyage over).

If by any chance you make a major purchase from a boutique that does not handle shipping, the concierge of your hotel will be able to make the necessary arrangements. Keep in mind that if you have your purchase (except for antiques that are 100 years old or more) shipped out of France, you automatically benefit from the *détaxe* and you do not have to process the tax forms at customs.

I've had clients fall in love with items but refrain from buying them because they already had to juggle two suitcases full of belongings. I recommend you travel lightly and bring over one empty suitcase (or collapsible bag) for carting purchases back home. French salespeople are very conscientious about protectively packaging goods for overseas travel.

If you decide to handle shipping arrangements yourself, contact the following international shippers (they speak English as well).

Napoléon Shipping
3 rue Ernest Renan
93500 Pantin; tel.: 48.46.72.28

Where to Rent

No, this section is not about real estate. It does, however, recommend a few places to go for renting formal attire. Certainly there are enough addresses in this book for buying eveningwear, but if you're on a strict budget, and you've just received an impromptu invitation to a ball at Versailles, here's where you may go.

Eugénie Boiserie

Eugénie Boiserie has been renting out couture-style cocktail and evening dresses for more than 30 years. Silk taffeta, chiffon, and satin frocks are at your disposal for about $160 (A $380 guaranty is required.). Credit cards are not accepted and you must call for an appointment.
32 rue Vignon, 9e;
tel.: 47.42.43.71; Métro: Havre-Caumartin

Au Cor de Chasse

This is Paris's most distinguished address for men's formalwear rentals. Tuxedos run about $85 with a $380 guaranty; accessories such as gloves, shirts, and cuff links must be purchased separately. The store also has a selection of formalwear for sale. No credit cards.
40 rue de Buci, 6e;
tel.: 43.26.51.89; Métro: Odéon
open Tuesday–Saturday 9 A.M.–noon
and 1:30–6 P.M.

Costumes de Paris

In addition to this establishment's up-to-date collection of women's eveningwear, they also specialize in every imaginable type of costume rental for men and women. This is the place to go to if you have to find a *déguisement* for a masked ball. Evening dresses rent out at about $140

(with a guaranty of $1000!); costumes run about $100 with a $380 guaranty.
21 bis rue Victor-Massé, 9e;
tel.: 48.78.41.02; Métro: Pigalle
open Tuesday–Saturday 9 A.M.–6:30 P.M.

Although most of the above addresses prefer that you call several days in advance, they will try to outfit you the day of your *soirée*.

Sizes and Size Conversion Chart

The following is a chart of U.S./French/British size conversions. Don't, however, refer to it as if it's the word of God. Not only are there a lot of size discrepancies between different labels and cuts, but I've found, for the most part, that it's extremely difficult to provide exact equivalencies for French sizes. In some stores you may be a 42, in others you may be a 40. Overall the salespeople are very helpful and quite effective with sizing you up. If you're buying for gifts, it's best to buy large—it can always be taken in later. If you're buying for yourself, it's a good idea to take the time to try on clothing and shoes.

Shopping for shoes can be a particularly difficult task in France (depending of course on your shoe size), because French shoes do not come in varying widths. Half sizes are not often easy to come by either and the selection of women's shoes drops off considerably for sizes 40 and 41. Large-sized women will have some difficulties shopping for clothing in Paris because most shops only carry up to size 44 (many only go up to size 42). The big-name boutiques are the best-supplied in 46s. You'll also find a lot of clothing (especially men's and women's shirts and sweaters) marked S,M,L, and XL for small, medium, large and extra large or 1, 2, 3 for small, medium, and large.

I've provided the conversions for children's shoe sizes, although clothing sizes are much easier to figure out. Children's clothing sizes run according to the age of the child; sizes run in months, for babies aged 3, 6, 12, and 18 months, and in years, for kids aged 2, 3, 4, 6, 8, 10, 12, 14, and 16 years.

·   **SIZE CONVERSION CHART**   ·

Women

Coats, Dresses, Blouses, Pants, and Skirts (*manteaux, robes, chemisiers, pantalons et jupes*)

USA	6	8	10	12	14	16
F	36	38	40	42	44	46
GB	8	10	12	14	16	18

Shoes (*chaussures*)

USA	5	6	7	8	9	10
F	36	37	38	39	40	41
GB	3½	4½	5½	6½	7½	8½

Men

Suits (*costumes*)

USA/GB	36	38	40	42	44	46
F	46	48	50	52	54	56

Shirts (*chemises*)

USA/GB	14	14½	15	15½	16	16½	17
F	36	37	38	39	40	41	42

Shoes (*chaussures*)

USA	6	7	7½	8½	9	10	11
F	39	40	41	42	43	44	45
GB	5½	6½	7	8	8½	9½	10½

Children

See above text for clothing sizes.

Shoes (*chaussures*)

USA	8	9	10	11	12	13	1	2	3
F	24	25	27	28	29	30	32	33	34
GB	7	8	9	10	11	12	13	1	2

Alterations

If you find something in a shop that you really like, don't hesitate to buy it because it needs to be altered. Alterations or *retouches* may be accomplished easily enough in most Paris boutiques and often in no time at all. Many shops require a week to ten days to carry out alterations, however, if they know that you're leaving tomorrow most establishments will carry out the job by the end of the day. This is particularly the case for the couture houses, and once the alteration has been made, they will have the item dropped off to you at your hotel. Unfortunately most of these big-name boutiques charge for alterations, whereas the smaller, lesser-known shops probably won't. Service has its price.

You and the French (Breaking Down the Myth)

Stop! Don't turn on your heels and walk out of a Parisian boutique because you have received a less than friendly welcome from a somewhat reserved French salesperson.

Breaking down the icy barriers that sometimes exist between Americans and French salespeople is not as difficult as you may think (or may have heard). Like much of life in France, it begins with a greater understanding of the French and their approach toward serving their clients. In the U.S., it is easy to enter a boutique anonymously and to browse freely at your own leisure. This is rarely the case in France, which explains why many Americans sometimes feel bothered or uncomfortable when dealing with French salespeople.

My CHIC PROMENADE boutique tours were partly created to help facilitate shopping experiences for visitors in the French capital. The presence of someone who not only speaks the language but, even more importantly, understands the little quirks that make the French shop owners and salespeople tick reassures the shopper that no one will ruffle their feathers along the way.

The innumerable experiences encountered with clients on CHIC PROMENADE shopping excursions have confirmed my theory that it's better to go with the grain than against it. Some of my (and my clients') most rewarding exchanges with French salespeople have occurred when I made the effort to engage in conversation with them. Some of you may balk at this idea, especially if you have ever been greeted by a rather snooty "bonjour, Madame." (Remember that the lack of a bubbly hello does not mean that the French are unfriendly—it's just a different approach.) If you feel slightly uncomfortable in a store because a salesperson is giving you the once-over, turn the tables around and warm up to them. In most instances your interactions with the salespeople will turn out to be a sort of game. For example, start off with comments such as "I've come to look at your new collection" (this only works at the beginning of the seasons), "I've heard you specialize in so and so," or even something so banal as "It's good to get in out of the rain." Compliments go even further in France than in the U.S., so if you start chattering about some element of the decor, you're halfway there. The more you share yourself with them, the more they'll open up to you.

If you don't feel comfortable uttering a few words in French (such as *cette lampe est superbe!*), say it in English, but remember that if you want to engage in English conversation with them, first ask whether or not they speak your language. Many Americans make the mistake of interpreting standoffishness as anti-American sentiment. *Au contraire!* The French not only have a perpetual love affair going on with Americans, but they also rely upon American tourists for part of their livelihood.

Now that I've explained a bit about the myth of the nasty Parisian salesperson, it's up to you to break down the myth of the ugly American. It is important to treat the Parisian shop owners and salespeople with the respect they merit. First of all, greetings and salutations are extremely important in France, and remember to always add *Monsieur* or *Madame* onto a hello, a thank you, or a good-bye—otherwise you may be considered impolite. Also keep in mind that in the big-name boutiques it is generally frowned upon to touch the merchandise and you should, instead, wait to be helped by one of the salespeople. Looking the part is key; if you go shopping on avenue Montaigne (the home of French couture), for example, try to look as elegant as the avenue itself. It's OK to dress down for sightseeing, but spiff up your look when shopping. Appearances count a lot in France and you should look as chic as the boutiques that you intend to visit. Accessorize, put on a dabble of makeup plus a few baubles, and remember to leave your Reeboks back at the hotel! Sneakers, though practical, still aren't part of being well dressed for shopping in Paris.

Le Look Français

Although I'm not a fashion consultant (and never would pretend to be one either), I thought that it would be of interest to some of you to learn more about *le look français* or in other words, the French look. The two questions my clients most frequently ask me are how do the French stay so slim (with all of their rich food and in particular, buttery pastries), and how do they afford to be so well dressed? The answer to both of these queries is quality, not quantity. If your goal is to return to the States with a newly aquired French look, the following tips should steer you in the right direction when planning your shopping itinerary.

- Pick up a few pieces of big, chunky costume jewelry. Large, round clips and long, bulbous earrings as well as weighty, gold, charm-like bracelets are sure to dress up the most basic little shift you have back home in your closet. Anything goes—as long as it's big.
- Buy a wool challis scarf or cashmere shawl that may be nonchalantly draped over one shoulder at cocktail parties. This one-shoulder effect also works well for daytime dressing and looks best worn casually over a wool jacket (great for covering up old, raggy ones as well).
- Invest in a few pairs of fantasy-like stockings such as the famous black, bow-print nets by Chantal Thomass ($37). These kinds of stockings may cost a lot, but they don't run easily and they can really jazz up a basic black dress. If you want to look *française* during the warm months, don't bother to wear stockings

(even to the office), but do make sure to have a nice Saint-Tropez tan—or at least a tube of self-tanning cream handy.

- Buy a silk scarf from one of the big-name boutiques that you will wear and treasure forever. Once you've bought it, the next step is to learn how to tie it (I swear the French women are born with this talent). Try asking the saleswoman to give you a demonstration.

- Hunt down a big, wide belt (with an equally big and impressive buckle) that may be used to accessorize your collection of jeans at home. You'll notice that the French mostly wear plain old Levis, but they never look scruffy because they know how to dress them up with sophisticated shirts, jackets, and a trendy pair of shoes. The French women wear as many (if not more) accessories with jeans as with an evening dress, which partly explains why the big, wide belt on a tight little waist has become *très à la mode*.

- Invest in a big, beautiful handbag that you love so much you'll never become tired of it. No matter how budget-minded a Frenchwoman may be, she'll inevitably plunk down a hunk of money for a handbag that will make a statement about who she is (or who she's trying to be). How do you think the Chanel, Louis Vuitton and Hermès bags became so popular? If you're not out to purchase *un sac* whose price tag teeters around the four figure mark, shops such as Didier Lamarthe, Jean Louis Imbert, Emilia, Soco and many more offer quality handbags at less earth-shattering prices.

- Pick up a pair or two of stylish, comfortable flats that may serve as an alternative solution to donning sneaks with skirts. The French do wear sneakers some of the time—but only the stylish kind, and only with jeans (except when they're doing sports, of course).

- The same rule applies for sweatsuits or *les joggings* as the French say. You never see fashion-concious French people wearing sweatsuits in public; instead, they wear jeans, or for women, comfortable leggings or stretchy pants.

- If you have an important event coming up at home such as a wedding or afternoon garden party, you may want to pay a visit to one of the many millineries mentioned in this book. French women often wear hats to such occasions, and, when I was married, most of them carted their little (and a few big) *chapeaux* across the Atlantic.

- Invest in a fashionable, well-cut blazer that you can sport with a simple round neck T-shirt (*à la* Hanes). This is also true for men, but instead, you may want to wear it with a polo shirt or for a more elegant look, with a handsome shirt and silk ascot.

- Buy a pair of classic bermudas or a short, tight skirt to wear around town during hot weather. The French always maintain a certain decorum in Paris and save shorts and other beachy-wear for resort-type areas.

Once again, think quality—not quantity. Even if you invest in only one of the items on this list, you'll be well on your way to dressing, and most importantly, thinking *à la française*. Don't set out to totally revamp your wardrobe—instead work with what you've got and accessorize!

Setting out on Your Shopping Promenade

Now that you know all of the essential information about shopping in Paris, you're probably eager to set out on your own. Although Paris is made up of a maze of centuries-old streets that don't bear even the slightest resemblance to the grid-like pattern of most major American cities, it is amazingly easy to find your way around.

The city is divided up into 20 districts or *arrondissements*. The first one is in the center of Paris near Les Halles; the others spin out in a spiral-like formation similar to that of a snail. As long as you know in which *arrondissement* an address is located, it is easier for you to visualize in what part of the city that establishment may be found.

One of the most efficient forms of transportation is the Paris subway (or Métro). Not only is it easy to figure out, but it also prevents you from being caught up in the city's frenzied traffic jams. Unless you plan on taking the subway at least twice a day for a month, your most economical solution to buying Métro tickets is to purchase 10 at a time (total cost 32.80 Fr for second class as opposed to 52 Fr for 10 individually purchased tickets); ask for a *carnet* (pronounced car-nay). You may also buy first-class tickets (49 Fr for the *carnet*, 7.80 Fr for individual tickets), which will help you to beat the crowded cars at rush-hour.

These same tickets may be used for the Paris city buses (sometimes you need two if you're going a distance) which may be picked up throughout the city. At each bus stop there is a map with the names of the stops on that bus's route; once you have determined whether that bus is going where you want to go, make sure that you pick it up in the right direction. Although slower and often less direct than the Métro, the bus is an excellent form of transportation in Paris because it lets you take in all of the beautiful sights as you travel to your destination.

Taxis are not as plentiful in Paris as in most major American cities, which means that you often have to wait for a while to get one. In most instances, you cannot halt a cab from just any street corner; instead you have to wait at one of the many taxi stations located throughout the city. Taxis take no more than three people (the front seat is saved for the drivers' dogs) and often charge extra for large bags and packages. Usually you tip them 5–10% of the total fare, and even though the service is included as in most restaurants and cafés, it is also customary to leave a few extra francs as a gesture of your appreciation.

Once you arrive in your desired shopping district, the best way to explore is by foot. The following promenades highlight the boutiques that I think are of most interest (it is by no means exhaustive), and I'm sure that once you start poking around, you'll discover more on your own.

Before you go, check to see whether you are bringing along the following things: passport (for *détaxe* and un-expected money exchanges), calculator, map of Paris (from your hotel reception desk), and even a tape mea-sure (comes in handy for measuring tablecloths, furniture, etc.). Last, but oh not least, don't forget your plastic and funds!

THE
≈
PROMENADES

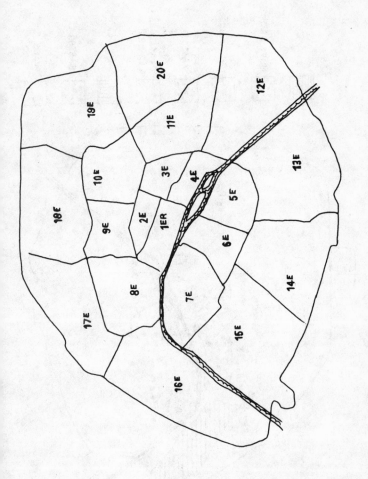

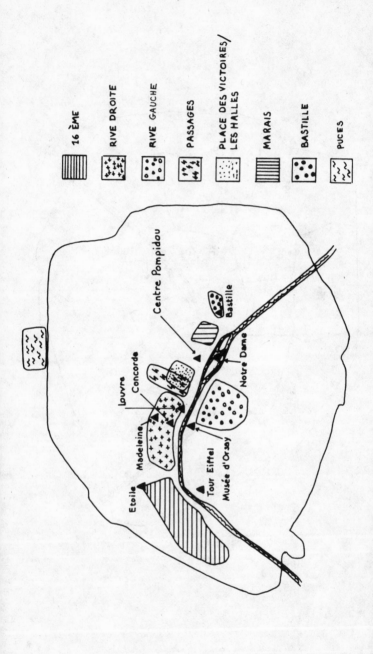

16 ÈME

RIVE DROITE

RIVE GAUCHE

PASSAGES

PLACE DES VICTOIRES/
LES HALLES

MARAIS

BASTILLE

PUCES

Etoile
Madeleine
Louvre
Concorde
Tour Eiffel
Musée d'Orsay
Centre Pompidou
Bastille
Notre Dame

· The Right Bank (The Big Names) ·

Newcomers to Paris often find it difficult to differentiate between the Left Bank and Right Bank, but once you become familiar with the French capital you realize how easy it is to tell the two apart—even if you don't know which side of the Seine you are on. Like the other areas of Paris, the Right Bank (the *Rive Droite*), touts a very distinct look—one that may be best described as chic, elegant, and, above all, luxurious. Here is where you stumble upon Paris's most beautiful stores, top luxury hotels, and even many of the city's best restaurants. Although areas such as place des Victoires, Les Halles, the Marais, and the Bastille are located on the Right Bank, the term *rive droite* is most often used for the area surrounding the Champs-Elysées as well as that of the rue du Faubourg–Saint-Honoré and the rue Saint-Honoré. The Sixteenth is also considered to be *très rive droite* because of the sort of people and places that are found there.

For the better part of this century the Right Bank has served as the world's window for designer fashions and, even more precisely, of the world of couture—that marvelous French fashion mechanism, which, because of its high standards of quality and creation, continues to influence designers and fashion-conscious people throughout the entire world. With the exception of Paco Rabanne, all of the 22 couture houses are located within the bustling confines of the 1st and 8th *arrondissements* that make up the Right Bank. The word *couture* refers to custom-made fashions, but in order to officially receive the title of Haute Couture (which is unpretentiously called couture) by the Fédération Française de la Couture, a couture house must fulfill the following requirements: create a collection consisting of at least 75 fashions each spring and fall; employ at least 20 workers in its couture atelier; show the collection with at least three live models; and present the collection at least 45 times a year, within its house, to its private clientele, which only consists of about 3,000 lucky women, most of whom are foreigners.

Each season is kicked off with a Haute Couture fashion show for the international press and buyers, taking place twice a year: in January (spring/summer) and in July (fall/winter). The collections are later presented to their private clientele within the couture houses' own salons during a month and a half following the press showing. Buyers are mainly interested in purchasing the patterns and the rights to reproduce certain models, whereas the press (at least 700 French and foreign journalists) represent the couture collections' real *raison d'être*: publicity. The pages of photos and articles that follow each couture presentation create exposure, prestige, and name recognition—all essential to the big names' survival. The bread and butter does not come from selling costly couture fashions, but from the various ready-to-wear, accessories, perfume, cosmetics, and housewares lines put out by the house. Licensing agreements only sweeten the pie and of course none of this would be possible without the glamour, gloss, and mystique that embody the couture scene.

Even though most of us can only afford to buy off the rack, there has been renewed interest and excitement in the world of couture ever since Christian Lacroix gave it a brisk new look with the opening of his couture house in the early 1980s. Other houses subsequently began to stir and have since dusted off the somewhat dowdy image that had settled in after their having sat a few too many years on their lofty laurels. New blood was called in to give life to many of Paris's first and most respected couture houses. Karl Lagerfeld has rejuvenated Chanel; Claude Montana has modernized Lanvin; and Gianfranco Ferre has added a touch of Italian flair to Dior. The renewed interest continues, and sleeping giants such as Rochas, Jacques Fath, and Balmain are beginning to take on a younger, fresher image through diversification into more image-building and lucrative domains such as deluxe ready-to-wear and accessories.

As such an important fashion reference, the Right Bank has its reasons for being intimidating and often downright snobby. If you stand straight and tall, throw your shoulders back, and assume the same air of authority as the French, you will have no qualms about crossing the thresholds of Paris's famous couture houses. Don't leave Paris without strolling along the glorious tree-lined avenue Montaigne, which (along with the rue François 1er and the avenue George V) makes up the luxury shop-laden neighborhood called the Golden Triangle. This is home to most of Paris's couturiers and even if you don't intend to buy a $10,000 couture dress, you may want to take a look at the stores' lovely accessories and more affordable ready-to-wear lines. The area is more prestigious than the rue du Faubourg–Saint-Honoré, which has lost a bit of its polish from the steady stream of tourists and motor coaches that flood that part of town. Stop into the ***Relais du Plaza*** at the Hôtel du Plaza Athénée on avenue Montaigne to have lunch or tea in an elegant Art Deco decor.

Look on the other side of the Champs-Elysées. (The street itself has been inundated with fast foods, tacky tourist traps, and crowds of people; however plans are in the works to restore it to its original splendor by the mid-1990s.) Here is the long and winding rue du Faubourg–Saint-Honoré which later turns into the rue Saint-Honoré. (I refer to this whole area as Saint-Honoré.) The high concentration of boutiques and glitzy store windows lure even the most uninterested passerby into high-style window shopping. Since there is so much traffic, it is easier to feel comfortable walking into these big-name stores, although once inside you may be treated more like a tourist here than if you were to enter one of the boutiques in the Golden Triangle. Keep in mind that most of the couture houses also have shops on the rue du Faubourg–Saint-Honoré and that although the settings vary considerably, the selections of merchandise are quite similar.

One of the most luxurious streets in Paris, the rue Royale runs perpendicular to the rue du Faubourg–Saint-Honoré and the rue Saint-Honoré. Beginning at the place de la Concorde and ending at the Madeleine, this 18th-century street harbors more sumptuous establishments including Maxim's, Lalique, Fred (the jewelers), and Paris's most exclusive florist, Lachaume. Further down the rue Saint-Honoré at the intersection of the rue de Castiglione, turn left onto the place Vendôme, home of the world's most prominent jewelers: Chaumet, Van Cleef and Arpels, Boucheron, and Mauboussin. After contemplating the monumental bronze column made from the melted-down cannons fired at Napoleon's victorious battle of Austerlitz, you may want to stop into the ***Ritz Hotel*** bar for tea or cocktails serenaded by lyrical harp music. Jewelers' Row continues up the rue de la Paix toward the Opéra where, like many others, Cartier's pristine windows dazzle your eyes and tempt you into entering to take a closer look at its enticing line of "musts."

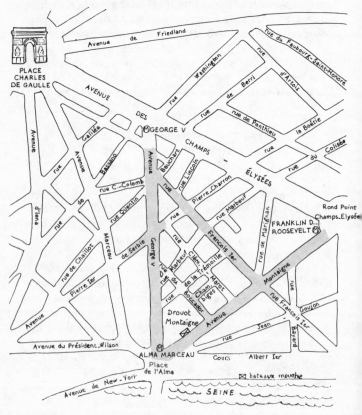

Parallel to the rue Saint-Honoré, the rue de Rivoli's sidewalks are covered with a seemingly endless series of 19th-century stone arcades, perfect for seeking cover from one of Paris's many impromptu rainstorms. Here the shopping consists largely of touristy-type shops that sell everything from Sorbonne T-shirts to Eiffel Tower key chains. In case you've missed the souvenir stands that surround all of the major monuments, this is a perfect place for picking up inexpensive memorabilia from gay Paree.

As you probably have already discerned, shopping on the Right Bank could take a month—if not a lifetime— and you can find just about everything here from a jewel-encrusted Fabergé egg to a copy of *The New York Times* at William H. Smith! With egg or paper in hand, once the shopping is done, I suggest you stroll over to the *Tuileries Gardens*, sit down, and contemplate all of the beautiful Parisian goods that continue to set the standards for fashion and luxury throughout the world—then you'll begin to have a greater sense of what shopping in Paris is all about.

Promenade Golden Triangle

This promenade is very easy to follow because it consists of three main streets that form a triangle: avenue Montaigne, rue François 1er, and avenue George V. I suggest you start at the beginning of avenue Montaigne, turn up onto rue François 1er, and walk down avenue George V to where you started the tour. The Métro stop for the beginning and the end of the promenade is Alma-Marceau. Note that the starting point for the *Bateaux-Mouches* (boat rides on the Seine) is just five minutes away from the Métro exit.

STREETS:

· ## Avenue Montaigne ·

Emanuel Ungaro

Large egg-shaped hollows make up the women's boutique, forming a luminous backdrop for the rich palette of colors that typifies this designer's three lines: Ungaro Parallèles, Solo Dona, and Ungaro Ter. Hot items include brightly colored silk print blouses from the Parallèle collection ($700–1100) and vivid silk scarves in a bouquet of floral prints ($175). The men's collection, considerably less flashy, features refined styles in a spectrum of earthy tones.

2 av Montaigne, 8e; tel.: 47.23.61.94;
Métro: Alma-Marceau
open Monday–Friday 10 A.M.–7 P.M.;
Saturday 10 A.M.–6:30 P.M.
58 rue du Faubourg–St.-Honoré, 8e (women only);
tel.: 47.42.16.06; Métro: Concorde or Madeleine
open Monday–Saturday 10 A.M.–7 P.M.

Harel

Looking for a pair of crocodile pumps? Try Harel, one of Paris's best kept secrets (you won't find them stateside), where you will discover a wide assortment of superbly crafted women's shoes and bags in crocodile, lizard, snake, ostrich, kid, and suede. Harel's timeless styles are shown in an undeniably chic range of colors. Fantastical apple greens, candy pinks, and sun yellows flirt with classic greens, burgundys, and browns.

Look upstairs for some spectacular sale items (30–50% off) during January–February and July–August. Friendly welcome.

8 av Montaigne, 8e; tel.: 47.20.79.01;
Métro: Alma-Marceau
64 rue François 1er, 8e; tel.:47.23.96.57;
Métro: Franklin-Roosevelt or George V
open Monday–Saturday 10 A.M.–6:45 P.M.

Pascal Morabito

12 av Montaigne, 8e; see rue du Faubourg–
St.-Honoré description p. 63

Isabel Canovas

Stepping into this jewel-like boutique means entering the world of the superfluous and the frivolous. There is nothing here that you need, but there may be a number of things that you absolutely can't live without—especially once you take a glimpse at all of the divinely precious handmade accessories tucked away in the many drawers of this tiny boutique.

Isabel Canovas draws inspiration from sources as wide and varied as Russian icons to primitive African art for her sophisticated collections of costume jewelry, shoes, bags, belts, gloves, hats, and scarves! Her creations are both flamboyant and extravagant, often tipped with feathers, fur, and beads, and not to be worn by the timid. As high as her prices may be (a pair of earrings may fetch as much as $1,200), they are still lower in Paris than in her Manhattan boutique.

16 av Montaigne, 8e; tel.: 47.20.10.80;
Métro: Alma-Marceau
open Monday–Saturday 10 A.M.–7 P.M.

Hanae Mori

17-19 av Montaigne, 8e; see rue du Faubourg–
St.-Honoré description p. 61

Valentino

These two boutiques house the elegant women's and men's fashions for which this Italian couturier is famous: Boutique, Miss V, Studio and the more basic line, Oliver (named after Valentino's dog). High quality fashions from each of the lines may be coordinated interchangeably for a look that is sure to be one of the classiest in town.

17 & 19 av Montaigne, 8e tel.: 47.23.64.61;
Métro: Alma Marceau
open Monday–Saturday 10 A.M.–7 P.M.

D. Porthault

Porthault's (pronounced *por-to*) light and airy garden-print cotton percale sheets and heavy hand-embroidered table linens have dressed some of the most famous beds and tables of the world, including those of the Duchess of Windsor, Jackie O., and Shah of Iran. A family-owned business that prides itself on custom work, the name Porthault is synonymous with quality, durability and, above all, beauty.

More dreamy self-indulgences include an exquisite collection of nightgowns, serving trays, and the plumpest towels in town. Don't miss the crisp white-and-pastel–colored baby clothes that are perfect for your most precious little darlings.

Items tend to vary with those sold stateside; here they only show the *crème de la crème.* Paris prices are the best and the bargains are even more tempting if you happen to be here for one of its January sales!

18 av Montaigne, 8e; tel.: 47.20.75.25;
Métro: Alma-Marceau
open Monday–Friday 9:30 A.M.–6:30 P.M.; Saturday
9:30 A.M.–6 P.M.; closed Monday and Saturday 1–2
P.M.

Guy Laroche

A rich landscape of colors, played upon a great variety of textures and volumes, greets you as you enter the Laroche boutique. The look is young, glamourous, and—most importantly—seductive.

With designer Angelo Tarlazzi now at the helm of the haute-couture collections, Guy Laroche couture continues to be one of the main attractions on the street. If one of their $10,000 creations is not within your budget, you may want to settle for a pair of faux-jewel–encrusted pendant earrings at $600 a crack!

29 av Montaigne, 8e; tel.: 40.69.69.50;
Métro: Alma-Marceau or Franklin-Roosevelt
open Monday–Saturday 9:30 A.M.–6:30 P.M.
30 rue du Faubourg–St.-Honoré, 8e; tel.: 42.65.62.74;
Métro: Concorde or Madeleine
open Monday–Friday 10 A.M.–6:30 P.M.; Saturday 10
A.M.–1 P.M. and 2:15–6:30 P.M.
9 av Victor Hugo, 16e; tel.: 45.01.82.75;
Métro: Etoile
open Monday–Saturday 10 A.M.–6:30 P.M.

Christian Dior

Renovated and enlarged a few years ago, the House of Dior is clearly the powerhouse on the block. The main boutique and its three offspring (Baby Dior, house linens, and its celebrated women's shoes) form the pearl-grey–and–white Dior empire that features everything from silk scarves to Limoges china. Even if you're just stopping in to pick up a bottle of Diorissimo, don't miss their women's and men's ready-to-wear lines as well as their *haute four-rure* department which shows some of the most magnificent furs in Paris.

30 av Montaigne, 8e; tel.: 40.73.54.44;
Métro: Alma-Marceau or Franklin-Roosevelt
open Monday–Saturday 10 A.M.–6:30 P.M.

Parfums Caron

The high point of this charming shop is not only Nocturnes de Caron, but also a dozen different perfumes bearing names such as French Cancan and Violette Précieuse. These scents, created in the first half of the 20th century, are sold exclusively in this boutique. Other heady items include shimmering scented candles and silky body powders.

34 av Montaigne, 8e; tel.: 47.23.40.82;
Métro: Franklin-Roosevelt
open Monday–Saturday 10 A.M.–6:30 P.M.

Céline

38 av Montaigne, 8e; see rue François 1er
description p. 43

Nina Ricci

Typified by bows, lace, and appliqué, Nina Ricci offers some of the prettiest and most feminine fashions on the street. In addition to its fanciful ready-to-wear line, this honey-colored boutique showcases their luxurious collection of house linens, lingerie, women's accessories, perfumes, and gift ideas for the home.

If you only have time to visit one couture house, come here because although Nina Ricci has opened a dozen boutiques in the Orient, it has not yet arrived stateside.

39 av Montaigne, 8e; tel.: 47.23.78.88;
Métro: Alma-Marceau or Franklin-Roosevelt
open Monday–Friday 10 A.M.–6:30 P.M.;
Saturday 10 A.M.–1 P.M. and 2:15–6:30 P.M.

22 rue Cambon, 1er; tel.: 47.03.35.91;
Métro: Concorde or Madeleine
open Monday–Saturday 10 A.M.–7 P.M.

Chanel

42 av Montaigne, 8e; see rue Cambon description
p. 85

Jean-Louis Scherrer

Glitzed up classicism is the trademark of this one-time
assistant to Christian Dior. Both Monsieur Scherrer's couture and ready-to-wear fashions are favorites among the
wives of many of the world's most famous dignitaries.
Luxurious fabrics cut in simple styles give way to sophisticated creations that herald state dinners, gala openings,
or the Academy Awards.
51 av Montaigne, 8e; tel.: 42.65.55.15;
Métro: Franklin-Roosevelt
open Monday–Saturday 9 A.M.–1 P.M. and 2–6:30
P.M.
31 rue de Tournon, 6e; tel.: 43.54.49.07;
Métro: Odéon
open Monday–Saturday 9:30 A.M.–7 P.M.
14 av Victor-Hugo, 16e; tel.: 45.01.71.53;
Métro: Etoile
open Monday 2–6:30 P.M.;
Tuesday–Saturday 10:30 A.M.–6:30 P.M.
29 av Ledru-Rollin, 12e (See Discount Shopping
p. 300)

Loewe

Loewe, Spain's leading leather-goods company, was established in 1845 and sold to Louis Vuitton in 1985. The
satiny feel of its high-quality (and expensive) leather products has remained the same, but now it is achieving worldwide fame.

Buttery leather bags, belts, shoes, gloves, and a luxurious collection of ready-to-wear in embroidered leather,
cashmere, and silk line the nut-colored paneled walls of
this handsome boutique.
57 av Montaigne, 8e; tel.: 45.63.73.38;
Métro: Franklin-Roosevelt
open Monday–Saturday 10 A.M.–7 P.M.

Escada

Recently opened, the Escada flagship store bears testimony to the soaring success experienced by this leading German manufacturer since the early 80s. Headed by Margaretha Ley, former Swedish model for Jacques Fath, the Escada look is one of high quality, elegance, and panache. With almost a thousand styles proposed in each collection, their astounding choice allows women to pull together many different looks from an assortment of brightly colored separates.

57 av Montaigne, 8e; tel.: 42.89.83.45;
Métro: Franklin-Roosevelt
418 rue St.-Honoré, 8e; tel.: 42.60.14.97;
Métro: Concorde or Madeleine
open Monday–Saturday 10 A.M.–7 P.M.

Noël

No, Noël does not specialize in Christmas decorations, but it does sell luxury linens for the home that you won't find stateside. Famous for its more than 10,000 hand-embroidered tablecloth designs, Noël also presents a less expensive (by their standards) line of bed and table linens, towels, and nighties that is sure to garnish your home in equally good taste and fine quality.

49 av Montaigne, 8e; tel.: 40.70.02.41;
Métro: Franklin-Roosevelt
open Monday–Saturday 10 A.M.–6:30 P.M.

Thierry Mugler

The most avant-garde designer in the neighborhood is Thierry Mugler, whose boutique (designed by the designer himself) looks like the entrance ramp into a spaceship from Mars. The ominous hum and glow from the halogen lighting enhances the futurist vibes that reverberate through your body as you descend the seemingly endless corridor, leading you to the sunken plateau that houses the womenswear in the back of the store.

Thirties melodrama with a sci-fi slant is what makes up the *femme fatale* look of the Mugler woman. Sculptural fashions composed of huge padded shoulders, wasp waists, and heavy metal trimmings make most women look as though they just stepped off a Hollywood set.

The men's fashions, which are punctuated with the same strong lines, radiate in sharp contrasts of day-glow colors and basic blacks.

49 av Montaigne, 8e; tel.: 47.23.37.62;
Métro: Franklin-Roosevelt
open Monday–Saturday 10 A.M.–7 P.M.
10 place des Victoires, 1er; tel.: 42.60.06.37;
Métro: Palais Royal or Etienne Marcel
open Monday 11–1 P.M. and 2–7 P.M.; Tuesday–
Saturday 10 A.M.–7 P.M.

S.T. Dupont

The perfect proportions and the streamlined shape of the Dupont lighter have made it one of those great symbols of *l'art de vivre.* You will find this handsome *objet* here in a variety of forms along with an inexhaustible collection of men's accessories and top-drawer ready-to-wear—not yet seen in the U.S. Expensive.

58 av Montaigne, 8e; tel.: 45.61.08.39;
Métro: Franklin-Roosevelt
open Monday–Saturday 10 A.M.–7 P.M.
84 rue du Faubourg–St.-Honoré, 8e; tel.: 42.66.05.33;
Métro: Champs-Elysées–Clémenceau
open Tuesday–Friday 10 A.M.–7 P.M.; Saturday
10:30 A.M.–6:30 P.M.

Louis Vuitton

Pass through the majestic Greco-Roman–styled portal to enter the world of luxury travel, Louis Vuitton style. If you're not knocked over by some of the bustling Japanese looking to complete their 10-piece sets of L.V. luggage, you will be able to browse around without too many problems. Prices on most articles run about 20% less than in the States. (If some of these prices are the same, that means that the U.S. pieces have been sown together in the U.S.) The minimum amount for the *détaxe* here is 1800 Fr, so if you just want to pick up a billfold—you're out of luck!

54 av Montaigne, 8e; tel.: 45.62.47.00;
Métro: Franklin-Roosevelt
78 bis av Marceau, 8e; tel.: 47.20.47.00;
Métro: Etoile
open Monday–Saturday 9:30 A.M.–6:30 P.M.

Torrente

The name may sound Italian, but this couturier is most definitely French. The Torrente look is one of sophistication and class; noble fabrics are draped into elegant silhouettes for some of Paris's most prominent *parisiennes*. Not only is this boutique small and intimate, but the saleswomen are also quite pleasant. Torrente does not have a boutique in the U.S.

60 av Montaigne, 8e; tel.: 42.56.14.14;
Métro: Franklin-Roosevelt
open Monday–Saturday 10 A.M.–7 P.M.

Rue François 1er

Ricci Club

The name is aptly chosen for Nina Ricci's newly opened menswear boutique. As you enter Ricci Club you feel as though you have discovered a distinguished men's club just off of London's Fleet Street. The handsome cinnamon-and-tan decor and the muffled atmosphere provide an ideal setting for the luxurious men's clothing, accessories, and toiletries on view in this exclusive boutique. Custom-made suits cost about $2,800.

19 rue François 1er, 8e; tel.: 47.23.78.88;
Métro: Franklin-Roosevelt
open Monday–Friday 10 A.M.–6:30 P.M.; Saturday
10 A.M.–1 P.M. and 2:15 –6:30 P.M.

Anita Oggioni

In the aftermath of the bra-burning women's-lib movement of the 70s, the 80s experienced a lingerie explosion. The 80s woman moved toward showing off her slimmer, trimmer body with silky niceties that would compensate for all of the bouncing and sweating on the gym floor.

Italian designer Anita Oggioni launched her made-in-France haute lingerie collection in the first part of the past decade, and her success has grown as rapidly as women's appetites for fine-quality frivolities. Madame Oggioni has continued her custom-made lingerie line and now sells

more affordable lacy creations as well as ultrafeminine
stockings and bathing suits.
19 rue François 1er, 8e; tel.: 47.20.74.76
4 rue de Marignan, 8e; tel.: 47.20.49.89
open Monday–Saturday 10–12:30 P.M.
and 1:30–7 P.M.
Métro for both stores is Franklin-Roosevelt.
30 rue de Grenelle, 7e; tel.: 45.49.27.61;
Métro: Sèvres-Babylone
10:30 A.M.*–12:30* P.M. *and 1:30–7* P.M.

Puiforcat

22 rue François 1er, 8e; see av Matignon
description p. 57

Fouquet

A family-owned business since 1852, Fouquet specializes
in handmade sweets that have conquered *gourmands*
throughout the entire world. This boutique, which has
been here since 1926, began to draw discerning clients
long before the neighboring couture houses set up shop.
Their mouth-watering chocolates make up only part of the
reason for their ongoing success; the shop's hard candies,
caramels, nougats, jams, jellies, and honeys maintain great
drawing power. If you happen to be in town at Eastertime,
you're particularly in luck because their pastel-colored,
melt-in-your-mouth *fondants* (creamy sugared sweets)
form the prettiest little Easter baskets that any bunny
would want to deliver. All of these goodies are presented
in beautiful gift packages, including their own multicolored hand-painted tins, which are ideal for friends
back home. In addition to sweets, Fouquet offers their
own exotic range of mustards, vinegars, spices, nuts, teas,
coffees, and many other delectables that are not sold
anywhere else in the world!
22 rue François 1er, 8e; tel.: 47.23.30.36;
Métro: Alma-Marceau of Franklin-Roosevelt
open Monday–Saturday 9:30 A.M.*–7:30* P.M.
36 rue Laffitte, 9e; tel.: 47.70.85.00;
Métro: Richelieu-Drouot
open Monday–Friday 10 A.M.*–6:30* P.M.

Céline

Although Céline shows smart collections of ready-to-wear for women and men, the name is best known for their classic women's accessories. Elegant leather bags, belts, and shoes in a range of timeless styles and colors provide a look that is distinctly Parisian. The styling of their heavy gold-metal chains, charm bracelets, hammered earrings, and silk scarves looks like a blissful marriage between Hermès and Chanel (what more could you ask for!).
24 rue François 1er, 8e; tel.: 47.20.22.83
38 av Montaigne, 8e; tel.: 49.52.08.79
Métro for both boutiques is Franklin-Roosevelt.
open Monday–Saturday 10 A.M.–7 P.M.

Rochas

An excellent address for luxurious gift ideas, this handsome store headlines the complete collection of Rochas fragrances as well as arts of the table, leather bags, and ultrathick towels and robes for the bath. The newly opened first floor features Rochas's elegant line of women's ready-to-wear designed by Scotsman, Peter O'Brien.
33 rue François 1er, 8e; tel.: 47.23.54.56;
Métro: Franklin-Roosevelt
open Monday 2:30–6:45 P.M.; Tuesday–Saturday
10 A.M.–6:45 P.M.

Ted Lapidus

Ever since son Olivier joined father Ted a couple of years ago, changes have been made in this world-renowned couture house. The masculine-like structural tendencies that made Ted Lapidus famous over 20 years ago have been softened by Olivier's shapely styling. The look is still well tailored but considerably less imposing, allowing a woman to please herself without having to adhere to current fashion dictums.

The men's fashions and accessories, which are known for their wide assortment and versatility, continue to be some of the most popular on the street.
35 rue François 1er, 8e; tel.: 47.20.56.14;
Métro: Franklin-Roosevelt
open Monday–Saturday 10 A.M.–6:45 P.M.

23 rue du Faubourg–St.-Honoré, 8e; tel.: 42.66.69.30;
Métro: Concorde or Madeleine
open Monday–Saturday 9:30 A.M.–7 P.M.

Victoire

38 rue François 1er, 8e; see place des Victoires/Les
Halles description p. 172

Courrèges

The 60s wouldn't have been the same without André Courrèges, the guy responsible for creating mod pant suits, go-go boots, and hip huggers and for baring our midriffs! Can he be forgiven!?! Only kidding.

Although today's Courrèges look is in tune with the 90s, the futuristic tone is still omnipresent; the women's and men's fashions shown in this boutique are less geometrical than past Courrèges creations yet still quite structural. To me, the boutique Courrèges is both a tease (as in last vestiges of the 60s) and a threat (daring to bring back the fashions from decades gone by).
40 rue François 1er, 8e; tel.: 47.20.70.44,
Métro: Franklin-Roosevelt.
open Monday–Saturday 9:45 A.M.–6:45 P.M.
46 rue du Faubourg–St.-Honoré, 8e; tel.: 42.65.37.75;
Métro: Concorde or Madeleine
open Monday–Friday 10 A.M.–7 P.M.; Saturday 10
A.M.–1 P.M. and 2–7 P.M.
49 rue de Rennes, 6e; tel.: 45.49.38.50;
Métro: St.-Germain-des-Près
open Monday 2:30–7 P.M.; Tuesday–Saturday 10
A.M.–7 P.M.
50 av Victor-Hugo, 16e; tel.: 43.01.70.18;
Métro: Etoile or Victor-Hugo
7 rue de Turbigo, 1er (see Discount Chapter p. 296)

Pierre Balmain

A lot of changes have taken place *chez* Balmain ever since business-whiz Alain Chevalier (formerly of Moët Hennessy) took over in 1989. Scotsman. Alistair Blair, has modernized the women's ready-to-wear line, and plans are now underway for the opening of a new, more luxurious ready-to-wear boutique. Wait and see. The company has also launched a casualwear line for men and women, as well as a new and more exciting jewelry and accessories line for *madame*. If you're thinking green these days, don't miss Vent Vert (green wind), a fragrance that contributed to the original success of the house that Monsieur Chevalier vied to relaunch in 1990.

44 rue François 1er, 8e; tel.: 47.20.35.34.
Métro: Franklin-Roosevelt
open Monday–Friday 10 A.M.–7 P.M.; Saturday 11 A.M.–1 P.M. and 2–7 P.M.
25 rue du Faubourg–St.-Honoré, 8e; tel.: 42.66.45.70;
Métro: Concorde or Madeleine
open Monday–Friday 10 A.M.–7 P.M.; Saturday 11 A.M.–7 P.M.

Francesco Smalto

One of the most important couturiers for men in Paris, Francesco Smalto has developed a winning combination of Italian styling and French *savoir-faire* in his elegant men's fashions and accessories. Monsieur Smalto's list of clients includes statesmen such as the king of Morocco and French celebs Jean-Paul Belmondo, Michel Sardou, and rocker Johnny Hallyday. What's the secret? High-quality fabrics fashioned into stylish men's apparel that swings with the times.

44 rue François 1er, 8e; tel.: 47.20.70.63;
Métro: Franklin-Roosevelt
5 pl Victor-Hugo, 16e (men's and women's); tel.:
45.00.48.64; Métro: Victor-Hugo
open Monday–Saturday 10 A.M.–7 P.M.

Bernard Perris

Bernard Perris's fashions, often considered to be among the most luxurious of all of the couturiers in Paris, are cut from high-quality fabrics and assembled with meticulous care. The look (especially for his eveningwear) is strikingly sophisticated—yet never too much.

The deluxe men's ready-to-wear line is also of the finest quality and workmanship. Prices throughout the shop are high but still about 20% less than in their U.S. boutiques.

48 rue François 1er, 8e; tel.: 47.20.55.62;
Métro: Franklin-Roosevelt
open Monday–Saturday 10 A.M.–7 P.M.

John Lobb

The name may sound English to you, but Hermès holds the reigns of the French marketplace for this famous English bootmaker. In London, John Lobb only sells custom-made men's shoes, however, in Paris, exquisitely crafted ready-to-wear shoes and boots for men and women are on view along with their famous tailormades. Prices are among the highest in town, but what can one expect with more than a 150 years of know-how and the finest quality leathers that go into John Lobb's *chausseurs*. Prices average about $440 for their classic-styled women's shoes; men's shoes fetch around $520. If you're in the market for one of the men's custom-mades (sorry ladies, only ready-to-wear for us) count on investing close to $2,750. Unfortunately you'll have to wait about 6 months for these beauties because they are entirely made by hand and it takes at least 40 hours of work to craft them. I'm sure they're worth the wait.

51 rue François 1er, 8e; tel.: 45.61.02.55;
Métro: Franklin-Roosevelt or George V
open Monday–Saturday 10 A.M.–7 P.M.

La Maison du Chocolat

No trip to Paris is complete without stopping at La Maison du Chocolat. Here you will savor the best chocolate in Paris (and all of France, for that matter). Many of you probably associate fine chocolate with Belgium or Switzerland, yet the true gourmets know that it is the French who regard it more like a treasured jewel than a candy. From the succulent texture of a mocha *ganache* to the exquisite packaging of a gold-embossed box, nowhere else in the world is chocolate so coddled and refined as in Paris.

Monsieur Robert Linxe, a spry, affable man whose enthusiasm for his chocolaty creations is dangerously contagious, is the *génie* behind La Maison du Chocolat. Monsieur Linxe's great dedication to quality is what distinguishes this chocolate shop from the rest. Top-quality chocolates are made from top-quality ingredients; Monsieur Linxe starts off with the finest *couverture* (the chocolate maker's raw material), blends it with fresh cream and natural flavorings (such as juicy ripe raspberries or

roasted almonds) in order to achieve chocolates of unparalleled taste. All of these chocolates, as well as their
pastries are made by hand in La Maison du Chocolat's
laboratoire just outside of Paris.

I suggest you stop into their cocoa-brown chocolate
salon for a heavenly cup of hot chocolate accompanied
by a scrumptious chocolate cake (and lots of glasses of
cool water). The peaceful atmosphere and energy-
inducing treats provide the perfect respite for shoppers'
weary souls.

The boutique is filled from top to bottom with delectable gift ideas including fixings for making your
own hot chocolate, fruit-jellied bonbons, liqueurs from the
provinces, and of course an endless selection of melt-in-
your-mouth chocolates—all packaged in elegant
chocolate-brown boxes (made by the same company that
manufactures Hermès's little orange boxes) that will keep
your candies fresh for nearly a month. *Bon chocolat!*
52 rue François 1er, 8e; tel.: 47.23.38.25;
Métro: Franklin-Roosevelt
225 rue du Faubourg–St. Honoré, 8e;
tel.: 42.27.39.44; Métro: Ternes
open Monday.–Saturday 9:30 A.M.–7 P.M.

Givenchy Gentlemen

56 rue François 1er, 8e; see av George V description
p. 48.

Harel

64 rue François 1er, 8e; see av Montaigne
description p. 34

▪ Avenue George V ▪

Gianfranco Ferre Homme

Just a few steps from the Champs-Elysées, this large and
spacious boutique is devoted entirely to superbly tailored
men's fashions and accessories by Gianfranco Ferre. If
you are a lover of this Italian designer's fine-quality menswear, don't miss this showcase boutique because the se-

lection goes above and beyond that which is sold to
selected stores in the U.S..
44 av George V, 8e; tel.: 49.52.02.74;
Métro: George V
open Monday–Saturday 10 A.M.*–7:30* P.M.

Motsch

I walked by this shop at least 50 times before I ventured
inside. Then one day I entered this century-old boutique
and discovered that the rich wood interior was in fact
as antiquated as the facade. To my surprise, however, the
shop was buzzing with activity and salespeople were either helping clients select just the right *chapeau* or busy
reshaping past purchases that had lost their pizazz. (This
is done in a very artisanal fashion with water, sponge, and
wooden forms.) Needless to say I have been won over
ever since by the charm and authenticity of this famous
hatter and now understand how they have been able to
remain in business since 1887.

Women and men shop at Motsch for quality and tradition. Nearly all of their more than 4,000 classically
fashioned hats have been made by hand in the finest
hand-dyed materials and are sold exclusively in this
shop.
42 av George V, 8e; tel.: 47.23.79.22;
Métro: George V
open Tuesday–Saturday 9:30 A.M.*–1* P.M.
and 2–6:45 P.M.

Manuel Canovas Boutique

30 av George V, 8e; see Left Bank description p. 110

Rochas

Women are not the only ones to be spoiled *chez* Rochas,
because this recently opened store is devoted entirely to
men's clothing and accessories—a first in the history of
Rochas. (Until now they only offered a few men's items.)
The Rochas man is one of sheer refinement and good
taste.
29 av George V, 8e; tel.: 47.20.90.13;
Métro: Alma-Marceau
open Monday–Saturday 10 A.M.*–7* P.M.

Kenzo

18 av George V, 8e; see place des Victoires/Les Halles description p. 170

Balenciaga

You don't hear as much about Balenciaga as you may have heard years ago, because Balenciaga is no longer considered a couture house (which of course means that the international press isn't as inspired to chat about them). Nevertheless, Balenciaga maintains a firm stronghold in the French fashion world and their couture-like line, Balenciaga Dix, is worthy of your recognition. Prices here also tend to run less than at other luxury goods houses in the golden triangle.

The Balenciaga fashions are still timelessly elegant, but now the boutique is also showing some younger, sassier items in an attempt to incite daughters to shop where Mom always has. The new trend seems to be working because Balenciaga has already opened the first of eight planned boutiques in Japan and is also talking about setting up shop in New York. In Paris, the Comtesse Tcherevkoff will welcome you with a smile.

10 av George V, 8e; tel.: 47.20.21.11;
Métro: Alma-Marceau
open Monday–Friday 10 A.M.–7 P.M.; Saturday 10 A.M.–1 P.M. and 2:30–7 P.M.

Givenchy

Entering Givenchy is like walking through a fresh garden of colors. Vibrant hues on classic forms yield fashions and accessories that a girl will never throw away. Long a favorite of Audrey Hepburn, Hubert de Givenchy has been designing clothing of aristocratic elegance ever since he first opened his couture house in 1952. Both this boutique and the men's on François 1er present a stunning collection of ready-to-wear and accessories. The av. Montaigne boutique specializes in a more upmarket selection of women's fashions.

8 av George V, 8e; tel.: 47.20.81.31
open Monday–Friday 9:30 A.M.–6:30 P.M.; Saturday 10 A.M.–1 P.M. and 2–6:30 P.M.
8 av Montaigne, 8e; tel.: 47.23.44.40

open Monday–Saturday 10 A.M.–7 P.M.
Métro stop for both boutiques is Alma-Marceau.
56 rue François 1er, 8e; (men's); tel.: 40.76.00.21
Métro: George V
open Monday–Saturday 10 A.M.–7 P.M.

Agnès Comar

Mixed in with all of the *grands couturiers* is home-decorating expert Agnès Comar. Having started out 20 years ago making luxurious pillows, Agnès Comar now features all of the interior dressings required to make your home look like a designer showcase. The Comar look is one of warmth and casual elegance. Trademark designs include Iberian-inspired motifs and unpretentious knots and bows. Her bed linens and throws are particularly rich and may easily be packed up and shipped stateside. Agnès Comar items are not yet sold in the U.S.

7 av Georges V, 8e; tel.: 47.23.33.85;
Métro: Alma-Marceau
open Monday–Saturday 10:30 A.M.–1 P.M.
and 2–7 P.M.

• Avenue Pierre 1er De Serbie •

Creed

Although practically nonexistent in the U.S., Creed has been making fragrances since 1760 and has been purveyor to many important figures over the years, including King George IV, Napoléon III, and Queen Victoria. Many of their fine scents may be used interchangeably by men and women, while the names tend to be nearly as exotic as the fragrances themselves: Ambre Cannelle, Santal Impérial, Bois de Portugal, and Fleur de Bulgarie.

The Creed fragrances are equally reknowned for their pure, medicinal-like *flacons;* clear cylindrical bottles and luxurious black glass "whiskey flasks" reek of understated elegance. Silky creams, bath oils, and gels may also be found as well as some very classic clothing items, such as silk ties and poplin shirts, which are favorites among the French.

38 av Pierre 1er de Serbie, 8e; tel.: 47.20.58.02;
Métro: Alma-Marceau or George V

open Monday 2:30–7 P.M.*; Tuesday–Saturday*
9:30 A.M.*–7* P.M.

· ## Rue de Boccador ·

Shirin Cashmere

You'll find more than twin sets in this small modern boutique. Designer Shirin gives a new meaning to cashmere in her stylish women's fashions that are intended to be mixed and matched together in the most sophisticated ways. A paprika-colored cashmere dress gains greater panache when tied together with a coordinating cashmere shawl (about $1,200 for both). Elegant cardigans look even more striking when trimmed in lace, pearls, or appliqué. It's best to buy these made-in-England items here—not only to benefit from the lower prices and *détaxe* but also because they're next to impossible to find stateside!
24 rue du Boccador, 8e; tel.: 49.52.03.60;
Métro: Alma-Marceau
open Monday–Saturday 10 A.M.*–7* P.M.

Sonia Farès

If you're shopping near Valentino on av Montaigne, this boutique is just a few minutes' walk up the rue du Boccador. Not yet available in the U.S., Sonia Farès is a name to watch out for. Her well-cut fashions are young, sexy, and dynamic—and priced considerably less than the other designerwear in the neighborhood. Short, tight or long, flowing jersey skirts and jackets in warm berry colors are softly tailored for a look that is *très jeune femme*.
5 rue du Boccador, 8e; tel.: 47.23.02.38;
Métro: Alma-Marceau
open Monday–Saturday 10 A.M.*–7* P.M.

· ## Rue Chambiges ·

Sepcoeur

Just a minute away from Sonia Farès is Sepcoeur's cunningly cute collection of women's handbags ($350–775) and belts ($160–290). Most of the shop's colorful creations are made of leather, others are fashioned out of grosgrain, satin, velvet, and denim—but all are dotted with gold and silver studs in the shape of buttons, hearts, butterflies, and stars.

3 rue Chambiges, 8e; tel.: 47.20.98.24;
Métro: Alma-Marceau
open Monday–Friday 10 A.M.–6:30 P.M.; Saturday 2–
6:30 P.M.

Rue Pierre-Charron

Hobbs

When Scotsmen start buying their cashmere sweaters in Paris, you know they must be good. Such is the case *chez* Hobbs where despite the English-sounding name, French owner Patrick Lifshitz prides himself on attracting clients north of the Channel as well as a few overseas celebs. Designed in France, made in Scotland—a winning combination that gives way to sweaters of not only the finest quality but great originality as well. Sure, Hobbs sells your standard V-necks in your basic colors, but the unique series of cashmeres (all hand-knit) inspired from cartoon characters, flags, and graphic designs have become *le dernier cri* of fashion-conscious Parisians. Prices run about $1,200 for their original models and around $550 for their classics—*très cher, mais très original.*

45 rue Pierre-Charron, 8e; tel.: 47.20.83.22;
Métro: Alma-Marceau or Franklin-Roosevelt
open Monday 2–7 P.M.; Tuesday–Saturday
10 A.M.–7 P.M.

Rue de Marignan

Sidonie Larizzi

Paris's posh women and international jet-setters come here to purchase Sidonie Larizzi's top-of-the-line shoes and accessories. If you don't find exactly what you are looking for, you may choose from one of the infinite colors of leather swatches and the store will make the shoes up especially for you; the shop works closely with the neighboring couturiers and will also cover your shoes in the same fabric as that of your newly purchased evening dress. A large and equally impressive selection of men's shoes is sold next door. Prices are steep.

8 rue de Marignan, 8e; tel.: 43.59.38.87;
Métro: Franklin-Roosevelt
open Monday–Saturday 10 A.M.–7 P.M.

How to Attend a Fashion Show

Certainly it is every other person's dream to attend one of the great Parisian fashion shows. However, it has unfortunately become increasingly more difficult to do this and only buyers, press, celebrities, and the couture house's loyal followers are able to squeeze in without having to blink an eye. Difficult as it is, it is not an impossible feat. The secret is to be in the right place at the right time. The main press shows held twice a year to present the new season's ready-to-wear and couture collections are the most difficult to attend, and you only have a shot at these if you have a contact with someone on the inside; the private couture shows (see p. 30), however, are far easier.

If you are in town at the time of the couture houses' presentations, you may reserve a seat at one of these private *défilés* either by calling up the couture house yourself or by having your concierge do it. Ask to speak with someone from the couture department (preferably *la directrice*) and explain that you are a devout follower of the designer and that you would enjoy seeing his or her new collection. If this does not work, you may still try to get in by strolling into the couture houses around 2:30 P.M. (The shows usually start at about 3 P.M. on Tuesdays and Thursdays during the months of February/beginning of March, September/beginning of October.) After you've browsed around the boutique a bit, casually ask if there is a show going on and if by any chance there might be an extra seat for you. Of course, you have

to have the right allure and the right savvy, but if all
goes well, you'll be in like a breeze. My friends and
I have tried these techniques numerous times, and
believe me—they work. If you still have struck out,
or if you happen to be in town during an off-season,
you may trying calling Dior because they run an excellent video showing year-round in their private couture salons. *Bonne chance!*

Promenade Saint-Honoré

Start at the lower end of the Champs-Elysées and take
avenue Matignon over to the rue du Faubourg–Saint-
Honoré. Walk down this street until you reach the intersection of rue Royale; here you may want to walk up
toward the Madeleine or down toward place de la Concorde. (Both areas are good places to pick up the promenade at the halfway point.) As you continue straight
down the rue Saint-Honoré toward the center of Paris,
the place Vendôme is on your left at the rue de Castiglione
intersection, and further down Saint-Honoré, also on your
left, is the place du Marché–Saint-Honoré. Stroll down
the rue de Rivoli en route to the *Louvre* or the *Tuileries
Gardens*. The Métro stop for the start of this promenade
is Franklin-Roosevelt.

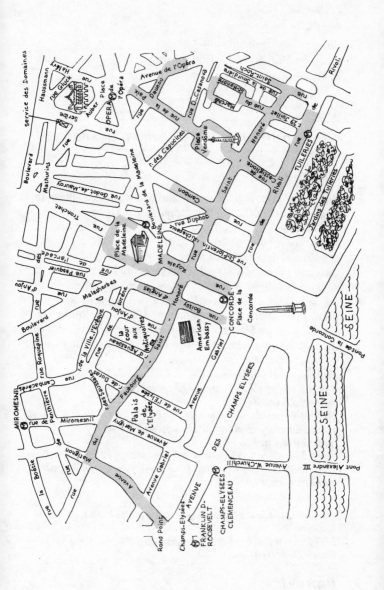

▪ Rond-Point des Champs-Elysées ▪

Carven

Enter the doorway at no. 6 and walk up one floor to discover yet another *couturier parisien*. The present Carven boutique is in need of a good face-lift and apparently plans are underway to do just that. Nonetheless this should not deter you from browsing through the racks of Carven's classically styled womenswear. The quality is of course excellent and the saleswomen are particularly cordial. Before you leave, be sure to take a look at the boutique's enchanting, handpainted Limoges birds (reproduced from Madame Carven's own private collection) that are also on sale. As you go out to the left, you'll pass in front of Carven's golf boutique which specializes in elegant sportswear for men and women.

6 rond-point des Champs-Elysées, 8e;
tel.: 42.25.66.50;
Métro: Franklin-Roosevelt
open Monday–Friday 9:15 A.M.–6:15 P.M.
(womenswear)
open Monday 2:30–6:30 P.M.; Tuesday–Friday 10
A.M.–6:30 P.M.; Saturday 10 A.M.–1 P.M. (men's and
women's sportswear)

Yves Saint Laurent Rive Gauche

12-14 rond-point des Champs-Elysées, 8e; see Left
Bank description p. 119

Lancel

Since 1885 the name Lancel has stood for quality and fine French styling. Glossy advertising campaigns within the

past few years have led to even greater worldwide recognition of their classic leather and faux-leather bags, luggage, and personal accessories. Excellent price/quality relationship on most of their goods.
4 rond-point des Champs-Elysées, 8e;
tel.: 42.25.18.35;
Métro: Franklin-Roosevelt
open Monday–Saturday 10 A.M.–7:30 P.M.
43 rue de Rennes, 6e; tel.: 42.22.94.73;
Métro: St-Germain-des-Prés
8 place de l'Opéra, 9e; tel.: 47.42.37.29;
Métro: Opéra
open Monday–Saturday 10 A.M.–7 P.M.

Avenue Matignon

Le Drugstore

One of the first things a newcomer to Paris should learn is that Le Drugstore is not a drugstore. Well, actually there is a small pharmacy within the store, which, needless to say, is only a very insignificant part of Le Drugstore itself. Aside from being a popular meeting spot on the "Champs," Le Drugstore is actually made up of a big jumble of restaurants and boutiques that sell every imaginable type of gift idea and take-out French delicacy. (Camembert, anyone?) Prices are high and the selection is spotty, but if it's midnight and you're leaving tomorrow, here's where you go to pick up a couple of last-minute gift items.
1 av Matignon, 8e; tel.: 43.59.38.70;
Métro: Franklin-Roosevelt
133 av des Champs-Elysées, 8e; tel.: 47.20.94.40;
Métro: Etoile
149 bd St.-Germain, 6e; tel.: 42.22.92.50.;
Métro: St.-Germain-des-Prés
open daily 9–2 A.M.

Puiforcat

Slightly off the beaten path lies Puiforcat (*Pwee-for-ca*), France's most distinguished sterling-silver company. This new, more contemporary-looking showcase store was the brainchild of Eliane Scali, the smart and savvy *parisienne* who took over this 170-year-old company in the early 1980s. In a luminous decor reminiscent of the Art Deco period (Puiforcat's *grande époque*), clients view tables and display cases set not only with Puiforcat silver, but also with a refined selection of china and crystal, selected by the boutique.

Downstairs highlights both original and reproduced works that master silversmith Jean Puiforcat designed in the 20s and 30s, as well as a fascinating collection of antique silver pieces that have served as inspiration for many of the company's creations throughout the years.

If the prices seem high *chez* Puiforcat, remind yourself that all of the sterling-silver pieces are still made entirely by hand. It wasn't until recently that the company started producing silverplate pieces—alas, times have changed and even the most well-to-do may no longer afford a superbly crafted 20-pound soup terrine in solid silver!

2 av Matignon, 8e; tel.: 45.63.10.10
open Monday–Saturday 9:30 A.M.–6:30 P.M.;
closed Monday and Saturday 1–2:15 P.M.
22 rue François 1er; tel.: 47.20.74.27;
Métro: Alma-Marceau or Franklin-Roosevelt
open Monday 2–6:30 P.M.; Tuesday–Friday 9:30 A.M.–
6:30 P.M.; Saturday 10 A.M.–6 P.M. Métro for both
boutiques is Franklin-Roosevelt.

Artcurial

A well-established contemporary art gallery, Artcurial offers one of Paris's richest selections of art books and modern prints at its bookstore.

9 av Matignon, 8e; tel.: 42.99.16.16;
Métro: Franklin-Roosevelt
open Tuesday–Saturday 10:30A.M.–7:15 P.M.

Anna Lowe

35 av Matignon, 8e; see Discount Shopping
description p. 298

▪ Rue du Faubourg–Saint-Honoré ▪

Miss Maud

90 rue du Faubourg–St.-Honoré, 8e; see Left Bank description p. 152

Louis Féraud

Hopefully their new boutique in New York is spiffier than their rue du Faubourg–St.-Honoré and rue Bonaparte establishments. If you look beyond the shabby decor, you'll discover this couturier's simple-cut ready-to-wear line which is punctuated by sharp contrasts of color and rhythmic patterns of black and white. The overall look is quite striking and undeniably *parisien*. Louis Féraud's true artistic talents (he dabbles as a painter in his spare time) particularly shine through in his dramatic collection of eveningwear, where each dress resembles a work of art.

88 and 90 rue du Faubourg–St.-Honoré, 8e;
tel.: 42.65.27.29;
Métro: Miromesnil or Champs-Elysées–Clémenceau
open Monday–Friday 10 A.M.–7 P.M.; Saturday 10:30 A.M.–7 P.M.
265 rue St.-Honoré, 1er; tel.: 42.60.08.08;
Métro: Concorde or Madeleine
open Monday–Saturday 10 A.M.–7 P.M.
47 rue Bonaparte, 6e; tel.: 46.34.57.96;
Métro: St.-Germain-des-Prés
open Monday–Saturday 10 A.M.–6:45 P.M.

S.T. Dupont

84 rue du Faubourg–St.-Honoré, 8e; see av Montaigne description p. 40

Walter Steiger

Walter Steiger chose this chic intersection as location for his flagship store that houses his luxurious collection of women's and men's shoes and accessories. The quality, craftsmanship, color choice, and price are as rich as the people who shop on this street!

83 rue du Faubourg–St.-Honoré, 8e; tel.: 42.66.65.08;
Métro: Miromesnil or Franklin-Roosevelt
open Monday–Saturday 10 A.M.–7 P.M.
5 rue de Tournon, 6e; tel.: 46.33.01.45;
Métro: St.-Sulpice
open Monday 2–7 P.M.; Tuesday–Saturday 10 A.M.–7 P.M.

Christian Lacroix

At certainly the most enchanting boutique on the street, the world of Christian Lacroix bathes you in sun-drenched harmonies from the couturier's native land, la Provence. Terra-cotta tile floors and pale-yellow walls, bordered in lush hues of orange and cherry form a theatrical backdrop as colorful as the folkloric fashions for which he is famous.

Even if you are not prepared to plunk down a couple of grand for one of his famous puffball skirts, don't miss his candy-colored selection of bags, shoes, belts, and scarves as well as his gold-encrusted baroque gems. His costume jewelry is among the best in town and, although the ready-to-wear baubles are sold all over the world, his couture pieces are sold only in this boutique. Signature Lacroix items include the Provençal cross (the couturier's fetish symbol), hearts, and stars. If all of this is just a bit too ornate (or expensive) for you, how about a bottle of C'est la Vie!—Christian Lacroix's recently launched celestial scent!

73 rue du Faubourg–St.-Honoré, 8e; tel.: 42.65.79.08;
Métro: Miromesnil or Champs-Elysées–Clémenceau
open Monday–Saturday 10 A.M.–7 P.M.

Sonia Rykiel

70 rue du Faubourg–St.-Honoré, 8e; see Left Bank description p. 104

Angelo Tarlazzi

Angelo Tarlazzi's seductive womenswear begs women to show off their curvy shapes. This Italian-born French designer has a knack for enveloping women's bodies in simple-cut knits that are either tight and clingy or softly draped. The result is deliciously cosmopolitan and tastefully naughty.

67 rue du Faubourg–St.-Honoré, 8e; tel.: 42.66.67.73;
Métro: Miromesnil or Champs-Elysées–Clémenceau
74 rue des Saints-Pères, 7e; tel.: 45.44.12.32;
Métro: Sèvres-Babylone or St.-Sulpice
open Monday–Saturday 10 A.M.–7 P.M.

Loris Azzaro

The name Loris Azzaro may be more familiar to you for their perfumes rather than for their glamorous eveningwear. The perfume division is actually a more recent addition to this French couture house which is best known in Paris for dazzling cocktail dresses and ball gowns. If you have an Ivana Trump pocketbook and a social schedule to match it, follow the mirrored stairway to the first floor where you will discover Azzaro's showstopper silhouettes. Here you may either buy off the rack or have a special number made up for you (takes three weeks).

65 rue du Faubourg–St.-Honoré, 8e; tel.: 42.66.92.06;
Métro: Miromesnil or Champs-Elysées–Clémenceau
open Monday–Saturday 10 A.M.–7 P.M.

Hanae Mori

After having started out designing costumes for film productions in Japan, Hanae Mori opened up a couture house in Paris. Her business has flourished tremendously and now Madame Mori is considered to be one of the top female designers in the world. Her feminine-like creations have great female appeal; the cuts are western but the exotic print and beaded fabrics have clearly drawn inspiration from her native land. The selection of women's ready-to-wear, accessories, and home gift ideas (lacquer boxes, etc.) in the rue du Faubourg–St.-Honoré is as bountiful as it is beautiful.

62 rue du Faubourg–St.-Honoré, 8e; tel.: 47.42.78.78;
Métro: Concorde or Madeleine
17-19 av Montaigne, 8e; tel.: 47.23.52.03;
Métro: Alma-Marceau
open Monday–Saturday 10 A.M.–7 P.M.

Chloé

Their peachy-colored boutique is small, elegant, and un-
derstatedly chic. Made out of the most luxurious fabrics,
this deluxe ready-to-wear collection is void of any excess
ornamentation; only the purity of line and fluidity of shape
define the subtle look that is distinctively Chloé.
*60 rue du Faubourg–St.-Honoré, 8e; tel.: 42.66.01.39;
Métro: Concorde or Madeleine
open Monday–Saturday 10 A.M.–7 P.M.*

Kalinger

Here is one of the hottest names in costume jewelry.
You're sure to be in vogue with a pair of chunky earrings
from Kalinger (average price $60). If you're like most
American women, your first reaction might be, "Oh, they're
too heavy for me." Kalinger's jewelry is in fact amazingly
light because all of their pieces are made out of resin
(even their elaborate gold-colored swirls and imitation-
ivory pieces). As with most costume jewelry in Paris these
days, the look is either baroque or exotic and of course
unabashedly big. Kalinger's creations are beginning to pop
up in major department stores in the U.S., but buy here
where the prices and selection are better.

  Before you go, take a peek upstairs where they display
their magnificent collection of one-of-a-kind jewel-like
vases—all are encrusted with their own luminous pieces
of costume jewelry!
*60 rue du Faubourg–St.-Honoré, 8e; tel.: 42.66.24.39;
Métro: Concorde or Madeleine
open Monday–Friday 10 A.M.–7 P.M.;
Saturday 10:30 A.M.–7 P.M.*

Pierre Cardin

The well-stocked Cardin men's boutique makes up most
of this prime location across from the Elysées Palace; the
women's ready-to-wear section is much smaller and far
less impressive. (I think that Monsieur Cardin is spending
too much time tending to his many licensing agreements.)
Plans are in the works for the opening of a huge Cardin
Euro-store on rue du Faubourg–St-Honoré in 1992.
*59 rue du Faubourg–St.-Honoré, 8e; tel.: 42.66.49.65;
Métro: Miromesnil
open Monday–Saturday 10 A.M.–6:30 P.M.*

Ungaro Parallèles

58 rue du Faubourg–St.-Honoré, 8e; see av Montaigne description p. 34

Frette

Take the elevator upstairs to the second floor to discover the luxurious linens of Italian big name, Frette. A stately 19th-century Parisian apartment serves as the selling place for Frette's rich collection of satiny cotton sheets, plush bath towels, silky lingerie, and lofty table linens. Known for over 100 years for their rich damask and jacquard patterns, Frette supplies not only the Italian embassies, but also many of the top hotels throughout the world. Although high, prices here are considerably less than in the U.S.

48 rue du Faubourg–St.-Honoré, 8e; tel.: 42.66.47.70; Métro: Concorde or Madeleine
open Monday–Saturday 9:45 A.M.–6:30 P.M.

Courrèges

46 rue du Faubourg–St.-Honoré, 8e; see rue François 1er description p. 44

Yves Saint Laurent Rive Gauche

38 rue du Faubourg–St.-Honoré, 8e; see Left Bank description p. 119

Pascal Morabito

Originally known for his watches and contemporary-styled costume jewelry, Pascal Morabito has since diversified into leather goods and perfumes. The trademark Morabito look (for his bags and women's and men's fragrance bottles) is highly architectural, sharp-edged, and shut with gold-plated rivets! Morabito does not have a boutique in the U.S., so if you are an angular sort of person, stop in here to see the complete Morabito offerings.

36 rue du Faubourg–St.-Honoré, 8e; tel.: 42.68.01.77; Métro: Concorde or Madeleine
12 av Montaigne, 8e; tel.: 40.70.97.45 (jewelry only); Métro: Alma-Marceau
open Monday–Saturday 11 A.M.–7 P.M.

16 place Vendôme, 1er; tel.: 42.60.30.76;
Métro: Tuileries or Concorde
open Monday–Saturday 9:30 A.M.–6:30 P.M.

Boutique Yves Saint Laurent

Once you drift across the plush emerald-green carpeting, you know that you have entered the world of enchantment, Yves Saint Laurent style. This newly opened boutique is a tribute to YSL couture, only you won't find any dresses here—only the accoutrement. The two floors of the boutique are filled with a gloriously rich collection of women's accessories: shoes, bags, belts, costume jewelry, scarves, shawls, and some heavenly soft cashmere tops. Most of the items come in a limited series (often not more than three) and they are sold only here and in Saint Laurent's mini couture boutique on avenue Marceau. Bring your American Express gold.

32 rue du Faubourg–St.-Honoré, 8e; tel.: 42.65.01.15;
Métro: Concorde or Madeleine
open Monday–Saturday 10 A.M.–7 P.M.

Guy Laroche

30 rue du Faubourg–St.-Honoré, 8e; see av
Montaigne description p. 36

Lancôme

The savings on Lancôme products will most certainly disappoint you because most of the Lancôme products sold in the U.S. are made by Cosmair and priced similarly to those in France. You may, however, turn up some new colors or products that aren't marketed in the U.S., which always makes the hunt more interesting. Upstairs is the divine Lancôme beauty institute; drop-ins are out of the question, but if you call two weeks in advance, you may be lucky enough to treat yourself to a heavenly facial and foot massage.

29 rue du Faubourg–St.-Honoré, 8e; tel.: 42.65.30.74;
Métro: Concorde or Madeleine
open Monday–Saturday 10 A.M.–7 P.M.

Léonard

Vibrant floral prints in the form of bathing suits, wraps, silk scarves, and dresses are the trademark of this celebrated French fashion house (little known to Americans). You may also purchase their heady fragrance, Léonard, here in the boutique.
28 rue du Faubourg–St.-Honoré, 8e; tel.: 42.65.54.54; Métro: Concorde or Madeleine
open Monday–Saturday 10 A.M.–7 P.M.

Krizia

Italian designer Maruccia Mandelli is the creative force behind this high-fashion womenswear label that has won the hearts (and pocketbooks) of many of the world's international jet-setters. The discrete charm and subtle sensuality of Krizia's earth-toned fashions create a young look that intimates sheer sophistication. Although the prices here are high, they are still less than in the U.S.
27 rue du Faubourg–St.-Honoré, 8e; tel.: 42.66.95.94; Métro: Concorde or Madeleine
open Monday–Saturday 10 A.M.–7 P.M.

Pierre Balmain

25 rue du Faubourg–St.-Honoré, 8e; see rue François 1er description p. 45

Hermès

You'll probably notice the beautifully decorated store windows before you even realize that you have arrived *chez* Hermès pronounced (*air-mess*—not *her-mies*). Once you walk inside, you won't be disappointed because Hermès is truly the warmest and most authentic of all of the luxury shops on this street.

Hermès began in 1837 as a harness maker, later took up saddle making, and now sells everything from ready-to-wear to arts of the table. (They recently acquired the centuries-old Cristal de Saint-Louis.) Although today they are only making about 450 saddles a year (mostly for American clients), the basic elements in horse-related accoutrement still serve as inspiration for virtually every article within the Hermès store.

I've found that what most Americans like to buy *chez* Hermès is their men's ties, their gloves, and of course their world-famous silk scarves. The problem is that every other person who walks into Hermès wants to buy their scarves, too, which of course creates massive traffic jams. I always recommend to my clients that they have an idea ahead of time of what color theme they prefer (the scarves are divided up accordingly) so that they don't have to waste much time with their selection. It's also best to go early in the morning because after noon the crowds are often three deep at the scarf counter. Prices generally run approximately $15 less than in the U.S. and if you benefit from the *détaxe* (a minimum of 1,800 Fr here) your savings are increased by about 15%. Be sure to ask for the booklet that shows the many glamourous ways to tie a scarf because the salesgirls don't always remember to slip it into your little orange box.

If you've planned a larger budget for Hermès, you can't go wrong with their classic leather items. Much of what is on sale in the boutique is handmade in their ateliers upstairs. These workshops will soon be relocated outside of the capital because the rising success of this celebrated leather-goods emporium has made it difficult for their craftsmen to keep up with production. Clients now have to wait nearly eight months for the delivery of their famous Kelly bag (the triangular-shaped handbag made popular by Grace Kelly). Even with this shift in fabrication, you can be guaranteed that future Hermès goods will be just as superbly handcrafted, because above all this is a house that is devoted to quality!

24 rue du Faubourg–St.-Honoré, 8e; tel.: 40.17.47.17; Métro: Concorde or Madeleine
open Monday–Saturday 10 A.M.–6:30 P.M.

Ted Lapidus

23 rue du Faubourg–St.-Honoré, 8e; see rue François 1er description p. 43

Lanvin

A lot of changes have taken place at Lanvin within the past couple of years. Wunderkind Claude Montana is now designing the couture line and Eric Bergère took over the women's ready-to-wear where Maryll Lanvin left off. The look, however, is still one of unadorned elegance and the lines possess the same sort of modernity as those of the 20s and 30s when the house was at its beginnings.

In 1926, Lanvin was the first couturier to launch a line of menswear, one that has been considered one of the most elegant of Paris (if not all the world) ever since. Don't be afraid to push open the door and walk inside. Their men's accessories department offers many exquisite gift ideas that would certainly be welcomed by the important man in your life. The rue Cambon address (on the rue de Rivoli) offers sportier, more affordable fashions for men.

22 rue du Faubourg–St.-Honoré, 8e (women's); tel.: 42.65.14.40
15 rue du Faubourg–St.-Honoré, 8e (men's); tel.: 42.65.14.40
Métro for both boutiques is Concorde or Madeleine.
2 rue Cambon, 1er (men's); tel.: 42.60.38.83; Métro: Concorde
open Tuesday–Friday 9:30 A.M.–6.30 P.M.; Monday and Saturday 10 A.M.–12:45 P.M. and 1:45–6:30 P.M.

Trussardi

If the name doesn't ring a bell, think of the ascot-wrapped greyhound (the company's logo). This Italian designer is a big seller in Paris—more for his immense collection of leather and plastified canvas bags than for his ready-to-wear. The Japanese are much better informed than we Americans (Trussardi has opened up boutiques there), because here you will most likely see them buying up Trussardi like crazy. The color range at Trussardi is far more varied than at L.V. (Louis Vuitton to you neophytes), which partly explains the Far Eastern influx. Take a look around—way to the back—and I bet you won't come out empty-handed!

21 rue du Faubourg–St.-Honoré, 8e; tel.: 42.65.11.40; Métro: Concorde or Madeleine
open Monday–Saturday 10 A.M.–7 P.M.

Karl Lagerfeld

Yes, Karl Lagerfeld was once the boy genius of Chloé and, yes, he is now the couturier of Chanel, but he also has his

own ready-to-wear and accessory lines that provide just
one more creative outlet for his brilliant talents. The look
chez Lagerfeld is elegant and discretely glamourous; the
designer uses soft pure lines that flow with the subtleties
of a woman's shape. His use of sober colors and sharp
blacks and whites often creates fashions that are strikingly dramatic.
17 rue du Faubourg–St.-Honoré, 8e; tel.: 42.66.64.64;
Métro: Concorde or Madeleine
open Monday–Saturday 10 A.M.–7 P.M.

Charles Jourdan

The main floor spotlights Jourdan's crayola-colored shoes
(a lot of high, high heels, ladies) with coordinating bags,
as well as a limited selection of seductive women's knit
and leather fashions. Downstairs features a considerably
more sober collection of men's shoes. Prices on all of these
fine-quality, well-styled shoes run slightly lower than in
the U.S.
12 rue du Faubourg–St.-Honoré, 8e; tel.: 42.65.35.22;
Métro: Concorde or Madeleine
open 9:45 A.M.–7 P.M.
39 rue de Grenelle, 7e; tel.: 42.22.55.60; Métro: Bac
open Monday–Saturday 10 A.M.–7 P.M.

Gianni Versace

Gianni Versace, who recently added one more feather to
his multimillion-dollar cap by launching a haute-couture
collection, designs some of the most modern and provocative women's and men's fashions on the street. His
choice of opulent materials and glittery designs is particularly theatrical (Versace is also a great costume designer
for the stage) in his women's-eveningwear collection. Like
the women's, Versace's menswear is highly constructed
and cut from exceptionally luxurious fabrics. Prices for
both collections are astonishing—but still a bit lower than
in the U.S.
11 rue du Faubourg–St.-Honoré, 8e; tel.: 42.65.27.04;
Métro: Concorde or Madeleine
open Monday 11 A.M.–7 P.M.; Tuesday–Saturday
10 A.M.–7 P.M.
67 rue des Saints-Pères, 7e; tel.: 42.84.00.40;
Métro: St.-Sulpice or Sèvres-Babylone

*open Monday 11:15 A.M.–7 P.M.; Tuesday–Saturday
10:15 A.M.–7 P.M.*

Carita

One of the most eye-catching and famous hair salons in
Paris, Carita is frequented by French film stars and members of the international jet set. This is where you should
come if you want a particularly trendsetting hair style that
will tell friends back home that you've been to Paris. Carita
also specializes in skin-care treatments and manicures
and sells a fashionable assortment of hair accessories.
Call ahead.
*11 rue du Faubourg–St.-Honoré, 8e; tel.: 42.65.79.00;
Métro: Concorde or Madeleine
open Monday–Saturday 9 A.M.–7 P.M.*

La Bagagerie

La Bagagerie is best known for their huge selection of
leather handbags. They also sell, however, a modest assortment of luggage, vinyl bags, gloves, small personal
accessories, and umbrellas. All of these moderately
priced (by Paris standards) items are featured in a rainbow-colored range of fashionable styles and shapes and
cost about 20% less than in their U.S. boutiques.
*11 rue du Faubourg–St.-Honoré, 8e; tel.: 47.42.79.13;
Métro: Concorde or Madeleine
open Monday–Saturday 10 A.M.–6:45 P.M.
41 rue du Four, 6e; tel.: 45.48.85.88;
Métro: St.-Sulpice
74 rue de Passy, 16e; tel.: 45.27.14.49; Métro: Muette
open Monday–Saturday 10:15 A.M.–7 P.M.*

Gucci

Gucci's selection of handsome real- and faux-leather bags,
accessories, and ready-to-wear is astounding. The only
problem is that most people leave the store even more
exhausted than when they entered because the boutique
is spread out over four different floors!
*2 rue du Faubourg–St.-Honoré, 8e tel.: 42.96.83.27;
Métro: Concorde or Madeleine
350 rue St.-Honoré, 1er; tel.: 42.96.83.27;
Métro: Tuileries*

open Monday–Saturday 9:30 A.M.–6:30 P.M. except
Wednesday 10:30 A.M.–6:30 P.M.

• ## Rue Boissy d'Anglas •

Territoire

This is probably as close as you'll come to a French country store. Territoire specializes in a hodgepodge of merchandise that has some kind of relationship to hobbies and leisure time. Here you're apt to unearth just about anything from delightfully pretty guest registers to a pair of vibrant batik-print bathing trunks! Sonorous notes of Vivaldi and Mozart fill this large, homey space, rendering Territoire an even more pleasant place for the discovery of eclectic French gift items.

Next door to the main entrance of Territoire is their children's boutique which houses a darling collection of typically French toys and games, many of which are handcrafted.

30 rue Boissy d'Anglas, 8e; tel.: 42.66.22.13;
Métro: Madeleine
open Monday–Saturday 10:30 A.M.–7 P.M.

Orient Express

The huge Venetian glass chandelier, the wood-paneled walls, and the overall small proportions of this boutique do indeed make you feel as though you are on your way to some distant land on the famed Orient Express. Nearly everything you behold on that luxury train is sold here in the boutique (except for the scenery of course), including towels, china, crystal, linen, silver, and even books and posters depicting the fine art of travel on the Venice Simplon Orient Express.

15 rue Boissy d'Anglas, 8e; tel.: 47.42.24.45;
Métro: Concorde
open Monday–Friday 10 A.M.–6:30 P.M.; Saturday
10 A.M.–1 P.M. and 2:15–6:30 P.M.

Au Bain Marie

This is one of those types of stores that is intrinsically Parisian—no one has ever duplicated it and no one will ever be able to either. Au Bain Marie's frightfully high ceilings, pale-pink walls, and white wedding-cake moldings showcase magnificently dressed tables in a Hollywoodian decor. These tables, as well as all of the beautiful collectibles that adorn them, are the fruit of owner Aude Clément's creative passion for *l'art de la table*. When working as a restaurant/food critic, Madame Clément learned where to unearth the rare linens and *objets* that give a table its soul and discovered that there was not one boutique in Paris that offered such an eclectic mix of tablewares. Hence, Au Bain Marie was born, and its success has created an entirely new look in the fine art of dining—one that has changed the face of table dressing throughout the entire world.

Asparagus plates, *trompe-l'oeil* dishes, Art Deco tea services, and multicolored cutlery are just a few of the items to which Aude Clément has given new meaning; countless versions of these antique pieces have been reproduced for the shop as well as exported abroad. Handsome old items (crystal, silver, etc.) that speak of long, luxurious dinners are presented in the glass cases displayed throughout the boutique. More contemporary versions of table-dressing chic, in the form of French bistro ware or Limoges china, are also sold at Au Bain Marie (ask for their mail order catalogue). Upstairs you'll discover a refined collection of antique house linens as well as some modern-day series that have been made expressly for the boutique. If you love to cook, take a look at their gastronomic book corner to the left of the boutique as you head out the door. *Bon appétit!*

12 rue Boissy d'Anglas, 8e; tel.: 42.66.59.74;
Métro: Concorde
open Monday–Saturday 10 A.M.–7 P.M.

Place de la Concorde

Boutique Crillon

Just around the corner from the rue Boissy d'Anglas is the Hôtel Crillon, one of Paris's most exclusive hotels. Inside to your left is the hotel's gift shop which sells the porcelain, crystal, bathwear, and faux-leather traveling bags that bear the Crillon's symbols: ivy and laurel. Before

you leave, why not toast your day's purchases with a glass of champagne from the hotel's bar.
10 place de la Concorde, 8e; tel.: 49.24.00.52;
Métro: Concorde
open daily 9 A.M.–10:30 P.M.

. ## Rue Royale .

Ken Lane

Well-made, eye-catching faux jewels are sold here for those of us who can't afford Place Vendôme–quality gems.
7 rue Royale, 8e; tel.: 42.66.28.85;
Métro: Concorde
14 rue de Castiglione, 1er; tel.: 42.60.69.56;
Métro: Tuileries or Concorde
open Monday–Saturday 10 A.M.–6:30 P.M.

Christofle

Christofle's 170-year-old reputation is based on having developed silverplate of the finest quality. There are many Christofle "pavillons" throughout Paris that are similar to those in the U.S. but shop here in the newly decorated rue Royale store where the selection is the best and the atmosphere is grander. Price wisely because the savings are practically non-existent on certain items (such as their jewelry), whereas with other pieces, you may save as much as 35% with the *détaxe*.

If you have time, ask to see their museum which traces the history of Christofle through the creation of some of their most significant pieces.
9 rue Royale, 8e; tel.: 49.33.43.00; Métro: Concorde
24 rue de la Paix, 2e; tel.: 42.65.62.43; Métro: Opéra
open Monday–Saturday 9:30 A.M.–6:30 P.M.
17 rue de Sèvres, 6e; tel.: 45.48.16.17;
Métro: Sèvres-Babylone
open Tuesday–Saturday 10 A.M.–7 P.M.
95 rue de Passy, 16e; tel.: 46.47.51.27; Métro: Muette
open Tuesday–Saturday 9:30 A.M.–7 P.M.

Lalique

Once a master jewelry maker, René Lalique switched to glass making in the early 1900s. From the beginning, Monsieur Lalique received great acclaim for his magnificent sculptural glass pieces, many of which embraced Art Nouveau and Art Deco designs. Since the founder's death in 1945, a few changes have taken place that have only enhanced the basic traditions of this celebrated house; Lalique's satiny masterpieces are now crafted in crystal rather than glass and some of the pieces are also presented in color (an innovation that Marie-Claude Lalique recently introduced to the firm).

The boutique on rue Royale is fairy-tale–like from the crystal door handles to the luminous display cases that present the frosted-sugar wonders in the most mouth-watering ways. The first boutique is devoted to home-decor items; the second (through the courtyard) specializes in arts of the table. Price savings run 15–25% and the boutique will gladly handle shipping.

11 rue Royale, 8e; tel.: 42.66.52.40; Métro: Concorde open Monday–Saturday 9:30 A.M.–6:30 P.M.

Bernardaud

Bernardaud, the whitest porcelain of the Limoges family, is also France's best-seller. This modern, recently opened boutique showcases many of Bernardaud's more than 200 patterns and shapes (all are available but all are not on display) on the glass shelves that line the black and white walls of the store. Prices are about 25–35% less than in the U.S. and the boutique takes care of shipping. Note: Orders are filled more quickly here (usually within a month) than at other stores that carry Bernardaud.

11 rue Royale, 8e; tel.: 47.42.82.66; Métro: Concorde open Monday–Saturday 9:30 A.M.–6:30 P.M.

Cristalleries de Saint-Louis

Numerous changes have taken place on the pristine rue Royale since the beginning of 1990: the opening of the Bernardaud boutique; Christofle moving across the street into new headquarters; and the most recent development, the opening of the flagship Saint-Louis store in a steel-grey, jewel-like interior. With this showcase setting, the Cristalleries de Saint-Louis should finally receive the worldwide recognition they deserve.

The company, which received its royal name from King

Louis IX, was actually founded in 1767 on the site of an old glassworks in Lorraine, dating back to 1586. The Cristalleries de Saint-Louis were the first to produce full lead crystal in France, and today, each piece is still made almost entirely by hand. Prices are considerably less than in the States and the shop will arrange shipping.

13 rue Royale, 8e; tel.: 40.17.01.74
Métro: Concorde or Madeleine
open Monday–Saturday 10 A.M.–6:30 P.M.

Bonpoint

Created just over a decade ago by Marie-France Cohen and Dominique Swildens (parfumeur Annick Gouthal's sisters), Bonpoint reeks of age-old charm and tradition. The store's pink-flowered carpeting and cream-colored walls form a perfect setting for their classically styled children's clothing, considered to be the most luxurious in all of Paris. Smocked dresses, grey flannel bermudas, and delicate lace-trimmed shirts are just a few of the elegant fashions featured *chez* Bonpoint. All of their timeless styles are of the finest quality, are beautifully made, and, needless to say, are terribly expensive (although still less so than in their New York boutique). Bonpoint does, however, represent the ultimate chic in childrenswear (ages 0–16 years). If you are looking to offer the perfect present for that special little one in your life—this is the place to shop.

15 rue Royale, 8e; tel.: 47.42.52.63; Métro: Concorde
67 rue de l'Université, 7e; tel.: 45.50.32.18;
Métro: Solférino
open Monday–Saturday 10 A.M.–7 P.M.

Ladurée

Shopping on rue Royale is not complete without a pause in Paris's most classic tearoom, Ladurée. If you aren't pushed aside by the eager people at the pastry counter to the left as you enter, you'll first notice the rich wood-paneled walls, the Boucher-styled ceiling paintings, and, above all, the little rectangular wooden tables that are set up so that all of the clients face out toward the entrance of this distinguished-looking tea parlor. This is of course typically French, because no matter where you go or how well or badly you are dressed, the French will take note of how you look in the most indiscrete manner. This perhaps is why Ladurée is so tremendously popular with Paris's little old ladies. If the waitresses try to hustle you upstairs to their extra salon, see if you can wait for a table on the main level, so that you may peoplewatch as well.

Interesting surroundings are not the only thing in which you may indulge at Ladurée, for their creamy pastries and buttery croissants are among the best in town. Delicious lunches consisting of grilled salmon and finger sandwiches are also served on silver trays that are as refined as the clientele. Ladurée offers scrumptious take-out goodies, too.

16 rue Royale, 8e; tel.: 42.60.21.79;
Métro: Concorde or Madeleine
open Monday–Saturday 8:30 A.M.–7 P.M.

Delvaux

For the past 160 years Belgian-based Delvaux has been handcrafting classically styled leather goods for discriminating clients, including members of Belgium's royal family. Enter the handsome stone-walled interior of Delvaux's recently opened Paris outpost to discover their elegant, and unfortunately terribly expensive line of high-quality, all-leather bags, briefcases, and personal accessories— not yet available stateside.

18 rue Royale, 8e; tel.: 42.60.85.95;
Métro: Madeleine
open Monday–Saturday 10 A.M.–7 P.M.

Villeroy & Boch

Best known for their *faïence* (refined earthenware), this centuries-old Luxembourgian company offers a charming selection of country-like dishes that are functional enough to use every day (dishwasher-safe). Some contemporary styles and porcelain services have also been added to the Villeroy & Boch line. Prices run about 20% lower than in the U.S.

21 rue Royale, 8e; tel.: 42.65.81.84;
Métro: Concorde or Madeleine
open Monday–Saturday 10 A.M.–6:15 P.M.

Carel

22 rue Royale, 8e; see Left Bank description p. 137

Rodier Homme

This rather small and unimpressive boutique can easily be missed as you stroll down the elegant rue Royale. However, if you are a fan of Rodier menswear, this is one of the best boutiques in Paris. All of their fine-quality knits and separates are sold here in great abundance at prices about 20–30% below those in the U.S.
22 rue Royale, 8e; tel.: 42.60.20.86;
Métro: Concorde or Madeleine
open Monday 10 A.M.–7 P.M.; Tuesday–Saturday
9:30 A.M.–7 P.M.

Façonnable

Elegant and classically styled men's ready-to-wear and accessories bearing the Façonnable label enrich the British-styled interior of this exclusive boutique.
25 rue Royale, 8e; tel.: 47.42.72.60; Métro: Madeleine
174 bd St.-Germain, 6e; tel.: 40.49.02.47;
Métro: St.-Germain-des-Prés
open Monday 2–7 P.M.; Tuesday–Saturday
10 A.M.–7 P.M.

Cerruti 1881

I can think of no happier marriage in the world of fashion than that of Italian quality with French styling. Such is the case for Nino Cerruti who developed his family's highly respected textile business into a house that is now considered one of Paris's frontrunners in deluxe men's ready-to-wear. The Cerruti look is one of sheer elegance and good taste; the designer's lines are smooth, well-tailored, and, most importantly, beautifully made. (Custom-mades take three to four weeks.) The store's suits, jackets, and pants collections, are located upstairs; the main floor presents a gorgeous selection of men's accessories, shirts, shoes, and their more sporty (and more moderately priced) line, Brothers.

27 rue Royale, 8e; tel.: 42.65.68.72;
Métro: Madeleine
open Monday 10 A.M.–1 P.M. and 2–7 P.M.; Tuesday–
Saturday 10 A.M.–7 P.M.

Place de la Madeleine

Le Peny

Next door to Cerruti, Le Peny is one of the best places in the neighborhood to stop for lunch or a quick *café crème*. Their menu includes fresh salads, cold plates, and delicious *plats du jour*. Don't miss their luscious desserts, especially their gooey coconut cake (called Peny coco) which is even better than Mom's back home! If the weather is nice, be sure to sit outside on their terrace where you'll have a spectacular view of the *Madeleine* church.

3 place de la Madeleine, 8e; tel.: 42.65.06.75;
Métro: Madeleine
open Monday–Saturday 7 A.M.–10 P.M.; Sunday
11 A.M.–10 P.M.

Odiot

If you can't drum up the nerve to walk inside, at least take a look at the museum-like display of magnificently crafted silver, gold, and vermeil pieces that embellish the windows of this distinguished boutique. Since 1690, Odiot has responded to the discerning needs of France's aristocracy and, later, upper upper class by creating, especially for them, their own patterns and by personalizing them with the coat of arms or initials of their families. If you do decide to enter this terribly discrete looking boutique, you may just discover a few treasures that are very much within your budget—how about a vermeil tumbler for $40?

7 place de la Madeleine, 8e; tel.: 42.65.00.95;
Métro: Madeleine
open Monday–Friday 9:30 A.M.–6:30 P.M.; Saturday
10 A.M.–1 P.M. and 2:15–6:30 P.M.

Baccarat

This new and luxurious store is quite a change from the
warehouse-like setting of the main Baccarat showroom
(see p. 280), but it does, however, provide a more appropriate setting for receiving Arab princes and other important personalities looking to replenish their supply of
this legendary crystal. As soon as you walk in the door,
you will most likely be greeted by an overzealous young
lady asking to assist you in some way; don't feel in-
timidated—she's just doing her job.

The two floors of the boutique are set up into individual
rooms, that make you feel as though you were inside a
small crystal-coated mansion on the *place de la Madeleine*.
If you want to look at glassware, go upstairs to the "dining
room," chandeliers are suspended in the stairway, etc.
The rosewood floors create an overall warm and cheery
decor which is of course sumptuous. The crystal, normally
considered to be a rather cold substance, is set off with
rich home accessories such as Limoges china, Christofle,
and a varied range of *objects*. The price savings on the
Baccarat run about 30–40% and, yes, they do ship.
11 place de la Madeleine, 8e; tel.: 42.65.36.26;
Métro: Madeleine
open Monday–Saturday 9:45 A.M.–6:30 P.M.;
see Paradise Street description p. 282

Cerruti Femme

15 place de la Madeleine, 8e; see Left Bank
description p. 155

Maison de la Truffe

If you are looking for the ultimate gourmet gift item, why
not bring home a small package of preserved truffles
(the ones that you find underground at the foot of oak
trees—not the chocolates)? La Maison de la Truffe also
offers a choice selection of canned foie gras, pâté, and

caviar to help you through French-food withdrawal once you've arrived back home.

19 place de la Madeleine, 8e; tel.: 42.65.53.22;
Métro: Madeleine
open Monday–Saturday 9 A.M.–8 P.M.

Hédiard

Most visitors to the French capital associate fine comestibles with the name Fauchon. However, the Parisians know that Hediard is also a good address for stocking up on gourmet items that you don't necessarily find in your corner *épicerie*. Special recognition goes to Hediard's exotic selection of teas and spices as well as their dangerously delicious *pâte de fruit* (sugared jellies made with real fruit flavorings). All of these delectable items come in an assortment of gift packages—perfect for friends back home. If you want to stop for a more substantial snack, don't miss Hediard's gourmet-styled restaurant at the place de la Madeleine address.

21 place de la Madeleine, 8e; tel.: 42.66.44.36;
Métro: Madeleine
126 rue du Bac, 7e; tel.: 45.44.01.98;
Métro: Sèvres-Babylone
76 av Paul-Doumer, 16e; tel.: 45.04.51.92;
Métro: Muette
open Monday–Saturday 9:15 A.M.–11 P.M.

Eres

If you shop at all of the fabulous food stores on the place de la Madeleine, you'll never be able to fit into the body-hugging *maillots* sold in this boutique. Eres is the Parisian specialist of swimwear; their fashions are soft, sophisticated, and always up-to-date (even when it's a 50s-styled number). In addition to bathing suits, Eres also shows a flattering collection of cover-ups, *paréos*, and assorted *maillots* that may just as easily be worn with a dressy suit as for a swim at the beach.

2 rue Tronchet, 8e (on the place de la Madeleine);
tel.: 47.42.24.55; Métro: Madeleine
open Monday–Saturday 9:30 A.M.–7 P.M.
4 bis rue du Cherche-Midi, 6e; tel.: 45.44.95.54;
Métro: St.-Sulpice
open Monday–Saturday 10:30 A.M.–7 P.M.

Fauchon

Foodie or not, every self-respecting visitor should set aside some time when in Paris to visit Fauchon. Fauchon pays homage to what the French people like to do most on earth: eat—and just not anything, mind you. From the minute you approach this large, bustling establishment, you see crowds of people, noses pressed up against the store's windows, oohing and aahing over the mouth-watering delicacies and exotic fresh fruits and vegetables that have been so exquisitely displayed before them.

Once you enter the store, you are confronted with the difficult decision of which direction to take: toward the frightfully rich pâté, foie gras, or jarred specialties section; onward to the superbly well stocked offerings from the cellar; upstairs to their divine selection of jams, jellies, and honeys; or across the street to an even more tempting assortment of sweets. As you pursue your hunt, don't overlook their seemingly endless parade of mustards or their exotic array of teas and coffees. If you plan to stay in Paris for Thanksgiving, be sure to pick up cans of pumpkin and cranberry sauce, too.

26 place de la Madeleine, 8e; tel.: 47.42.60.11;
Métro: Madeleine
open Monday–Saturday 9:40 A.M.–7 P.M.

Rue Saint-Honoré

Grès

Grès is back in full swing—not with Madame Grès at the helm, but instead, headed up with a talented young Japanese designer and backed by a group of adept Japanese businessmen. The person in charge, however, is a French-woman, Jill Soudant, and the look is one of sheer Parisian elegance. With prices starting at the $1,000 mark for a simple cocktail dress, this is not the place to go for an ordinary frock. Yet this is the only place where you may find the Grès luxury ready-to-wear line (another line is sold through licensing agreements in Japan) as well as their exclusively-designed accessories. If this is all a little too much for you, you may still content yourself with a considerably more reasonably priced bottle of Cabochard.

422 rue Saint-Honoré, 8e; tel.: 42.60.72.00;
Métro: Madeleine or Concorde
open Monday—Saturday 10 A.M.—7 P.M.

Cassegrain

Since 1919, the name Cassegrain has been synonymous with high-quality engraving and paper products. Stop at this fashionable Parisian address to purchase elegant stationery, handsome leather desk accessories, and self-indulgent writing instruments by big names: Mont-Blanc, Waterman, and Shaeffer.

422 rue St.-Honoré, 8e; tel.: 42.60.20.08;
Métro: Concorde or Madeleine
open Monday—Saturday 9:30 A.M.—6:30 P.M.
81 rue des Saints-Pères, 6e; tel.: 42.22.04.76;
Métro: Sèvres-Babylone
open Tuesday—Saturday 10 A.M.—7 P.M.

Escada

418 rue St.-Honoré, 8e; see av Montaigne
description p. 39

Au Nain Bleu

The F.A.O. Schwarz of Paris, Au Nain Bleu first opened its doors in 1836 at the onset of the golden age of porcelain-faced dolls. These magnificent dolls may still be found here today along with an adorable collection of doll clothing, stuffed animals, miniature porcelain tea sets, wooden sailboats (the ones that the French children sail in the Tuileries fountains), games, and hundreds of other luxurious gift ideas from Paris's most famous toy store!

408 rue St.-Honoré, 8e; tel.: 42.60.39.01;
Métro: Concorde
open Monday—Saturday 9:45 A.M.—6:15 P.M.

Laurèl

Laurèl, like its parent company, Escada, is also beginning to take the Parisian ready-to-wear scene by storm. The same unbeatable fashion formula holds suit: highly stylish quality fashion separates that may be coordinated in a multitude of forms.

402 rue St.-Honoré, 1er; tel.: 42.60.13.89;
Métro: Concorde
open Monday–Saturday 10 A.M.–7 P.M.

Emilio Robba

392 rue Saint-Honoré, 1er; see Passages description
p. 205

Gucci

350 rue St.-Honoré, 1er; see rue du Faubourg–St.-
Honoré description p. 69

Georges Rech

Georges Rech is one of those popular French women's
ready-to-wear manufacturers that you don't hear much
about in the U.S. Although classically styled, Georges
Rech's clothing possesses just the right fashion know-how
to give it a distinctly Parisian flair. The quality is fine and
the prices are lower than at the neighboring designer boutiques.
273 rue St.-Honoré, 1er; tel.: 42.61.41.14;
Métro: Concorde
54 rue du Bonaparte, 6e; tel.: 43.26.84.11;
Métro: St.-Germain-des-Prés
23 av Victor-Hugo, 16e; tel.: 45.00.83.19;
Métro: Etoile
open Monday 11 A.M.–7 P.M.; Tuesday–Saturday 10
A.M.–7 P.M.

Louis Féraud

265 rue St.-Honoré, 1er; see rue du Faubourg–
St.-Honoré description p. 59

Max Mara

265 rue St.-Honoré, 1er; see Left Bank description
p. 134

Laura Ashley

I've found that savings on a lot of Laura Ashley's English
country fashions tend to be rather hit-or-miss. Basically

you have to be price-savvy—certain items may be marked about 10% lower in France, others may cost considerably more than in the U.S. The January sales, however, are always a sure bet, especially since you'll probably pick up something that will never go out of fashion.

The savings on the Laura Ashley home-decorating materials are more consistent. You may look around at their home-decorating showroom on the rue de Grenelle, but if you want to make a purchase, go to Coolman. (See Coup de Foudre description p. 281)

261 rue St.-Honoré, 1er; tel.: 42.86.84.13;
Métro: Concorde
94 rue de Rennes, 6e; tel.: 45.48.43.89; Métro: Rennes
open Monday noon–7 P.M.; Tuesday–Saturday 10
A.M.–7 P.M.
34 rue de Grenelle, 7e; tel.: 45.48.84.48 (home-
decorating showroom); Métro: Bac
open Monday–Friday 10 A.M.–1 P.M. and 2–6:30 P.M.

Alexandre de Paris

For those of you who remember the outrageous hairdos worn by Marisa Berenson and photographed by Richard Avedon in the *Vogue* magazines of the 60s and 70s, you may recall that the star coiffeur was Alexandre. Now you no longer have to refer to the pages of magazines to indulge yourself in the illustrious talents of this famed hairdresser.

The Alexandre de Paris boutique, which specializes in luxurious hair accessories, offers just about everything for your curly locks except Alexandre's magical scissors. The day I discovered the beautiful hair ornaments that glorify the three floors of this boutique, I longed to have once again the shoulder-length coif of my high-school years. Whether you're looking for headbands, combs, barrettes, scungees, clips, or a gold-threaded snood, you will find it all here in the most refined styles and materials, including taffeta, satin, leather, suede, velvet, and hand-embroidered wonders by Lesage. The prices, although high, are not as lofty as you would imagine for such fine-quality pieces that remain exclusive to Paris. If you're like me and have hair so short that it wouldn't hold a comb, you can always content yourself with one of their satin evening bags or Art Nouveau–inspired hand mirrors.

235 rue St.-Honoré, 1er; tel.: 42.61.41.34;
Métro: Concorde or Tuileries
open Monday–Saturday 9:45 A.M.–7 P.M.

Goyard

Parisians' most exclusive address for travel bags, Goyard offers an ultraluxurious collection of baggage in plastified canvas printed with their famous trademark design of light grey and gold herringbone on black background. An excellent address for the discriminating traveler who does not like to overtly promote signature brands, this family-owned business has been making quality leather goods since 1850. In addition to their more esoteric selection of library trunks, hat boxes, and dog carriers, Goyard also offers a handsome choice of leather handbags and personal items.
233 rue St.-Honoré, 1er; tel.: 42.60.57.04;
Métro: Tuileries
open Monday–Saturday 10 A.M.–6:30 P.M.

Didier Lamarthe

Didier Lamarthe, a name that has gained great momentum in recent years, is known for their classically designed fine-quality leather and faux-leather bags, luggage, and accessories. The fabrication is French and in the States you will find them at Bendell's for much much more.
219 rue Saint-Honoré, 1er; tel.: 42.96.09.90;
Métro: Palais-Royal
open Monday–Saturday 10 A.M.–7 P.M.
19 rue de l'Echaudé, 6e; tel.: 43.29.47.03;
Métro: St.-Germain-des-Prés or Odéon
open Monday–Saturday 10 A.M.–7 P.M.;
Sunday 2:30–6 P.M.

Il Pour l'Homme

Imagine a store entirely devoted to every imaginable type of men's gift idea. At Il Pour l'Homme you don't have to imagine any longer because they specialize in providing clients with endless gift-giving possibilities for those of the *masculin* sex. Here you will not only find a classic assortment of ties, sweaters, and shirts but also hundreds of gadgets and accessories that include everything from

mini manicure sets to Eiffel Tower–emblazoned silk boxer shorts.
209 rue St.-Honoré, 1er; tel.: 42.60.43.56;
Métro: Tuileries
open Monday–Saturday 9:30 A.M.–7 P.M.
13 rue du Roi-de-Sicile, 4e; tel.: 42.76.01.81;
Métro: St-Paul
open Tuesday–Saturday 11 A.M.–2 P.M. 2:30–7 P.M.
68 rue de Grenelle, 7e; tel.: 45.44.98.27; Métro: Bac
open Monday 2–7 P.M.; Tuesday–Saturday 10:30
A.M.–1:15 P.M. and 2:30–7 P.M.

▪ Rue Saint-Florentin ▪

Jean Patou

Recently opened, this contemporary-looking, polished-oak–paneled boutique pays a handsome tribute to one of France's greatest couturiers, Jean Patou. The star attractions are not couture dresses, but rather very up-to-date women's accessories that intimate 1930s style and grace. Colorful costume jewelry handmade from Bakelite (a hard plastic used during the Art Deco period) and elegant leather bags are a few of the creations sold exclusively in this boutique. An equally striking selection of silk and chiffon scarves, men's ties, and a unique collection of Patou perfumes (created between 1925 and 1964) make up the list of items that are difficult to find elsewhere. Other Patou legends such as Joy and 1000 are also sold here for considerably less than in North America.
7 rue St.-Florentin, 8e; tel.: 42.60.36.10;
Métro: Concorde
open Monday–Saturday 10 A.M.–7 P.M.

▪ Rue Cambon ▪

Chanel

Just across from the service entrance of the Ritz Hotel is the sight where Mademoiselle Chanel first opened her couture house in 1928. Couture and ready-to-wear designer Karl Lagerfeld perpetuates the Chanel legacy in his updated versions of timeless chic; Mademoiselle's same braid-trimmed boxy-styled jackets, faux-pearl earrings, and long swingy gold chains work just as well in the 90s as they did in the first half of this century. The *grande dame* look has softened up, and now Chanel chic comes in the shape of everything from jeans to leather-trimmed watches.

I prefer the Cambon boutique to that of avenue Montaigne because the selection often seems better and the help is friendlier. Price savings are not as fantastic as we all would like. If you benefit from the *détaxe*, you may be able to save about 25% on certain items. Their famed earrings start at $95 for a basic pearl and go on up to $1,200 for a more elaborate pair of evening dangles. Unfortunately virtually nothing is on display, so as at many other Parisian boutiques, here you have to ask to be shown the coveted merchandise that has been hidden away.

31 rue Cambon, 1er; tel.: 42.86.28.00;
Métro: Concorde
open Monday–Saturday 9:30–6:30 P.M.
42 av Montaigne, 8e; tel.: 47.20.84.45 or 40.70.12.33
(watches);
Métro: Alma-Marceau
open Monday–Friday 9:30 A.M.*–6:30* P.M.*; Saturday*
10 A.M.*–1* P.M. *and 2–6:30* P.M.

Apostrophe

Apostrophe is one of those leading French womenswear manufacturers that is practically unknown to Americans. The store basically carries two different collections; one is classically styled and womanly; the other is young and swingy. Both are fashioned out of fine-quality fabrics. Prices reach those in the name-brand–designer category.

24 rue Cambon, 8e; tel.: 42.61.30.81;
Métro: Concorde or Madeleine
open Monday–Saturday 10 A.M.*–7* P.M.
54 rue Bonaparte, 6e; tel.: 43.29.08.38;
Métro: St.-Germain-des-Prés
open Monday–Saturday 10:30 A.M.*–7:30* P.M.

Gianfranco Ferre Femme

All of the grace and elegance that made this Italian designer worthy of being delegated the couturier *chez* Dior is demonstrated in Monsieur Ferre's deluxe ready-to-wear line. The boutique spotlights a selection of high-quality womenswear and accessories that is incomparable to those sold stateside.

23 rue Cambon, 1er; tel.: 42.61.97.27;
Métro: Concorde
open Monday–Saturday 10 A.M.–7 P.M.

Nina Ricci

22 rue Cambon, 1er; see av Montaigne description
p. 37

Sartore

14 rue Cambon, 1er; see Left Bank description
p. 140

• ## Rue de Castiglione •

Annick Goutal

Whenever any of my clients mentions a desire to purchase French perfume in Paris, I automatically recommend Annick Goutal. Once you enter the cream-and-gold interior of this jewel-like boutique, you will understand why.

To me, the Annick Goutal products embody a perfectly balanced harmony of Parisian refinement and French savoir faire. Former concert pianist Annick Goutal turned her musical virtuosities into the fine-tuned sense of smell that is required to become a "nose." The talent must have been innate, because since the beginning of the company in the early 80s, Annick Goutal has grown from 3 fragrances in one Paris boutique to 16 fragrances in over a half a dozen boutiques throughout France. These scents, which are blends of mostly natural extracts (as opposed to synthetic), have been developed by the artist herself on the *orgue* (or organ, which refers to the organ-like arrangement of the thousands of bottles of extracts that are needed in the creation of a new scent) located upstairs in the rue de Castiglione boutique.

The real showstopper, however, is the packaging. No one knows better than Annick Goutal that people buy fragrances and beauty products as much for the sight as for the smell. Who would ever think of offering just one bar of soap as a gift to someone? *Chez* Annick Goutal you may, because each bar of soap is individually wrapped in heavy gold paper, placed in a glossy white bag, and tied with a glittery gold ribbon—just dripping with class.

Prices which are competitive with the other big-name fragrances sold in Paris, are 25% lower (about 40% with the *détaxe*) than those stateside! Although Annick Goutal products are sold in a few prestigious department stores in the U.S., they still have an exclusive side to them that whispers of true Parisian chic.

14 rue de Castiglione, 1er; tel.: 42.60.52.82;
Métro: Tuileries or Concorde
16 rue de Bellechasse, 7e; tel.: 45.51.36.13;
Métro: Solférino
open Monday–Saturday 10 A.M.–7:30 P.M.

Ken Lane

14 rue de Castiglione, 1er; see rue Royale
description p. 72

Catherine

The boutique is so tiny that if you're not paying attention, you may walk right by it—but don't because Catherine's offers some of the best discount perfume, cosmetics, and beauty-products savings that exist in Paris. If you purchase a minimum of 1500 Fr worth of merchandise, price reductions (including *détaxe* of course) run up to 40%. French residents benefit from a 30% reduction. Ask for information about their mail-order service in case you need to replenish your supply once back home.

6 rue de Castiglione, 1er; tel.: 42.60.81.49;
Métro: Tuileries or Concorde
open Monday–Saturday 9:30 A.M.–7:30 P.M.

Jacqueline Perès

Jacqueline Perès has been dressing distinguished women for the past 20 years. Inside this bright and airy space you may choose from Madame Perès's collections and have your choice made up especially for you, in your desired color and size, within just 48 hours. It is this formula, halfway between couture and ready-to-wear, that has allowed Madame Perès to meet the needs of discriminating women who expect quality and fine workmanship, but who don't have the time for fussy fittings. Styles *chez* Madame Perès range from casual sportswear to dressy eveningwear; the look is one of subtle elegance. Needless to say, you won't find it elsewhere.

4 rue de Castiglione, 1er; tel.: 42.60.67.42;
Métro: Tuileries or Concorde
open Monday–Saturday 10 A.M.–7 P.M.

Place Vendôme

Guerlain

You may be disappointed to learn that Shalimar costs only slightly less in France than it does in America. This is the case for most of Guerlain's fragrances because Guerlain ships their extracts over to the U.S. where they are mixed, blended, and bottled for the American market. Some of you will be happy to learn, however, that certain scents, that are difficult (if not impossible) to find stateside are sold in all six of Guerlain's elegant perfume emporiums found throughout the French capital.

If you are able to plan ahead (one to two weeks), treat yourself to a lavish skin-care treatment at Guerlain's beauty institutes on rue de Sèvres and the Champs-Elysées.

2 place Vendôme, 1er; tel.: 42.60.68.61;
Métro: Tuileries or Concorde
29 rue de Sèvres, 6e (boutique and beauty center);
tel.: 42.22.46.60; Métro: Sèvres-Babylone
68 av des Champs-Elysées, 8e; (boutique and beauty
center); tel.: 45.62.52.57; Métro: Franklin-Roosevelt
93 rue de Passy, 16e; tel.: 42.88.41.62; Métro: Muette
open Monday–Friday 9:30 A.M.–6:45 P.M.; Saturday
9:45 A.M.–7 P.M.

Giorgio Armani

As you enter the mirrored cubicles that make up the museum-like setting of this Armani boutique, you have the impression that the clothing inside is more for hanging on your wall than for wearing on your back. The effect is quite dramatic, and if the finely woven linen suits are out of your budget, don't miss the artist's silk and chiffon scarves priced at $220.

At the opposite end of place Vendôme is the Emporio Armani boutique which features more affordable Armani creations in a far less intimidating setting.

6 place Vendôme, 1er; tel.: 42.61.55.09;
Métro: Tuileries or Concorde
25 place Vendôme, 1er; tel.: 42.61.02.34 (Emporio Armani); Métro: Opéra
open Monday–Saturday 10 A.M.–7 P.M.

Lesage/Schiaparelli

Located in the former residence of famed couturière Elsa Schiaparelli, this enchanting boutique offers a wonderful glimpse at Lesage's 120-year-old history of high-style embroidery. Luminous gilt frames set into an all-black decor provide a theatrical setting for the beaded and embroidered women's accessories that shimmer from within this small boutique. Most of the pieces, whether jewelry or evening bags, are one-of-a-kinds and all are handmade. You'll probably never see anything like them anywhere else. Prices start at $175 and go up to $5,800.

21 place Vendôme, 1er; tel.: 40.20.95.79;
Métro: Opéra
open Tuesday–Friday 10 A.M.–6:30 P.M.; Saturday 10 A.M.–1 P.M. and 2–6:30 P.M.

Charvet

Although best known for their top-quality men's shirts, both ready-made and custom-made, Charvet also offers one of the most distinguished and least expensive gift ideas for men that exists in Paris: their braided-knot cuff links (three pairs for $30). These cuff links, which come in a fabulously rich range of colors, have come to act as a sort of trademark for this 152-year-old French company which represents the epitomy of elegant menswear.

28 place Vendôme, 1er; tel.: 42.60.30.70;
Métro: Opéra
open Monday–Saturday 9:45 A.M.–6:30 P.M.

• Rue de la Paix •

Daum

Although in existence since 1870, Daum (pronounced *Dome*) has become familar to many Americans in just the past few years. In 1986, artistic director Clotilde Bacri thoroughly rejuvenated the look of this reputable crystal company by commissioning contemporary artists Hilton McConnico, Phillippe Starck, and Salvadore Dali to create special works for the then fledgling Daum. The cactus series by American Hilton McConnico took off like wildfire and soon the crystal carafes with cactus-shaped *pâte de verre* (molten glass) stoppers were appearing in every other fashion and home-decorating magazine from New York to Tokyo. This new-found success prompted more works inspired by nature as well as a series of porcelain plates of the same theme. Most of Daum's pieces, whether jewelry, table arts, or objects, are highly sculptural and evoke subjects as wide and varied as superslick race cars to Art Deco–inspired vases. Prices run 20–30% lower than in the U.S.

4 rue de la Paix, 2e; tel.: 42.61.25.25;
Métro: Opéra
open Monday–Saturday 10 A.M.–7 P.M.

Paloma Picasso

Just as I was putting the last touches on this book I got wind of the upcoming opening of the world's first Paloma Picasso boutique. I can't give you my firsthand impressions since the workmen were still hammering away as we went to print, but I do know that here you can expect to see Paloma's exclusive collection of luxury fashion accessories and table arts as well as her world-renowned perfume and cosmetics.

5 rue de la Paix, 2e; tel. 42.86.02.21;
Métro: Opéra
open Monday–Saturday 10 A.M.–P.M.

Ermenegildo Zegna

Now that Zegna (*Zen-ya*) has opened their three-floor blockbuster store in New York, this superior-quality, Italian menswear label has begun to conquer the hearts, minds, and wallets of well-dressed American males. The recently expanded rue de la Paix boutique is the flagship store for the highly styled men's ready-to-wear and accessories line that was launched about ten years ago by this centuries-old Italian textile manufacturer. Paris prices (especially with *détaxe* and without New York sales tax) are considerably more interesting than those encountered stateside.

10 rue de la Paix, 2e; tel.: 42.61.67.61;
Métro: Opéra
open Monday–Saturday 10 A.M.–7 P.M.

Dunhill

Smoking, with all of the paraphernalia that enhances this ritual, is alive and well in France. English smokemaster Alfred Dunhill set up this Paris branch at the turn of the century and it continues to be one of the French capital's most reputable shops for the purchase of superior-quality tobaccos, cigars, pipes, lighters, cigar boxes, and many other distinguished-looking men's gift ideas.

15 rue de la Paix, 2e; tel.: 42.61.57.58;
Métro: Opéra
open Monday 10:30 A.M.–6:30 P.M.; Tuesday–
Saturday 9:30 A.M.–6:30 P.M.

Michel Swiss

Another good address for buying discounted perfumes and big-name accessories, this spacious boutique is located upstairs at 16 rue de la Paix. Plan to spend at least an hour here because the place is usually so crowded, and there is so much from which to choose, that stop-and-go shopping becomes next to impossible.

16 rue de la Paix, 2e; tel.: 42.61.61.11;
Métro: Opéra
open Monday–Saturday 9 A.M.–6:30 P.M.

Alain Figaret

Alain Figaret is one of the leading shirtmakers in France today. The selection is astronomical. For men, clients may choose from five different collars, three different sleeve lengths, two different cuffs, and countless styles in several different types of quality cottons! The women's selection is equally impressive and just as classically styled. The sales staff will readily help you with size equivalents. In addition to the shirts, the boutique sells a handsome collection of traditional men's and women's accessories including silk ties and bows.

21 rue de la Paix, 2e; tel.: 42.65.04.99;
Métro: Opéra
open Monday–Saturday 10 A.M.–7 P.M.
99 rue de Longchamp, 16e; tel.: 47.27.66.81;
Métro: Pompe or Trocadéro
open Monday 3–7 P.M.; Tuesday–Saturday 10 A.M.–7 P.M.

Repetto

Just a few toe steps away from the Opéra Garnier (which now stages primarily ballet performances rather than opera) is Repetto, France's most celebrated dancewear specialist. This is where long lithe *danseuses* and wide-eyed *petits rats* (the youngest members of the Paris Opera ballet company) come to pick up a fresh leotard or a new pair of ballet shoes. Repetto's selection equals their reputation for quality. If you know a little girl back home who dreams of becoming a prima ballerina, why not start her off with a rosy pink *maillot* from Repetto?

22 rue de la Paix, 2e; tel.: 47.42.47.88;
Métro: Opéra
open Monday–Saturday 10 A.M.–7 P.M.

Rue Danielle-Casanova

Maupiou Accessoires

Just next door to the reputable Maupiou silk-fabric emporium is this superstylish and trendy boutique of the same name. Maupiou Accessoires showcases mainly costume jewelry from many of Paris's hottest designers, including Patrick Retif, Dominique Aurientis, Migeon and Migeon, and Van Der Straeten—the ever-evolving list goes on ...

28 rue Danielle-Casanova, 2e; tel.: 42.61.16.66;
Métro: Opéra
open Monday–Saturday 10 A.M.–7 P.M.

Tassinari et Chatel

One of the most reputable silk houses of Lyon, Tassinari et Chatel has woven exquisite silk upholstery fabrics for the past two centuries. Purveyors to Europe's royal families during the 18th and 19th centuries, Tassinari's highly refined works have since been used to beautify interiors throughout the world. The firm's designs are as wide and varied as their clientele; modern graphic patterns by artists such as Dufy and Giraldon are shown along with more traditional motifs of spring flowers, *fleur-de-lys*, and classic stripes in order to create a well-composed selection of materials catering to a medley of tastes. Indeed, if you are looking to cover all four walls of your living room with one of their silken fabrics, the prices may seem a bit extravagant. However, if you are only interested in upholstering a favorite armchair or two, you will be pleasantly surprised with how affordable these sumptuous fabrics may be.

26 rue Danielle-Casanova, 2e; tel.: 42.61.74.08;
Métro: Opéra
open Monday–Friday 9–noon and 2–6 P.M.

■   **Rue Daunou**   ■

Harry's Bar

This landmark gathering spot for American residents and out-of-towners includes a few French people too. Harry's famous bloody Marys, bourbons, and hot dogs have comforted such legendary greats as Ernest Hemingway, F. Scott Fitzgerald, and Gloria Swanson since its beginnings in 1911. Live piano music is played in a dimly lit decor downstairs from 10 P.M. on.

5 rue Daunou, 2e; tel.: 42.61.71.14;
Métro: Opéra open daily 10–2 A.M.

* ## Avenue de L'Opéra *

Brentano's

If you're only halfway through your trip and you've run out of reading material, stock up at Brentano's. Prices here are of course more than those at home, but keep reminding yourself that all of the English-language publications in this famous bookstore are imports.

37 av de l'Opéra, 2e; tel.: 42.61.52.50;
Métro: Opéra
open Monday–Saturday 10 A.M.–7 A.M.

* ## Rue du 29 Juillet *

Destinations

If you're like a lot of other weary tourists and are tired of the junk-filled souvenir shops that line the rue de Rivoli, it's time to go to Destinations. This bright and spacious boutique is attractively stocked with the most innovative souvenir-type gift items that Paris has to offer, many of which have been designed exclusively for the shop under the artful eye of owner Jean Huèges. The boutique sells some traditional items such as authentic French berets and models of the Eiffel Tower, but the real fun begins with their more funky versions of typical French memorabilia, including glasses of faux Beaujolais wine, Eiffel Tower suspenders, pieces of glass from the *Pyramide du Louvre*, watches made out of old French stamps ($175) and floating Arc de Triomphes, croissant magnets shaped in real croissant dough ($4.75) as well as postcards, T-shirts, and prints made from Destinations's own fun-loving designs. Don't miss it!

9 rue du 29 Juillet, 1er; tel.: 49.27.98.90;
Métro: Tuileries
open Monday–Saturday 10:30 A.M.–7:30 P.M.

• Rue du Marché—Saint-Honoré •

> ### *Le Rubis*
>
> Stop into this small, rustic-looking wine bar for a piping hot *plat du jour,* a fresh cheese platter, or a hearty wedge of pâté—accompanied with a ruby-red glass of wine.
>
> *10 rue du Marché–St.-Honoré, 1er; tel.: 42.61.03.34; Métro: Tuileries*
> *open Monday–Friday 7 A.M.–10 P.M.*

• Place du Marché—Saint-Honoré •

Philippe Model

As you make your way around the place, stop into some of the up-and-coming designer boutiques which include Michel Léger, Corinne Cobson, Toile de Fond, and Dô. The place du Marché–St-Honoré has always served as a starting block for many of Paris's most inventive fashion designers. Philippe Model is no exception and his ingenious millinery talents have won him the reputation of one of Paris's most creative hatmakers. Monsieur Model's high-style look is further accentuated in his smart collection of gloves, bags, and shoes.

33 place du Marché–Saint-Honoré, 1er;
tel.: 42.96.89.02;
Métro: Tuileries
open Monday–Friday 10 A.M.–7 P.M.; Saturday 1–7
P.M.

Jean-Charles de Castelbajac

Probably Paris's most witty *créateur,* Jean Charles de Castelbajac boasts fashions and home accessories for those who have a sense of humor and who like to show it. Bright and colorful creations inspired by Warhol's Campbell soup can, the Betty Boop comic strip, Schultz's Snoopy, and even a koala-covered winter coat have helped to win people's hearts throughout the world. If your tastes tend to be less eccentric, don't miss the designer's celebrated blanket plaid sportswear that offers comfort and practicality without sacrificing style.

31 place du Marché–St.-Honoré, 1er;
tel.: 42.60.78.40;
Métro: Tuileries
open Monday–Saturday 10:30 A.M.–7 P.M.
5 rue des Petits-Champs, 1er, tel.:42.60.37.33,
Métro: Pyramides
open Monday 10 A.M.–1 P.M. and 2–7 P.M.; Tuesday–
Saturday 10 A.M.–7 P.M.

Elizabeth de Senneville (children's)

38 place du Marché–St.-Honoré, 1er;
see place des Victoires/Les Halles
description p. 189

Rue Saint-Roch

Renaud Pellegrino

Like neatly wrapped gifts or candy-colored treats, Renaud Pellegrino's handbags come in many different irresistible shapes and styles. The two things that remain the same, however, are their small size and jewel-like quality. Leather, satin, and grosgrain are fashioned into cute little geometric shapes and trimmed with bows, embroidery, feathers, and gold buttons. These charming and delightfully elegant bags have won the hearts of accessory connoisseurs throughout the world including Catherine Deneuve and Paloma Picasso. Although lower than in the U.S., prices are in the collectors'-item range.

10 rue St.-Roch, 1er; tel.: 42.60.69.36;
Métro: Tuileries
15 rue du Cherche-Midi, 6e; tel.: 45.44.56.37;
Métro: St.-Sulpice or Sèvres-Babylone
open Monday–Saturday 10:30 A.M.–1 P.M. and
1:45–7 P.M.

L'Heure Bleue

In one of the most unassuming Art Deco stores in Paris, Martine and Vincent Raderscheidt present their fruits of 20 years of collecting. In a long and narrow space, L'Heure Bleue highlights an eclectic mix of home-decor items such as vases, lamps, and some furniture along with an extensive collection of *objets* from the 20s and 30s.

17 rue St.-Roch, 1er; tel.: 42.60.23.22;
Métro: Tuileries
open Monday–Friday noon–7 P.M.; Saturday 2–
6:30 P.M.

Rarissime

If you take a close look at this cupboard-sized shop, you'll notice that it was built right into the thick stone walls of the majestic Saint Roch church. From 1630 until the mid-1970s, this tiny space played host to some of Paris's best-known *coiffeurs*, and legend has it that the fellows on their way to the nearby guillotine were first brought in here for their last "cut and shave." Today Rarissime has been taken over by the La Brosse family and its extraordinary charm has fortunately remained intact. The shop now boasts a small, but selective collection of antiques consisting largely of paintings and prints (there's not enough floor space for too much else) from the past couple of centuries.

18 rue St.-Roch, 1er; tel.: 42.96.30.49;
Métro: Tuileries
open Tuesday–Saturday 2–7 P.M.

• ## Rue de Rivoli •

William H. Smith

British-based William H. Smith has been satisfying the literary needs of English-speaking visitors and residences since 1903. The store offers a plentiful supply of English and American books, magazines, newspapers, and greeting cards including a well-stocked selection of maps and travel books for those of you who run astray in the City of Lights.

248 rue de Rivoli, 1er; tel.: 42.60.37.97;
Métro: Concorde
open Monday–Saturday 9:30 A.M.–7 P.M. except
Tuesday 10 A.M.–7 P.M.

Angelina's

I tend of feel that Angelina's is the most overrated tearoom in all of Paris. It is however, conveniently located across from the Tuileries gardens and not far from other major attractions such as the *Louvre* and the *place de la Concorde*. Their lunches, pastries, and legendary hot chocolate are quite good, but if you insist upon reasonably fast, efficient and cordial service, you might be better off going elsewhere.
226 rue de Rivoli, 1er; tel.: 42.96.47.10;
Métro: Tuileries
open Monday–9.30 A.M.–7 P.M.; Saturday and
Sunday 9:30 A.M.—7:30 P.M.

Galignani

Considered to be the oldest English-language bookstore in Europe, this 300-year-old, wood-paneled establishment provides a serene setting for perusing their large selection of English, American, and French publications. The store will gladly obtain long–sought-after books and ship them to you anywhere in the world.
224 rue de Rivoli, 1er; tel.: 42.60.76.07;
Métro: Tuileries
open Monday–Saturday 9:30 A.M.–7 P.M.

Gault

Some of the best-quality souvenir-type items in Paris, Jean-Pierre Gault's handmade ceramic houses enable you to bring back a piece of French architecture into your own home. Gault's miniature creations capture the spirit of Paris neighborhoods including Montmartre, Ile Saint-Louis, and the Marais, as well as the sunny region of Provence and other European cities such as Amsterdam and Venice. Each house averages about $90 and since you

need at least six to make up a little village, prices tend to add up fast. Détaxe minimum is 2,000 francs.
206 rue de Rivoli, 1er; tel.: 42.60.51.17;
Métro: Tuileries
open Monday–Saturday 10 A.M.–7 P.M.; Sunday
11 A.M.–7 P.M.
5 rue Norvins, 18e (at Montmartre); tel.: 46.06.23.38;
Métro: Abbesses
open daily 10 A.M.–midnight

· The Left Bank (The Parisians' Paris) ·

You have not experienced shopping in Paris until you have shopped on the Left Bank. I like to look at the Left Bank as the soul of Paris and the Right Bank as the showcase. The Left Bank is as casual and unpretentious as the Right Bank is formal and cool. There is a sense of free spirit on the Left Bank or *Rive Gauche*. Students have always had a stronghold on this area and it is still considered to be the center of intellectual activity and artistic expression. (L'Ecole des Beaux-Arts is located on the rue des Beaux Arts, and music from the neighborhood jazz clubs rings out long into the night.) Although the Right Bank does not have as much tradition deeply embedded into its streets, it does have one very solid reputation to uphold: the world's window on the *haute couture*.

Once you've realized this, you'll understand why Yves Saint Laurent went Rive Gauche in 1966 with his collection of high-fashion ready-to-wear (before then, France's best-dressed women only wore couture), and thus the fashion world began to look at the Left Bank in another light. Saint Laurent's Left Bank boutique is still there and many other big names such as Sonia Rykiel, Claude Montana, and Nino Cerruti have since set up shop on the rue de Grenelle, the Left Bank's most prestigious street for designer clothing. Even in these big-name boutiques the ambiance is warmer and more relaxed than on the other side of the river.

The real beauty of the Left Bank, however, is that it has remained the Parisians' Paris. Sure there are a lot of tourists, but not nearly as many as on the rue du Faubourg–

Saint-Honoré. Small, quaint hotels have replaced the need
for more glitzy palaces, but most of all, these are the streets
where many of the Parisians *live*. The ground floors may
be filled with scintillating storefronts, but the rest of the
buildings have for the most part remained residential,
which means that some of the boutiques' best business
comes from their neighbors. It's also nice to see that mixed
in with all of the fashion boutiques are neighborhood
grocers, butchers, and bakers as well as centuries-old
antique shops, interior-decorating showrooms, and newly
founded art galleries.

Visitors often think that they're "doing" Left Bank shopping when they're on the boulevard St.-Germain, the big
boulevard that horizontally cuts the Left Bank in two. Well,
you are and you aren't; boulevard St.-Germain can be a
great starting or stopping place, but the most interesting
boutiques are found on the little side streets that weave
in and out on either side of the boulevard. Most of the
shops directly on the boulevard are geared toward the
student crowd from the nearby Sorbonne, l'Ecole de Médecine, and l'Ecole des Sciences Politiques. The two
promenades that I have outlined for you cover the interesting streets to the north and south of the boulevard St.-
Germain.

No matter what route you take, if you follow my itinerary or make your own—don't miss the St.-Germain-des-
Prés church, Paris's second oldest church and one of the
finest examples of Romanesque architecture. Across from
the church is the *Café les Deux Magots* and next door
to that is the *Café de Flore*, Paris's two most famous
cafés, where writers the likes of Camus, Sartre, and Hemingway once conferred. You can sit here for hours with a
café au lait and watch the incredibly diverse types of
people come and go. As you leave, step into *La Hune* at
170 boulevard St.-Germain, Paris's most well known bookstore for literature, history, and art-history books. They're
open until midnight (except for Saturday and Sunday)
and, even though they don't have any books in English,
it is fun still to go and have a look around.

You'll notice that the streets that I have marked off for
you don't go as far as the place St-Michel, the very core
of the Latin Quarter. Although it's interesting to walk
through these winding old streets that conjure up images

of a Medieval past, the shops and restaurants here are tacky tourist traps.

The shopping along the *quais* (the riverbanks) can be pretty touristy too, but if you walk on the Seine side of the street you'll find yourself next to some of the world's greatest peddlers, the *bouquinistes*. Here in makeshift wooden storefronts you'll meet book salespeople as interesting as their eclectic assortment of goods: dusty old 19th-century novels by Flaubert, past issues of *Paris Match* magazine, turn-of-the-century postcards of Paris, engravings of Napoléon (France's greatest leader), and much, much more. If you become tired of looking at old bric-a-brac, just look toward the banks of the Seine for one of the world's most magnificent views!

Promenade North of the Boulevard Saint-Germain

I suggest that you start this tour at the St.-Germain-des-Prés church and head down the boulevard to the rue des Saints-Pères and then to the rue du Pré-aux-Clercs. From there, work your way northerly toward the Seine and then easterly toward the rue de Seine. Aside from the stores that I have indicated, enjoy exploring all of the gorgeous antique shops, decorators's showrooms, and art galleries that punctuate this part of the city. The tour ends at the colorful open-air market at rue de Buci. The Métro stop for the beginning of this promenade is St.-Germain-des-Prés or Odéon.

STREETS:

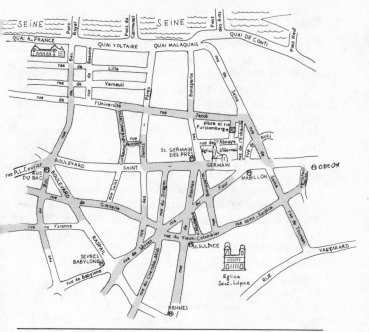

• Boulevard Saint-Germain •

Daniel Hechter If you're a Daniel Hechter fan, you'll love this handsome boutique filled with a prodigious amount of moderately priced classic and sporty fashions for men and women. It's a good address for traditional women's and men's apparel (Monsieur Hechter stopped designing children's clothing a few years ago.) Shop in this newly decorated Right Bank boutique where the setting is far more homey (Daniel Hechter has tried to re-create the clubby-type ambiance of a French yuppy's interior) than that of the Left Bank outlet.

146 bd St.-Germain, 6e; tel.: 43.26.96.36;
Métro: Odéon
2 pl de Passy, 16e; tel.: 42.88.01.11; Métro: La Muette
open Monday–Saturday 10 A.M.–7 P.M.
66 rue François 1er; tel.: 40.70.94.38;
Métro: George V or Alma-Marceau
open Monday—Saturday 10:30 A.M.–7:30 P.M.
Daniel Hechter

Kashiyama

Kashiyama shows many of the most sophisticated international designers of the moment: Romeo Gigli, Martin Margela, Dolce & Gabbana, Sybilla, Ozbek, John Galliano, and Byblos. The names are constantly changing, and those who are "in" this year may not necessarily be "in" the next. Since the mid-1980s, however, they have continued to show a nice selection of Ramosport and Ramowear winter coats and raincoats. The boutique near Les Halles shows the designers that are even more on the cutting edge of fashion.

Don't miss their selection of lingerie (mostly Italian) and stockings downstairs. I have never seen such an efficient way of displaying lingerie in all of Paris. Instead of your having to ask to be shown certain items, they are all right there in front of you, attached to a series of wooden panels that you can flip through at your own leisure.

147 bd St-Germain, 6e; tel.: 46.34.11.50;
Métro: St.-Germain-des-Prés
open Monday 11 A.M.–7 P.M.; Tuesday–Saturday 10
A.M.–7 P.M.
80 rue Jean-Jacques–Rousseau, 1er;
tel.: 40.26.46.46; Métro: Etienne-Marcel
open Monday–Friday 10 A.M.–12:30 P.M. and 1:30–7
P.M.; Saturday 11 A.M.–12:30 P.M. and 1:30–7 P.M.

Façonnable

174 bd St.-Germain, 6e; see Right Bank description
p. 76

Sonia Rykiel

I'm sure that the fashion world is grateful that Sonia Rykiel finally moved out of her cubbyhole headquarters on the rue de Grenelle into this considerably larger, more spacious location on the Saint-Germain. Here amidst a bright blondwood decor, you may admire all of the luxurious knits that have made this designer famous throughout the world. The entire space is devoted to Madame Rykiel's women's fashions and accessories as well as her signature house linens, cosmetics, and gourmet-quality comestibles.

175 bd St.-Germain, 6e; tel.: 49.54.60.60;
Métro: St.-Germain-des-Prés

70 rue du Faubourg–Saint-Honoré, 8e;
tel.: 42.65.20.81; Métro: Concorde
open Monday–Saturday 10 A.M.–7 P.M.

· Rue des Saints-Pères ·

Junko Shimada

You may not already know about Junko Shimada because this Japanese designer does not yet have a boutique in the U.S. The look in the rue des Saints-Pères boutique is considerably different from the more high-fashion approach used on the clothes shown at the rue Etienne-Marcel address.

Here, many of the young and fun styles have been inspired from more traditional clothing. Shimada's solid and striped casual jackets look as though they're direct spin-offs from our classic American baseball jackets. (The Japanese do love that sport, don't they?) Another collection boasts very stylish short skirts, tightly fitted jackets, and leather-trimmed plastified canvas bags—all in brightly colored tartan plaids. Except for the skirts and a few of the jackets, most of the amusing sportswear in this boutique is interchangeable between guys and gals. Prices run moderate to expensive.

34 rue des Saints-Pères, 7e; tel.: 42.22.58.55;
Métro: St.-Germain-des-Prés
54 rue Etienne-Marcel, 1er (women's);
tel.: 42.36.36.97 Métro: Etienne-Marcel
open Monday 2–7 P.M.; Tuesday–Friday 10 A.M.–7
P.M.; Saturday 11 A.M.–7 P.M.

Debauve & Gallais

In 1800, chocolate had a somewhat dubious reputation. People were unclear as to whether it should be treated as a drug or a sweet. The problem was solved easily enough when Debauve & Gallais, a pharmacist and a chocolate maker, teamed up to open one of Paris's first chocolate shops. The myth surrounding the miraculous healing effects of chocolate has since disappeared (or at least diminished), but the jewel-like packages containing flavor-

ful, full-bodied chocolate candies have remained at Debauve & Gallais.
30 rue des Saints-Pères, 6e; tel.: 45.48.54.67;
Métro: St.-Germain-des-Prés
open Tuesday–Saturday 10 A.M.–1 P.M. and 2–7 P.M.

- ## Rue Perronet •

Sonia Rykiel Homme

Paris had to wait a long time—until 1989—for the arrival
of this Sonia Rykiel boutique exclusively consecrated to
men. This warm and intimate shop is stocked from hardwood floor to ceiling with an inexhaustible supply of
men's jackets, pants, shirts, sweaters, bathrobes, and accessories that include ties, belts, socks, and travel bags.
The Rykiel man is dressed for any sort of romantic adventure in these clothes that are handsomely styled in an
array of plush, modern colors.
3 rue Perronet, 6e; tel.: 45.44.83.19;
Métro: St-Germain-des-Prés
open Monday–Saturday 10 A.M.–7 P.M.

- ## Rue du Pré-aux-Clercs •

Isadora

Danielle Poulain is the craftswoman of the Art Deco–
inspired costume jewelry that illuminates this shop. Each
of her creations is hand-carved in brightly colored Bakelite, a hard, synthetic plastic, characteristic of the Art
Deco era. Both figurative and geometric designs reign in
a variety of fun and flamboyant forms: fantasy-like necklaces composed of multicolored parrots; New York's
looming skyline; and an orange artist's palette line one
wall; the other displays pieces that are unique in their
choice of geometric shapes and vivid colors. A glass case
displays an equally exciting selection of earrings, pins,
and rings, many of which are on sale at the Los Angeles
Museum of Art for considerably more. Prices start at $60
for a pin and go up to $350 for some of the larger neck-
laces.

10 rue du Pré-aux-Clercs, 7e; tel.: 42.22.89.63;
Métro: St.-Germain-des-Prés
open Monday 2–7 P.M.; Tuesday–Saturday 11 A.M.–7
P.M.

Irié

At the beginning of sale time, the line is so long at this fashionable boutique that you're guaranteed at least a 15-minute wait. What's the big attraction? Reasonably priced, up-to-the-minute women's clothing that will most likely still be in fashion next year. Irié creates modern styles out of both natural and synthetic fabrics. They're just trendy enough to be in this year and classic enough to bear the test of time.

For more stylish, affordable togs, peek in across the street at the recently opened Anvers boutique.
8 rue du Pré-aux-Clercs, 7e; tel.: 42.61.18.28;
Métro: St.-Germain-des-Prés
open Monday–Saturday 10 A.M.–7 P.M.

Michel Klein

The ambiance is much more serene next door *chez* Klein than *chez* Irié because this French designer primarily uses four colors in his collections: blue, brown, black, and white—with the addition of one other that changes according to the season. Nevertheless, Klein's classically cut clothes still evoke a strong sense of excitement and panache. Don't miss his stylish leather skirts and jackets.
6 rue du Pré-aux-Clercs, 7e; tel.: 47.03.93.76;
Métro: St.-Germain-des-Prés
open Monday–Saturday 10 A.M.–7 P.M.

•   Rue Jacob   •

Petit Faune

Petit Faune has created a very original style of children's clothing (ages 0–6), and it's no surprise that this is one of Parisians' favorite addresses for beautifully made children's fashions. Their *tour de force* lies in their use of unusual colors and motifs that are not normally found in childrenswear, such as a tan-and–teal-blue flower print dress trimmed in a coordinating polka-dot collar. Another one of their trademarks is their fine wool knit outfits, which come in a variety of genteel colors for baby. Be sure to take a look at their sumptuous silk and embroidered party dresses for little girls (average price: $130).

Petit Faune's clothing is as practical as it is beautiful and all of their natural fabrics are made to hold up in the washer. Although they're considered expensive, about $115 for a little dress, you can bet that they cost at least 20% more in their new boutique in the States.

33 rue Jacob, 6e; tel.: 42.60.80.72;
Métro: St.-Germain-des-Prés
open Monday–Saturday 10:30 A.M.–7 P.M.

Brocante Store

This boutique came to my rescue once when one of my clients told me that he was looking for something to add to his banister-ball collection. We didn't have time to go to the flea markets and I had nary an idea of where I could find that sort of thing in town. At the Brocante Store, we came up with about 10 different kinds of glass and crystal banister balls and everyone was of course very happy. Other interesting kinds of antiques include glass paperweights, old-fashioned corkscrews with a brush on one end (for dusting off the old wine bottle, *bien entendu*), and hundreds of superbly polished brass lamps, candlesticks, frames, letter holders, whistles, and bathroom and fireplace accessories!

31 rue Jacob, 6e; tel.: 42.60.24.80;
Métro: St.-Germain-des-Prés
open Tuesday–Saturday 10:30 A.M.–7 P.M.

La Villa

Everyone is talking about Paris's latest and trendiest hotel. Stop into "le bar" for a very slick, streamlined cocktail.

29 rue Jacob, 6e; tel.: 43.26.60.00;
Métro: St.-Germain-des-Prés
open daily from 6 P.M. to at least midnight

A la Bonne Renommée

1 rue Jacob, 6e; see Marais description p. 231

• Rue Bonaparte •

Vicky Tiel

American designer Vicky Tiel experienced her first big break when Woody Allen asked her to design the costumes for *What's New Pussycat?* Then followed 10 years of outfitting Hollywood stars (Kim Novak, Elizabeth Taylor, and Ursula Andress) before she finally set up this Left Bank shop.

Her popularity has grown and now she has clients such as Ivana Trump, Joan Collins, and Goldie Hawn knocking at her door. And understandably so—her dresses are so glamourous that you have to have someplace equally as glamourous to go to wear them. Her dressy suits, cocktail dresses, and ballgowns are cut close to the body and serve to show off what a girl has to show off. Her silky creations fall somewhere between couture and ready-to-wear. You may either buy off the rack or have a dress made for you, which takes about two weeks. Her Paris prices (about 25% lower than in the U.S.) start at $1600 and go to about $4,900 for a beaded gown.

21 rue Bonaparte, 6e; tel.: 46.33.53.58;
Métro: St.-Germain-des-Prés
open Monday–Friday 10 A.M.–7 P.M.; Saturday
noon–7 P.M.

• Rue de Furstenberg •

Patrick Frey

Patrick Frey is the son of the famed textile designer Pierre Frey, and his boutique is found upstairs from the Pierre Frey showroom. Many of the elegant Pierre Frey fabrics are immortalized here in the shape of breakfast sets, serving trays, pillows, damask tablecloths, silk and wool-

blend shawls, and various-sized women's and men's canvas traveling bags. If you're looking for a considerably
less pricey typically Parisian gift idea, take a look at their
Okiasis scented candles. They come in seven exotic fragrances and they're used to perfume the most luxurious
homes in town. To purchase Pierre Frey fabrics, see Coolman description p. 293.
2 rue de Furstenberg, 6e; tel.: 46.33.73.00;
Métro: St.-Germain-des-Prés
47 rue des Petits-Champs, 1er; tel.: 42.97.44.00;
Métro: Pyramides
open Tuesday–Saturday 10 A.M.*–6:45* P.M.

•　　　　　　Place Furstenberg　　　　　　•

Manuel Canovas Boutique

Tucked into Paris's most charming little square is this
bright and cheery boutique (this one is more quaint than
the Right Bank Store) that sells bed and table linens,
cotton toiletry bags, canvas totes, bath towels, nightgowns,
bathrobes, and kimonos—all in Manuel Canovas's fresh
and airy prints! His use of color is either crisp and delicate
or bold and decorative; dainty bouquets of violets shower
a snow-white towel, and a huge yellow and pink flower,
in full bloom, encompasses an entire placemat.

Nearly everything is made out of Egyptian cotton, one
of the world's finest cottons, whose beauty lies in the fact
that it wrinkles less than ordinary cotton and practically
never wears out. Their divinely soft, silk and cashmere-
blend shawls also make for important purchases that
you'll have forever. Canovas shows a ready-to-wear collection in the spring and summer that is equally as colorful.
To purchase Manuel Canovas fabrics, see Coolman description p. 293.
5 place Furstenberg, 6e; tel.: 43.26.89.31;
Métro: St.-Germain-des-Prés
30 av George V, 8e; tel.: 49.52.00.36;
Métro: George V or Alma-Marceau
open Monday–Saturday 10 A.M.*–6:30* P.M. *(until 7*
P.M. *in the summer)*

Rue de Seine

Jeanne Do

Glittering fantasy is sold in a treasure trove of forms in this enchanting shop. Costume jewelry from the 20s as well as other Art Deco–inspired gems, many in sterling silver, are delightfully presented alongside Jeanne Do's own baroque-looking creations. Her jewelry is feminine and poetic, based on themes such as flowers, butterflies, and stars. Other high-quality costume jewelry includes sculptural pieces from Spanish designer Carrera. (There is only one other boutique in Paris that shows his creations.)

If costume jewelry is not your thing, you may be more interested in some of the marvelous *objets de collection* that adorn the shop. Jeanne Do also creates one-of-a-kind, whimsical-looking, furry cat statues—each one dressed in a different manner. Hand-blown glasses and vases, which were very much in fashion during the 30s, have become one of Paris's most recent art forms and Madame Do has made it a point to show some of these colorful creations here in her boutique.

67 rue de Seine, 6e; tel.: 46.33.48.94;
Métro: Mabillon
open Tuesday–Saturday 11 A.M.–7 P.M.; Monday
2:30–7 P.M. except during January and February

Autour du Monde

54 rue de Seine, 6e; see Marais description p. 221

Rue des Canettes

Kookaï

If you've been in France lately or at least leafed through a few French fashion magazines, you may have noticed the sassy and insolent Kookaï girls who flaunt their stuff in this clothing manufacturer's million-dollar ad campaigns. The Kookaïettes (as they're called) embody the look of France's precocious teens, who still aren't sure whether they want to dress with Chanel chic or as school-girl vamps. These coquettish styles, which consist largely of reasonably-priced skintight knits, have hardly arrived stateside.

3 rue des Canettes, 6e; tel.: 40.46.04.58;
Métro: Mabillon
106 rue de Longchamp, 16e; Tel.: 45.53.30.10.
open Monday–Saturday 10 A.M.–7:30 P.M.

Naf Naf

5 rue des Canettes, 6e; See Place des Victoires/Les Halles description p. 184

· **Rue de Beaune** ·

Les Nuits des Thés

Stop in at the Left Bank's most elegant tea salon before or after you weave in and out of the neigh-borhood's antique-shop–filled streets. Located in an old *boulangerie* (bakery), this pink-marble–floored, white-lacquered–chair salon specializes in tasty salads, quiches, and, of course, succulent desserts.

22 rue de Beaune, 7e; tel.: 47.03.92.07;
Métro: Bac
open Monday–Saturday noon–7 P.M.

Promenade South of the Boulevard Saint-Germain

This side of the boulevard is made up of a maze of streets just loaded with all different kinds of boutiques. Pick and choose before you decide to tackle every one of them. I suggest you start your promenade at the Carrefour de l'Odéon (Métro: Odéon) and sweep across in a westerly direction toward the rue du Bac via the rue St.-Sulpice, rue du Vieux Colombier, and rue de Grenelle, picking up the side streets as you go along. The last part (first part according to the numbers) of the rue du Bac crosses over to the other side of the boulevard St.-Germain. One last word: if you like *santons* (figurines for the manger at Christmastime), there is a whole series of boutiques specializing in them across from the St.-Sulpice church. Have fun!

STREETS:

Rue Saint-Sulpice

Mandarina Duck

Mandarina Duck is to bags as Ferrari is to cars. The slick, streamlined look of these Italian bags has positioned them at the top of the Italian marketplace, and their success is catching on throughout all of Europe. In the U.S., however, their merchandise can only be found in a few select stores. Their innovative design, their wide product range, their light yet durable materials (mostly nylon and rubber), their attractive color assortment (ever-popular black but also red, grey, and green), and their sleek metal handles and clasps on their shoulder bags, briefcases, travel bags, and accessories appeal to all different types of people for use in business, travel, school, or a spin around town. Prices start at $19 for a key case, $70 for an umbrella, $235 for an attaché case, and on up to $535 for a garment bag.

6 rue St.-Sulpice, 6e; tel.: 46.33.40.08; Métro: Odéon
open Monday–Saturday 10 A.M.–1 P.M. and 2–7 P.M.
7 bd de la Madeleine, 1er; tel.: 42.86.08.00;
Métro: Madeleine
open Monday–Saturday 10:30 A.M.–7:30 P.M.

La Chambre Claire

A must for camera buffs, this is Paris's best-known photography bookstore. The world's greatest photographers are all here in black and white, and color: Penn, Avedon, Snowdon, and French celebrities Cartier Bresson, Dominique Issermann, and Bettina Rheims. Enjoy leafing through the many books in French, English, and German, but know your prices if you decide to buy—the American editions cost 30–50% more here than in the States.

14 rue St.-Sulpice, 6e; tel.: 46.34.04.31; Métro: Odéon
open Tuesday–Saturday 11 A.M.–7 P.M.

Agnès B.

22 rue St.-Sulpice, 6e (men's); see Place des
Victoires/Les Halles description p. 186

Anne Marie Beretta

Well-structured, architectural clothes for self-assured men and women. The use of well-defined, almost severe cuts, and strong, earth-tone colors allows the person— not the clothes—to make the statement. A tailored women's olive-green and grey, pin-striped wool jacket and pants ($1,225) is equally as effective for the office as for an important lunch.

Madame Beretta's leather and sheepskin coats for men and women, manufactured by French big name Mac-Douglas, are extremely handsome and of excellent quality.

24 rue St.-Sulpice, 6e; tel.: 43.26.99.30; Métro: Odéon
open Monday 2:30–7 P.M.; Tuesday–Saturday 10:30
A.M.–7 P.M.

Galerie d'Amon

This art gallery/boutique showcases glassworks from some of Europe's finest craftspeople. These variously priced pieces range from sculpture to arts of the table, and the exhibitions change regularly.
28 rue St.-Sulpice, 6e; tel.: 43.26.96.60;
Métro: Odéon or St.-Sulpice
Tuesday–Saturday 11 A.M.–7 P.M.

Beauté Divine

As you enter this boutique, dim lighting, deep-purple walls, and translucent, pastel-colored, Art Nouveau hanging lamps give the impression that you have just set foot into a very feminine-looking turn-of-the-century *boudoir*. Madame Régine de Robien has created the perfect ambiance for selling her unique accessories for *la toilette*, antique perfume bottles, and various other *objets* for the home and bath, both old and new. Collectors come (or call) from all over the world in search of a rare *flacon* by Baccarat or Lalique or perhaps an Arpège atomizer from the 20s. Distinguished-looking mirrors, tortoise-shell comb-and-brush sets, fine linen towels, Art Deco soap boxes, and fragrant bath-oil beads make for very Parisian gift ideas.
40 rue St.-Sulpice, 6e; tel.: 43.26.25.31;
Métro: St.-Sulpice
open Monday 2–7 P.M.; Tuesday–Saturday 10 A.M.–1 P.M. and 2–7 P.M.

Rue de Tournon

Emmanuelle Khanh

Women's-clothing designer Emmanuelle Khanh has at least a dozen boutiques in France yet still remains a well-kept secret to most Americans. Her collections are soft and feminine, often pronounced by a few sophisticated cuts and embroidered appliqués, adding a note of interest to a particular dress, suit, or coat. Prices are moderate to expensive; a chestnut-colored wool jacket with a collar-like leaf appliqué recently sold for $575, and a midnight-blue taffeta evening ensemble with a jagged-cut neckline sold for $800.

2 rue de Tournon, 6e; tel.: 46.33.41.03; Métro: Odéon
45 av Victor-Hugo, 16e; tel.: 45.01.73.00;
Métro: Etoile or Victor-Hugo
open Monday–Saturday 10:15 A.M.–7 P.M.

Walter Steiger

5 rue de Tournon, 6e; see Right Bank description
p. 59

Ségriès

Since the 17th century the town of Moustiers, located in
the Alps of Haute-Provence, has been reputed for its superb *faïence* (refined earthenware). In 1979, Monsieur
Tonia Peyrot created Ségriès, an atelier in Moustiers
Sainte-Marie, where 25 highly skilled artisans make by
hand all of the faïence sold in their delightful Rive Gauche
boutique and exported throughout the world. Many of the
forms and themes of the Ségriès plates, bowls, vases,
planters, and candlesticks are based on 17th- and 18th-
century designs; others are patterned after the fauna and
flora that surround their workshop in Provence. Autumn
leaves, spring bouquets, and hot-air balloons hand-
painted on pure white, okra, and cornflower-blue back-
grounds create a crisp, airy, French country-looking ceramic.

  In the U.S., Ségriès *faïence* is sold in New York at Barney's, Pierre Deux, and their other boutique, Solanée. Unfortunately, their Paris prices are only slightly better than
those in New York (a plate costs about $45), yet with the
détaxe you can squeeze out another 15% off (if the items
don't need to be shipped). Nevertheless, their vast Paris
selection, tastefully displayed on Provençal-style wood
and wrought-iron furniture (also for sale), definitely merits a stop on your shopping promenade.
13 rue de Tournon, 6e; tel.: 46.34.62.56;
Métro: Odéon
open Monday–Saturday 9 A.M.–7 P.M.

Yves Saint Laurent Diffusion

21 rue de Tournon, 6e; see Left Bank description
p. 119

Ursule Poney

Ursule Poney has earned a nice reputation among many Parisians for delicately embroidered, hand-finished silk blouses that can just as easily be worn with a pair of jeans as with a velvet skirt. Count on spending about $385 for a silk *chemisier*, $680 for an embroidered violet-blue floral-print velour top, and $700 for an absolutely stunning cream-colored silk vest embroidered with dusty pink flowers and ivy vines.

29 rue de Tournon, 6e; tel.: 46.34.26.39;
Métro: Odéon
open Monday–Saturday 3–7 P.M.

Jean-Louis Scherrer

31 rue de Tournon, 6e; see Right Bank description p. 38

Rue de Seine

Clémentine

A superb address, *très parisienne,* for achieving that well-heeled, polished look. Classic forms, graced with pure and simple lines, and just a hint of sophistication are the secret to this womenswear label. The Clémentine collections are created in the most noble fabrics: silk, cashmere, and wool—primarily in solid colors.

The beauty of the boutique lies in the possibility to have any piece of clothing from the collection (or even previous ones) made up for you in your own color choice or size. Each *couture* item takes about 10 days, at no additional cost from the boutique price. Silk blouses start at $290. Prices go on up to $700–1070 for a wool suit. Knits and an assortment of accessories (belts, hats, shoes) coordinate each collection. Clémentine also boasts a limited, but gorgeous, selection of eveningwear and wedding dresses.

101 rue de Seine, 6e; tel.: 43.26.64.80; Métro: Odéon
open Monday–Saturday 10 A.M.–1 P.M. and 2–7 P.M.

Fabrice Karel

A couple of smart shoppers from Scarsdale helped me discover this boutique a few years ago and it has since

become a favorite shop for quality women's knits. Each year's collection is complete with a lot of mix-and-match skirts, tops, sweaters, and dresses in an ever-changing array of colors (smoke brown, raspberry sherbet, moss green, and basic reds, blacks, and whites). Prices range from $165 to $280 for the sweaters; skirts are about $120.
95 rue de Seine, 6e; tel.: 46.34.26.97;
Métro: Mabillon
39 av Victor-Hugo, 16e; tel.: 45.00.59.22;
Métro: Victor-Hugo
open Monday–Saturday 10:30 A.M.–7 P.M.

Pixi & Cie

"You don't play with our toy soldiers, you dream with them," exclaims the daughter of the founder of Pixi & Cie. And as you peer into glass cases neatly lined with lead figurines, depicting not only wartime heros (Napoléon, Caesar, Alexander the Great), but also figures from our everyday lives (a doctor, a violinist, a magician, a cartoon character, a painter, each portrayed in its own lifelike setting), you realize that these little statuettes do indeed feed the world of the imaginary.

All of the miniatures are artisanally made and hand-painted in the Pixi & Cie workshop in Normandy. Their success has been tremendous with both collectors and amateurs alike since 1983, when the store first opened. Already many of the figurines are exported throughout the world. Their biggest rage has been the minimannequins depicting the Paris haute-couture designers. Selling for $29, they are attractively displayed in laquered boxes and perfect for light, easy-to-carry gifts for friends back home.
95 rue de Seine, 6e; tel.: 43.25.10.12;
Métro: Mabillon or Odéon
open Tuesday–Saturday 10:30 A.M.–1 P.M. and 2:30–7 P.M.

Souleiado

The minute you walk in the door, vivid color tones of warm red, marigold, and *bleu gitane* muster up images of sunny Provence, that wonderfully rich region in the south of France. Endearing Provençal (or what Americans often call French Provincial) prints flourish in a variety of timeless motifs and fashions: bags, table linens, fabrics, bathrobes, gypsy-like skirts and blouses, and an unlimited supply of cotton, wool, and silk scarves and shawls. Don't miss the men's French "ranchero-look" shirts ($85) that are also great for women; I became hooked when my husband and I made our first trip to Camargue (France's wild, wild west) and now every time we go, we ritually bring back a shirt from Arles or Saintes-Maries-de-la-Mer, France's gypsy capital.

You may be somewhat familiar with this terrific French country look from the Pierre Deux boutiques in the U.S. that are franchises of Charles Demery—the original designer and company name of Souleiado. The warm, friendly ambiance of the Paris boutiques, however, is much different from the upscale marketing approach used stateside. Basically the Paris Souleiado boutiques resemble Provence whereas Pierre Deux looks more like Madison Ave. Everyone in the Left Bank boutique is quite friendly, speaks English, and is capable of helping out with size equivalents.

78 rue de Seine, 6e; tel.: 43.54.62.25;
Métro: Mabillon
open Monday–Saturday 10 A.M.–7 P.M.
83 av Paul-Doumer, 16e; tel.: 42.24.99.34;
Métro: La Muette
open Monday 2–7 P.M.; Tuesday–Saturday
10 A.M.–7 P.M.

Place Saint-Sulpice

Yves Saint Laurent

Probably no other couturier embodies Parisian style as completely as master-designer, Yves Saint Laurent. Innovator, genius, and one-time rebel, this ex-assistant to Christian Dior was the world's first designer to set up a ready-to-wear boutique. He did it here on the *Rive Gauche* and this same store has remained the most heartwarming of all of his *Rive Gauche* outlets. Signature Saint Laurent trademarks include superbly-cut, elegant silhouettes, sophisticated man-tailored tuxedos for women, and vibrant bursts of striking color combinations. Indulge. The Diffusion line is priced a bit less.

6 pl Saint-Sulpice, 6e (women's); tel.: 43.29.43.00
12 pl Saint-Sulpice, 6e (men's); tel.: 43.26.84.40
the Métro for both boutiques is Saint-Sulpice
21 rue de Tournon, 6e (Diffusion only);
Métro: Odéon
open Monday–Saturday 10 A.M.–7 P.M.
12–14 rond-point des Champs-Elysées, 8e (women only);
Métro: Franklin-Roosevelt
open Monday–Saturday 10:30 A.M.–7 P.M.
19/21 av Victor Hugo, 16e; tel.: 45.00.64.64;
Métro:Etoile
open Monday–Saturday 10 A.M.–7 P.M.

▪ Rue Bonaparte ▪

Boutique Go

This enchanting shop provides an interesting contrast with the surrounding fashion boutiques by bringing you back to the roaring 20s—if only for a few minutes. Every inch of the place is covered with antique-lace house linens and undergarments, beaded evening bags and shawls, Art Nouveau lamps, frames, and jewelry (some reproductions). The owner once told me that most of her merchandise comes from little old ladies from the neighborhood who decide to sell off parts of their no-longer-needed trousseaus.

70 rue Bonaparte, 6e; tel.: 43.54.21.45;
Métro: St.-Sulpice
open Monday–Saturday 10:30 A.M.–1 P.M. and 2–6:45 P.M.

Joseph Tricot

Although "Joseph" originated in London and has a couple of boutiques in New York, their Paris boutiques are still worth visiting since the styles and designers shown vary from city to city. There are actually two boutiques at rue Bonaparte. One is devoted to women's casual wear: big, ethnic-looking, heavy-knit sweaters and sweater-dresses in the winter plus cool, breezy, cotton T-shirts and dresses in the summer (all at honest prices). The other shop consists of sophisticated women's suits by Joseph and a part

of Azzedine Alaïa's collection for pencil-thin shapes. Joseph's Les Halles boutique offers much of the same with a slightly larger selection of knits.
68–70 rue Bonaparte, 6e; tel.: 46.33.45.75;
Métro: St.-Sulpice
44 rue Etienne-Marcel, 1er; tel.: 42.36.87.83;
Métro: Etienne-Marcel
open Monday–Saturday 10:30 A.M.–7 P.M.

L'Observatoire

A stately, modern boutique that shows very "in" fashions by three international labels: Callaghan (Italian), Helmut Lang (Austrian), and Katherine Hamnett (English) at prices much better than those found stateside. A lot of romantic silk and cotton blouses with interesting detail in exciting colors à la Romeo Gigli. Friendly, laid-back welcome.
70 bis rue Bonaparte, 6e; tel.: 43.54.43.06;
Métro: St.-Sulpice
open Monday–Saturday 10:30 A.M.–7:30 P.M.

River

With the same owner as L'Observatoire, River focuses entirely on Italian designer Moschino, whose fun clothes (at expensive prices) jazz up any wardrobe. Moschino's three women's-clothing lines—couture, cheap and chic, and jeans—don't take fashion seriously and amusingly poke fun at many of the big names—a Hermès-like scarf is casually sewn onto the shoulders of a plain, navy top; a classic-looking, grey flannel suit is striped with labels marked 100% wool in French, English, and Italian; and a taxi-cab–yellow wool coat, trimmed with black and white checks, says "follow me" on the back.
68 rue Bonaparte, 6e; tel.: 43.26.35.74;
Métro: St.-Sulpice
open 10:30 A.M.–7:30 P.M.

Saponifère

Take your time exploring this delightful boutique filled with some of Europe's finest toiletries and bathroom accessories. The left-hand side wall gleams with elegant toilet waters and beauty creams: England's most-reputed perfume makers, Floris and Penhaligon's, and France's oldest and most exclusive *parfumeurs* Creed (1760) and Coudray (1822). Comptoir Sud Pacifique's exotic-smelling, vanilla scents and Nicole Houques's sophisticated-looking *flacons*, whose smells of Provence's *garrigues* (scrublands) permeate from within, are not to be missed either.

Eloi Pernet, the Cadillac of manicure sets, attracts customers from every corner of the earth who are willing to pay up to $900 for an ostrich case containing five impeccably crafted gold and tortoise-shell instruments—all made by hand. White, tan, and black badger-tufted shaving brushes are also big items and can cost up to $350 for one of pure white—the rarest of them all. The French paintbrush company Raphael, which experienced its first success with the Impressionists, also fashions makeup brushes in every imaginable size and shape.

If you still haven't hit upon that perfect gift after having seen all of these exquisite products, you're certain to find happiness in a silky-rich bar of handmade, cedar-smelling soap from the south of France ($4.50).

59 rue Bonaparte, 6e; tel.: 46.33.98.43;
Métro: St.-Sulpice
open Monday–Saturday 10:15 A.M.–7:15 P.M.
Forum des Halles, 1er; tel.: 40.39.92.14;
Métro: Les Halles
open Monday–Saturday 10:30 A.M–7 P.M.

Soco

Although this French leather manufacturer has been around for a while, it's only within the past few years that Soco has taken off like a rocket. Their well-made, western-styled bags have become one of Paris's most trendy fashion accessories. These traditionally shaped bags, which blend brightly colored leather with warm mud tones, are stitched in rodeo-like designs!

56 rue Bonaparte, 6e; tel.: 40.51.78.76;
Métro: St.-Germain-des-Prés or St.-Sulpice
open Monday 11 A.M.–7 P.M.; Tuesday–Saturday
10:30 A.M.–7 P.M.
9 place des Petits-Pères, 2e; tel.: 42.60.12.80;
Métro: Bourse

*open Monday 2–7 P.M.; Tuesday–Saturday 10:30
A.M.–7 P.M.*

Elizabeth de Senneville (children's)

*55 rue Bonaparte, 6e; see Place des Victoires/Les
Halles description p. 189*

Olivier Strelli

Olivier Strelli's subtle-colored women's fashions project
an aura of cool elegance. Fine-quality fabrics are cut into
sophisticated shapes that are neither too trendy nor too
classic. Expensive.
*55 rue Bonaparte, 6e; tel.: 46.34.54.85;
Métro: St.-Germain-des-Prés or St.-Sulpice
open Monday–Saturday 10:30 A.M–7 P.M.*

Georges Rech

*54 rue Bonaparte, 6e; see Right Bank description
p. 82*

Fabrice

One of my favorite Paris addresses for sophisticated costume jewelry. Big, chunky bracelets, necklaces, and pins
are fashioned out of copper, silver, resin, lizard, crocodile,
and gold. The result is *très mode* and it's no wonder they
have conquered the fashion editors from almost every
magazine in France!

They also have a boutique at 33 rue Bonaparte that is
more roomy and offers a better selection of their fine
jewelry and sumptuous silk chenille scarves—perfect for
eveningwear.
*54 rue Bonaparte, 6e; tel.: 43.26.09.49;
Métro: St.-Germain-des-Prés
open Monday–Saturday 10 A.M.–7 P.M.*

Apostrophe

*54 rue Bonaparte, 6e; see Right Bank description
p. 86*

Chipie

Good old apple-pie American fashion with a French twist. It never ceases to amaze me how the French can turn our American basics, such as blue jeans, football sweaters, and knapsacks, into something incredibly chic and fun. Chipie does exactly that and in its 20-years of existence has sold well over a million pair of jeans! A little bit of humor and good quality go a long way in their 20-some boutiques throughout France that sell clothing and shoes to kids of all ages. Their secret to success: a girl can *chipe* (pick or borrow) anything from a guy and of course he can do the same. So don't ask where are the women's clothes—they're all the same.

49 rue Bonaparte, 6e (children); tel.: 43.29.21.94;
Métro: St.-Germain-des-Prés
22 rue des Halles, 1er (adults); tel.: 42.36.05.57;
Métro: Châtelet
129 rue de la Pompe, 16e (children and adults);
tel.: 47.27.60.01;
Métro: Pompe
open Monday–Saturday 10 A.M.–7 P.M.
16 rue du Four, 6e (adults and shoes);
tel.: 46.34.62.32;
Métro: Mabillon
open Monday–Saturday 10:30 A.M.–7:30 P.M.
31 rue de la Ferronnerie, 1er (children);
tel.: 45.08.58.74;
Métro: Châtelet
open Monday 11 A.M.–7 P.M.; Tuesday–Saturday 10 A.M.–7 P.M.
5 rue St.-Opportune, 1er (shoes); tel.: 40.26.12.03;
Métro: Châtelet
open Monday 2–7 P.M.; Tuesday–Saturday 10:30 A.M.–1 P.M. and 2–7 P.M.

· **Rue du Vieux-Colombier** ·

Miki House

No, this is not Eurodisneyland's outpost for Mickey Mouse gift items—but rather a Japanese-brand children's-clothing store for ages 0–8 years. About 120 Miki Houses are scattered throughout Japan, but so far, nary a boutique in the U.S. (Their clothing can only be found in a few selected stores.) Yet word is catching on fast in Europe. Their first Paris boutique appeared several years ago in the oh so chic place des Victoires neighborhood, followed by the opening of this Left Bank boutique in 1989. One of the saleswomen boasted that "Not many Americans figure within our clientele because they don't like paying these kind of prices," without even trying to hide the fact that Miki House is *cher*, even by Paris standards. The very least expensive outfit (sweater and boxer shorts) costs $160, and most of the others are in the $300 category (for a cute skirt and blouse). And why is this brand so pricey? Beautifully made clothing with unique designs and adorable themes (ranging from cars and planes to Santa Claus), plus brightly colored cottons and wools of excellent quality that hold up in the wash are just a few of the reasons—and the French love them.

1 rue du Vieux-Colombier, 6e; tel.: 46.33.77.55;
Métro: St.-Sulpice
1 place des Victoires, 1er; tel.: 40.26.23.00;
Métro: Bourse
open Monday–Saturday 10 A.M.–7 P.M.

Naj-Oleari

The name sounds like a cross between Japanese and Irish, but is in fact Italian. This textile manufacturer, firmly implanted in Italy, opened its first boutique in Paris a couple of years ago and has been going strong ever since. It's hard not to fall for their adorable, whimsical motifs that look as though they just walked out of a Keith Haring tableau. Fabrics, clothes for women and babies, as well as accessories for you and your home serve as excellent vehicles for these very original prints—perfect for people who refuse to take themselves seriously.

1 bis rue du Vieux-Colombier, 6e; tel.: 40.46.00.43;
Métro: St.-Sulpice
130 av Victor-Hugo, 16e; tel.: 47.55.67.45;
Métro: Pompe
open Monday–Saturday 10 A.M.–7 P.M.

Chantal Thomass

Chantal Thomass's ready-to-wear is as quintessentially feminine as her lingerie. In fact, different elements of lingerie (lace and many of the forms) are often incorporated into her clothes. This is one of the best addresses for *bustiers*—those, form-fitted, long-line, strapless bras that are not meant to be covered up, unless with an evening jacket. Seductive-looking *bustiers* ($140–230) and *bustier* dresses abound in a variety of colors and materials—trimmed with jet tassles, old-fashioned lace, velvet ribbons, and a few inevitable sequins!

Most of the evening clothes are upstairs. Downstairs is stocked with many lovely and not-so-outrageous clothes for daytime wear. Tassles and bows, either knitted or printed directly into the fabric, are popular themes in the many suits, dresses, and blouses sold in this shop.

5 rue du Vieux-Colombier, 6e; tel.: 45.44.07.52;
Métro: St.-Sulpice
12–14 Galerie du Rond-Point, 8e (ready-to-wear
and stockings); tel.: 43.59.87.34;
Métro: Franklin-Roosevelt
open Monday 11 A.M.–7 P.M.; Tuesday–Saturday 10
A.M.–7 P.M.

Formes

Their maternity clothes are so beautiful that you almost wish you were pregnant just to be able to wear them! There are already three Formes in Paris, licensing agreements with the Japanese, and rumors floating around about an eventual boutique in New York. What's the secret to all of this success? Fashionably designed clothing in fine-quality fabrics (100% cotton, wool, linen, and silk), all in attractive colors. Thank goodness someone has finally developed a smart look for pregnant women—all at reasonable prices ($175–310 for an elegant suit).

5 rue du Vieux-Colombier, 6e; tel.: 45.49.09.80;
Métro: St.-Sulpice
7 rue d'Aboukir, 2e; tel.: 40.26.09.95; Métro: Sentier
open Monday–Saturday 10:30 A.M.–7 P.M.
1 rue de Sontay, 16e; tel.: 45.01.72.78;
Métro: Victor-Hugo
open Monday–Saturday 10:30 A.M.–2 P.M. and 2:30–
7 P.M.

Fil à Fil

The first time I seriously thought about starting up a Paris shopping service was in the mid-1980s when I brought a friend of mine to Fil à Fil. She was so impressed by the quality of their 100% cotton shirts for men and women that she decided to purchase all of the gifts for her family and friends in this one small shop. There's no doubt that shirt quality in France is often superior to that found in the U.S. (Even the Arrow shirts sold in France are of a much better quality than those made in the U.S.) In its decade of existence Fil à Fil has opened over 70 boutiques throughout the world, two of which are in the U.S. The average price of shirts in France is $80 as opposed to $90 in the States. (Buying them *détaxe* can save you another 15%.)

The look of their shirts is French preppie, cut large— so most Americans don't have any problems with the sizes; the salespeople are usually quite helpful with providing size equivalents. A variety of silk accessories complement the many different shirt styles: ties and *pochettes* (those marvelous little silk hankies that men tuck into the breast pocket of their jackets in order to achieve that suave, European look) as well as some very classic bows for women.

14 rue du Vieux-Colombier, 6e; tel.: 42.22.58.74;
Métro: St.-Sulpice
11 rue Pierre-Lescot, 1er; tel.: 45.08.81.24;
Métro: Etienne-Marcel
140 av Victor-Hugo, 16e; tel.: 47.04.55.74;
Métro: Pompe
open Monday–Saturday 10:30 A.M.–7:15 P.M.
and seven other addresses as well!

Marcel Lassance

One of the best stores in Paris for elegant men's wear. French cinema people and politicians (including President Mitterand) shop here for very stylish, somewhat classic clothing. There's not a bit of stodginess in this shop, and their success lies in the exquisite wools, cashmeres, and linens selected by Monsieur Lassance, a former textile designer. Dresden blue, malachite green, and tile red contribute to a modern look, as quality fabrics and exclusive styles dictate investment-level prices. Monsieur Lassance recently opened a shop in Tokyo and there is rumor that one may open in New York within a year or two.

17 rue du Vieux-Colombier, 6e; tel.: 45.48.29.28;
Métro: St.-Sulpice
open Monday–Saturday 10 A.M.–7 P.M.

21 rue Marbeuf, 8e; tel.: 49.52.09.01;
Métro: Franklin-Roosevelt
open Monday–Saturday 10:30 A.M.–2:30 P.M. and
3–7 P.M.

Claudie Pierlot

Femininity without frills is the Claudie Pierlot look. Her clothing is worn by both young and mature women (small-sized) who prefer a neat, subtle approach to a more sophisticated fashion statement. Her favorite colors (blue, black, and white) as well as her flannel suits, velour tops, and jersey dresses reflect just a hint of French preppy, but the note of fantasy given to each of the collections prevents her clothes from being labeled classic. In the summer, cool linen suits and delicate prints flourish—all at fairly reasonable prices. Claudie Pierlot's clothing is similar to Agnès B.'s, however the quality tends to be better and costs are lower.

23 rue du Vieux-Colombier, 6e; tel.: 45.48.11.96
Métro: St.-Sulpice
4 rue du Jour, 1er; tel.: 42.21.38.38;
Métro: Les Halles
open Monday 1–7 P.M.; Tuesday–Saturday 10:30
A.M.–7 P.M.

■ ## Rue Madame ■

Chantal Thomass

This boutique sells the "ultimate" in French lingerie. Chantal Thomass designs ultrasexy stockings and lingerie that dare a woman to be both a schoolgirl charmer and a vamp. Flirtatious designs reign throughout the shop. A Scottish tartan-print corset and panties, stockings that lace up behind the calves, and a peach, ruffly-type number with frills in the most surprising places all catch your eye. The stockings, priced at $55 and $90, tend to run on the small side.

Alongside all of this "provocation" is a rack of comfortable-looking play clothes and pajamas for children—all in imaginative prints and priced at $90–135.

11 rue Madame, 6e; tel.: 45.44.07.52;
Métro: St.-Sulpice
open Monday 11 A.M.–7 P.M.; Tuesday—Saturday 10
A.M.–7 P.M.

Victoire

1 rue Madame, 6e; see place des Victoires/Les Halles description p. 172

· # Rue de Rennes ·

Lancel

43 rue de Rennes, 6e; see Right Bank description p. 56

Guy Laroche

47 rue de Rennes, 6e; see Right Bank description p. 36

Courrèges

49 rue de Rennes, 6e; see Right Bank description p. 44

J.M. Weston

These superbly crafted French men's shoes (limited selection for women) have people coming to this boutique in droves. The prices are so steep, averaging between $290 and $350, it's a wonder they have so much appeal, but a pair of Westons will almost never wear out. The styles and colors are all very classic and there is a wide assortment from which to choose. Don't be surprised if you see a lot of young people in the boutique. Westons are just as popular with French high schoolers as with high-level executives.

49 rue de Rennes, 6e; tel.: 45.49.38.50;
Métro: St.-Sulpice
open Monday 2:30–7 P.M.; Tuesday–Friday 10 A.M.–7 P.M.
114 av des Champs-Elysées. 8e; tel.: 45.62.26.47;
Métro: George V
open Monday 10 A.M.–7 P.M.; Tuesday–Saturday 9:30 A.M.–7 P.M.
97 av Victor-Hugo, 16e; tel.: 47.04.23.75;
Métro: Victor-Hugo
open Monday 2–7 P.M.; Tuesday—Saturday 10 A.M.–7 P.M.

Burberrys

It rains almost as much in Paris as in London so if you forgot to bring your raincoat or are in need of a new one, keep in mind that Paris has two lovely Burberrys stores. The Paris prices on their classic trench coats are a bit higher than those in the U.K., but still less than in the U.S.
55 rue de Rennes, 6e; tel.: 45.48.52.71;
Métro: St.-Sulpice
8-10 bd Malesherbes, 8e; tel.: 42.66.13.01;
Métro: Madeleine
56 rue de Passy, 16e; tel.: 42.88.88.24;
Métro: Muette
open Monday 2–6:45 P.M.; *Tuesday–Saturday 10* A.M.*–6:45* P.M.

Céline

58 rue de Rennes, 6e; see Right Bank description p. 43

Kenzo Studio

All of Kenzo's vibrant colors and floral prints bloom in this delightfully refreshing boutique devoted solely to his more youthful, sporty lines. Not only the young buy here. So do many women in search of more affordable Kenzo creations than those sold in his other Paris boutiques. The boutique shows three different Kenzo labels: "City," a neat, cosmopolitan look; "Jungle," a lot of fun knitwear; and "Jeans," perfect for casual weekend dressing.
60 and 62 rue de Rennes, 6e; tel.: 45.44.27.88;
Métro: St.-Sulpice
open Monday 11 A.M.*–7* P.M.; *Tuesday–Saturday 10* A.M.*–7* P.M.
See place des Victoires/Les Halles description p. 170 for more on Kenzo.

Et Vous

Et Vous has taken off like a rocket within the past few years. Their men's and women's Left Bank clothing emporium presents their moderately priced country-looking fashions so tastefully that you can already envision yourself wearing them—and yes, there's a hint of Ralph Lauren in the air. Embroidered shirts, nubby sweaters, corduroy

pants, and prairie skirts in creamy beige, pink, and caramel create a very soft look for city dwellers.
*62 and 64 rue de Rennes, 6e; tel.: 45.48.56.93 and
45.44.23.75;*
Métro: St.-Sulpice
15 rue des Francs-Bourgeois, 4e; tel.: 48.87.48.98;
Métro: St.-Paul
open Monday–Saturday 10:30 A.M.–7:30 P.M.

Tartine et Chocolat

One nice thing about the French is that they dress their
children like children even if the parents themselves look
like fashion victims. Tartine et Chocolat's top-quality, pastel-colored baby and children's clothes (ages 0–12) are
classically designed without an inch of froufrou; their
most popular item, the *salopettes* Nicolas (powder-pink
or baby-blue striped, cuddly soft cotton overalls for $90)
has been sold since they launched their first collection
more than 10 years ago.

The whole first part of the boutique is lined with shelf
after shelf of stuffed animals wearing their trademark
salopettes as well as neatly displayed packages of their
children's fragrance, Ptisenbon (little one smells good).

Future moms can also outfit themselves in the same
Tartine et Chocolat stripes or their equally popular prints.
A peony-flowered maternity dress runs about $235.
90 rue de Rennes, 6e; tel.: 42.22.67.34;
Métro: St.-Sulpice
open Tuesday–Saturday 10 A.M.–7 P.M.

Laura Ashley

*94 rue de Rennes, 6e; see Right Bank description
p. 82*

Geneviève Lethu

A little over 10 years ago, Geneviève Lethu opened her
first store in La Rochelle. Now she has over 70 boutiques
throughout France devoted to the kitchen and the table.
Homey-looking, brightly colored dishes, ideal for everyday use, attractively displayed with coordinating glassware, cutlery, and table linens are her strongpoint. Usual
and unusual kitchen utensils such as spaghetti tongs, min-

iature whips, and wooden butter molds make excellent gift ideas for budget-minded shoppers.

95 rue de Rennes, 6e; tel.: 45.44.40.35;
Métro: St.-Sulpice or Rennes
open Monday 11 A.M.–*7* P.M.; *Tuesday–Saturday*
10:15 A.M.–*7* P.M.
1 rue Pierre-Lescot, 1er; tel.: 40.39.95.94;
Métro: Etienne-Marcel
open Monday–Saturday 10:30 A.M.–*7:30* P.M.
1 av Niel, 17e; tel.: 45.72.03.47;
Métro: Ternes
open Monday 2–7 P.M.; *Tuesday–Saturday 10* A.M.–*7*
P.M.

Culinarion

Culinarion has over 30 boutiques in France specializing in very practical kitchen equipment. Traditional French cooking pans, pie plates, couscous pots, and terrine molds are mixed in with more unusual gadgets such as scissors for cutting cheese and rubber gloves to wear when opening oysters—all at fairly reasonable prices.

99 rue de Rennes, 6e; tel.: 45.48.94.76;
Métro: Rennes
83 bis rue de Courcelles, 17e; tel.: 42.27.63.32;
Métro: Péreire
open Monday 11:15 A.M.–*7* P.M.; *Tuesday–Saturday*
10:15 A.M.–*7* P.M.

• # Rue du Four •

Lario 1898

You may not already know about this Italian shoemaker since they don't have a store in the U.S, but if you are partial to ultrasupple, classic women's shoes, then this is the place for you. Most of their basic pumps, loafers, and cyclist shoes (they were making them long before the trend) are crafted out of *agneau plongé* (specially treated lambskin), the softest of leathers used in shoe manufacturing.

Lario is also well known for their preppy-looking, bow-tipped, quilted leather and suede *ballerines* (flats) that come in about 10 different colors each season.

56 rue du Four, 6e; tel.: 45.48.44.65;
Métro: St.-Sulpice
open Monday noon–7 P.M.; Tuesday–Saturday 10
A.M.–7 P.M.

Marina Rinaldi

Ivory-colored walls and a glossy marble floor and staircase create an elegant ambiance in this spacious boutique
that specializes in chic fashions for larger-sized women.
The use of quality fabrics in stylish creations has largely
contributed to the success of this Italian designer's label's
popularity with France's *belles rondes.*
56 rue du Four, 6e; tel.: 45.48.61.57;
Métro: St.-Sulpice
open Monday–Saturday 10:30 A.M.–6:45 P.M.

La Bagagerie

41 rue du Four, 6e; see Right Bank description
p. 69

Le Garage

40 rue du Four, 6; see Marais description p. 221

Descamps

A beautiful selection of house linens and bath accessories
in delicious colors and cheerful prints—all priced lower
than in America. The saleswomen are particularly helpful
in providing you with U.S.-size equivalents for bed and
table linens. Hot items include lovely floral-print sheets
designed by Primrose Bordier; country French linen and
cotton tablecloths by the Jacquard Français; and the
grand voile—those marvelous cotton throws in colorful
paisleys, designed to cover up that old sofa that you just
can't bear to give away. Their bathrobes and towels also
come in luscious colors and two different textures, but I
was once told by the owner of a famous Paris bath shop
that she would never sell anything but our own, U.S.-made
Martex towels, whose weight and quality are superior.
There are Descamps boutiques in almost every district of
Paris.

38 rue du Four, 6e; tel.: 45.44.22.87;
Métro: St.-Sulpice
52 av Victor-Hugo, 16e; tel.: 45.00.70.22;
Métro: Victor-Hugo
44 rue de Passy, 16e; tel.: 45.25.28.25;
Métro: Muette
open Monday–Saturday 10 A.M.–7 P.M.

Max Mara

Max Mara is firmly implanted in Italy with over a hundred women's clothing stores, and their success in France is growing rapidly. The selection and quality of their clothes is excellent. Six different lines cater to a variety of tastes for both daytime and evening dressing: Max Mara (classic ready-to-wear), Pianoforte (couture-like chic), I Blues (comfortable sportswear), Sportmax (trendy fashion), Weekend (elegant casualwear), and Blue's Club (romantic separates). If you plan to go to Italy, then buy there where prices run about 20% lower than in Paris; their Paris prices, however, are still better than boutique prices in San Francisco if you benefit from the tax refund.
37 rue du Four, 6e; tel.: 43.29.91.10;
Métro: Mabillon
open Monday–Saturday 10:30 A.M.–6:45 P.M.
265 rue Saint-Honoré, 1er; tel.: 40.20.04.58;
Métro: Palais Royal
open Monday–Friday 10:15 A.M.–7 P.M.; *Saturday 10* A.M.–7 P.M.

Caroll

Although the quality is better and the styles are more classic, this French womenswear manufacturer is best likened to Italy's Benetton. Priced lower than in the U.S., the Caroll knits represent good value and wearability. This is only one of many Caroll boutiques in Paris.
33 rue du Four, 6e; tel.: 43.26.68.38;
Métro: St.-Sulpice
open Monday–Saturday 10 A.M.–7 P.M.
85 rue de Passy, 16e; tel.: 45.27.08.05;
Métro: Muette
open Monday 11 A.M.–7 P.M.; *Tuesday–Saturday 10* A.M.–7 P.M.

Free Lance

If you can't make it over to check out the far-out decor of the Jean-Paul Gaultier boutique in the Galerie Vivienne, then this is the next best thing. The friendly folks at Free Lance aptly refer to their boutique as "the recycled shop." Tin watering cans illuminate the facade; rusted metal machine parts and tools ornament the door; and more rusty old drawers and storage bins are used to contain their huge supply of men's and women's punkish-style shoes. Their industrial-stitched and riveted footwear, elevator pumps, and tractor-soled clodhoppers are the rage with all of Paris's *branchés* (plugged-in) types. Nearly all of the shoes, including the Junior Gaultier's, are made by Free Lance, a French manufacturer. The boutique also sports a line of western-like shirts, sweaters, and jeans.

30 rue du Four, 6e; tel.: 45.48.70.61; Métro: Mabillon
open Monday–Saturday 10:30 A.M.–7:30 P.M.
22 rue Mondétour, 1er; tel.: 42.33.74.70;
Métro: Etienne-Marcel
open Monday–Friday 10:30 A.M.–7 P.M.; Saturday
10:30 A.M.–7:30 P.M.

Pom d'Api

The same manufacturer as Free Lance, Pom d'Api sells the most inventive shoes for children (ages 0–14) in all of Paris. Although Pom d'Api carries a classic line, most people come to them for their fun, gold-lamé baby slippers, imitation crocodile loafers, blue suede pointed shoes, fake leopard-skin sneakers, or even for a pair of multicolored, court-jester–inspired boots! Prices start at $38 for a pair of booties and go on up to $235 for a pair of lizardly cowboy boots. You'll have to look hard to find them stateside.

28 rue du Four, 6e; tel.: 45.48.39.31; Métro: Mabillon
open Monday–Saturday 10 A.M.–7 P.M.
13 rue du Jour, 1er; tel.: 42.36.08.87;
Métro: Les Halles
open Monday–Friday 10:30 A.M.–7 P.M.; Saturday
10:30 A.M.–7:30 P.M.
6 rue Guichard, 16e; tel.: 46.47.40.05;
Métro: Muette
open Monday 2–7 P.M.; Tuesday–Saturday 10 A.M.–7
P.M.

Utility-Bibi

When I first came to Paris, I didn't like this boutique. I guess I found their enormous baubles and beads just too overwhelming. But as I quickly became "Frenchified," I learned to appreciate this little shop and now consider it to be one of Paris's best addresses for avant-garde costume jewelry.

There's no doubt that one has to be the right sort of person to pull off wearing the big, chunky pieces shown here, but if you can, you'll discover a gold mine of creations from some of the best designers that Paris has to offer: Migeon and Migeon, Spok, Dominique Aurientis, Gaultier, and Montana, to name a few. After you've been to this boutique, you'll understand why Frenchwomen often consider their accessories to be more important than the clothes they are wearing.

27 rue du Four, 6e; tel.: 43.25.53.77; Métro: Mabillon open Monday–Saturday 10 A.M.–7 P.M.

Blanc Bleu

With well over 50 shops throughout France, this casual-wear manufacturer is another success story grown out of Paris's garment district. Blanc Bleu is best known for having transformed America's basic clothing innovation, the sweatshirt, into a snazzy unisex fashion element for French kids and teens. Although often plastered with somewhat nonsensical sayings (at least to us), Blanc Bleu's inexpensively priced fashions create a fresh, sporty look that is somewhere between West Coast surfer and Ivy League preppie!

25 rue du Four, 6e; tel.: 43.54.50.02;
Métro: Mabillon or St.-Germain-des-Prés
open Monday–Saturday 10:30 A.M.–7 P.M.
8 rue des Francs-Bourgeois, 4e; tel.: 40.27.05.27;
Métro: Saint-Paul
open Monday 11:30 A.M.–7:30 P.M.; Tuesday–
Saturday 10:30 A.M.–7:30 P.M.
14 pl des Victoires, 1er; tel.: 42.96.05.40;
Métro: Palais-Royal or Etienne-Marcel
open Monday–Saturday 10 A.M.–7 P.M.

Néréides

A very attractive boutique twinkling with costume jewelry by other hip Parisian designers that you probably won't find next door at Utility-Bibi (their prices are less frightening as well). Gold-encrusted gems by Edouard Rambaud, ultralight, colored resin earrings by Poggi, and miniature, beaded, baroque chandelier earrings by Julian Anryon are just a few of the wonders displayed alongside more classic jet necklaces and various-sized, silver hoop earrings.

23 rue du Four, 6e; tel.: 43.26.33.55; Métro: Mabillon open Monday 10 A.M.–7 P.M.; Tuesday–Friday 10 A.M.–7 P.M.; Saturday 10 A.M.–7:30 P.M.

Chevignon

Their leather *blousons* patterned after American flight-bomber jackets from the 50s, have been so popular these past few years that they have French high schoolers scraping together every last franc to buy one—and those who didn't have the money were literally ripping them off the backs of their fellow students!

Things have calmed down a bit, but the Chevignon jackets, priced between $675 and $970, are still the rage. Frontier-like fashions and rugged shirts, sweaters, and jeans also have teens and adults flocking to the four Chevignon boutiques throughout Paris. Prices here run 15–20% lower than in the U.S.

18 rue du Four, 6e; tel.: 43.54.59.97; Métro: Mabillon 5 rue Turbigo, 1er (children's); tel.: 45.08.14.79; 5 place des Victoires, 1er; tel.: 42.36.10.16; 49 rue Etienne Marcel, 1er; (megastore); tel.: 40.28.04.67 Métro: Etienne-Marcel 72 rue de Passy, 16e; tel.: 42.88.22.43; Métro: Muette 4 rue des Rosiers, 4e (megastore); tel.: 42.72.42.40 Métro: St. Paul open Monday–Saturday 10:15 A.M.–7 P.M.

Chipie

16 rue du Four, 6e (adult clothing and shoes); see Left Bank description p. 124

Carel

Carel is a classic. A good many French women have at least one pair of Carel shoes in their closet. I recently read about one French woman who had a collection of about 600 pairs of Carel shoes and I'm sure that Imelda Marcos had a few, too. The great variety of colors and styles of their charming flats and pumps invites you to buy them not just to go with something you already have, but to go out and buy something to go with them. A bejeweled satin slipper or ballerinas ornamented with a cute mouse face or with a "man in the moon" instantly become irresistible. The rue du Four boutique is less fashion-oriented than the boutique at rue des Saints-Pères.

12 rue du Four, 6e; tel.: 43.54.11.69; Métro: Mabillon
20 av Victor-Hugo, 16e; tel.: 45.00.84.21;
Métro: Etoile
open Monday–Saturday 10 A.M.–7 P.M.
78 rue des Saints-Péres, 6e; tel.: 42.22.71.65;
Métro: St.-Sulpice
open Monday 11 A.M.–1 P.M. and 2–7 P.M.; Tuesday–Friday 10 A.M.–1 P.M. and 2–7 P.M.
22 rue Royale, 8e; tel.: 42.60.23.06;
Métro: Madeleine
open Monday 11 A.M.–7 P.M.; Tuesday–Saturday 10 A.M.–7 P.M.

Rue du Cherche-Midi

Un Après-Midi de Chien

Pink walls, hardwood floors, and red gingham curtains set just the right tone for the cutesy women's clothes that are sold in this shop. Delicately embroidered shirts and petticoats are perfect for today's grown-up women who still have a little girl's heart.

2 rue du Cherche-Midi, 6e; tel.: 45.44.05.32;
Métro: St.-Sulpice
10 rue du Jour, 1er; tel.: 40.26.92.78;
Métro: Les Halles
open Monday–Saturday 10:30 A.M.–7:15 P.M.

Eres

4 rue du Cherche-Midi, 6e; see Right Bank description p. 79

Robert Clergerie

If you're familiar with Clergerie in the States, then you might be surprised to find that the Paris shops don't have nearly as many high, high heels as those in the U.S. The shoes do, however, cost about 15–25% less in Paris, and the collections tend to show more flats and *masculin*-like tie shoes and boots, along with their very fashionable pumps. Some of the shoes are made by hand and their excellent quality and perfection of design almost make it worth paying between $151 and $410 a pair.

5 rue du Cherche-Midi, 6e; tel.: 45.48.75.47;
Métro: St.-Sulpice
46 rue Croix-des-Petits-Champs, 1er; tel.:
42.61.49.24; Métro: Palais-Royal
open Monday 11 A.M.–7 P.M.; Tuesday–Saturday 10
A.M.–7 P.M.

Soleil de Provence

A mixture of warm smells of olive oil, honey-based soap, and *herbes de Provence* greet you as you push open the door to this little shop, specializing in products from the Provence region of France. Several huge terra-cotta urns containing extra-virgin olive oil and aromatic olives take up one side of the boutique, while the other side displays artisanally made soaps and honeys in a variety of *parfums*: lavender, mint, and rose. A charming boutique for finding very inexpensive gift items.

6 rue du Cherche-Midi, 6e; tel.: 45.48.15.02;
Métro: St.-Sulpice
open Tuesday–Saturday 10 A.M.–8:30 P.M.

Accessoire

Sober-looking, fashionable women's shoes that look their best when matched with clothes from Agnès B., Comme des Garçons, and many of the hip, new Japanese designers. Accessoire is best known for their ankle-length, lace-up boots and for their very colorful (about 12 different hues each season) line of stretchy leather and suede flats ($130) that are great for both fashion and comfort.

6 rue du Cherche-Midi, 6e; tel.: 45.48.36.08;
Métro: St.-Sulpice
8 rue du Jour, 1er; tel.: 40.26.19.84;
Métro: Les Halles

open Monday–Saturday 10 A.M.–7 P.M.
36 rue Vieille du Temple, 4e; tel.: 40.29.99.49;
Métro: St.-Paul
open Monday–Saturday 11 A.M.–7 P.M.;
Sunday 3–7 P.M.
9 rue Guichard, 16e; tel.: 45.27.80.27; Métro: Muette
open Monday 2–7 P.M.; Tuesday–Saturday 10 A.M.–1
P.M. and 2–7 P.M.

Poilâne

Lionel Poilâne's rustic sourdough bread has gained so much snob appeal that it has become fashionable to wait in line just to buy it! Although you may not want to cart around one of their heavy, round loaves of bread, if the line isn't too bad, I suggest you stop in for a fresh apple tart or some of their nearly as famous *sablés* (shortbread cookies).

8 rue du Cherche-Midi, 6e; tel.: 45.48.42.59;
Métro: St.-Sulpice
open Monday–Saturday 7 A.M.–8 P.M.

Sartore

Very stylish, western-looking shoes and boots made in France. Slick pointed-toe, lizard-like cowboy boots cost about $555—enough to make you get back on your horse and head back to the real wild, wild west.

13 rue du Cherche-Midi, 6e; tel.: 45.48.90.50;
Métro: St.-Sulpice
open Monday 2–7 P.M.; Tuesday–Friday 11 A.M.–
7 P.M.
14 rue Cambon, 1er; tel.: 40.15.00.24;
Métro: Concorde
open Monday 2–7 P.M.; Tuesday–Saturday 10 A.M.–7
P.M.

Au Chat Dormant

If you like kitty cats, you'll love this boutique. Cat paintings and drawings, cat postcards, cat statues, cat clocks, cat pillows, cat key rings, and cat earrings are just a few of the feline fetishes that adorn this shop.

13 rue du Cherche-Midi, 6e; tel.: 45.49.48.63;
Métro: St.-Sulpice
open Monday 2–7 P.M.; Tuesday–Saturday 11 A.M.–7
P.M.

Renaud Pellegrino

15 rue du Cherche-Midi, 6e; see Right Bank description p. 97

Il Bisonte

It took an Italian leather designer—a former architect—to incarnate the handsome and rugged traveling bags from 19th-century America. Wanny di Filippo aptly chose the bison, symbol of peace and strength, as the trademark for his good-looking leather bags, accessories, and men's and women's coats and jackets (designed by Mrs. di Filippo).

It Bisonte leather goods only get better with age—natural shades of tan, olive, and burgundy darken with use as the leather softens. And the styles never go out of fashion. Much of what is currently shown at Il Bisonte was designed 10 years ago.

In the U.S., Il Bisonte can be found at some of the finer department stores and in their SoHo boutique in New York. Paris prices tend to represent about a 15% savings (30% if you benefit from *détaxe*). (See p. 211)
17 rue du Cherche-Midi, 6e; tel.: 42.22.08.41;
Métro: St.-Sulpice
7-9 galerie Véro-Dodat, 1er; tel.: 45.08.92.45;
Métro: Louvre
open Tuesday–Saturday 10:30 A.M.–1:30 P.M. and 2:30–7:30 P.M.

Jule des Prés

The artist's name is Jule and all of the glorious sculptural bouquets that she creates are indeed composed of dried flowers, herbs, and spices from *les prés* (the meadows) of France. Poppy trees, wheat bundles, clove balls, rose-petal potpourris, cinnamon-stick wall hangings, and spice gardens made up of bay leaf, lavender, and juniper berries exude heady, sensual aromas reminiscent of fresh-cut hay, the fields of Provence, or an old-fashioned Christmas at home. The arrangements come in a variety of sizes. Prices start at $30 for a potpourri and go on up to about $700 for some of the bigger, more impressive pieces. Aside from their divine smell, the bouquets serve as decorative items that work harmoniously with many different types of interiors.

19 rue du Cherche-Midi, 6e; tel.: 45.48.26.84;
Métro: St.-Sulpice
46 rue du Roi-de-Sicile, 4e; tel.: 48.04.79.49;
Métro: St.-Paul
open Monday–Saturday 11 A.M.–7 P.M.

Le Cherche-Midi

Stop here for lunch (or for dinner at the end of your shopping) for bistro fare with Italian flare! The ambiance is always lively and the restaurarant is filled with a lot of neighboring "celebs". (I once dined next to Françoise Sagan and French actor Michel Blanc.)
22 rue du Cherche-Midi; tel.: 45.48.27.44;
Métro: St-Sulpice
open every day 12:15–2:30P.M.; and 8:15P.M.–
midnight

Paco Rabanne

Recent recipient of the *dé d'or* (golden thimble—Paris's most prestigious award for couture excellence), Paco Rabanne's creations are always unique, theatrical, and sometimes downright outlandish. Monsieur Rabanne has just invested in 3 floors of shop space filled with selected offerings of men's and women's fashions, as well as up-to-the minute accessories full of glitter and gleam.
7 rue du Cherche-Midi, 6e; tel.: 42.22.87.80;
Métro: St.-Sulpice or Sèvres-Babylone
open Monday–Saturday 10 A.M.—7 P.M.

J. Fenestrier

Fenestrier has been superbly handcrafting men's shoes since 1895. It's not surprising to learn that they are the maker of Robert Clergerie's shoes for women. The men's shoes, like the women's, are based on solid, streamlined forms or, in other words, more stylish versions of the classics. Most of the men who buy here are young and prefer putting their money toward a pair of Fenestriers than a pair of Westons. Now that the status-symbol Westons are in such demand, it is said that their quality is inferior to those *chez* Fenestrier. The average price for a pair of shoes at Fenestrier is about $270.

23 rue du Cherche-Midi, 6e; tel.: 42.22.66.02;
Métro: St.-Sulpice
open Monday 11 A.M.–12:30 P.M. and 1:30–7 P.M.;
Tuesday–Friday 10 A.M.–12:30 P.M. and 1:30–7 P.M.;
Saturday 10 A.M.–7 P.M.

Les Contes de Thé

Every nook and cranny of this adorable shop is filled with tea or tea-related paraphernalia. Eighty different blends of traditional and exotic teas with names such as Marco Polo (raspberry-vanilla-, and licorice-flavored) in violet-, almond-, and bordeaux-colored canisters line one wall; hundreds of cute and collectible teapots decorate the other; and more classic clay and cast-iron teapots crowd the center table. Almost every imaginable type of teapot is here, arranged according to theme: birds, animals, houses, cars, fruits and vegetables, and special events that depict a married couple, Santa Claus in his sleigh, and a maiden voyage in a hot-air balloon! Most of the teapots are imported from England; others are made in France.

60 rue du Cherche-Midi, 6e; tel.: 45.49.45.96;
Métro: Rennes or Sèvres-Babylone
open Tuesday–Saturday 10:30 A.M.–7:30 P.M.

Rue de Sèvres

Jet-Set

My French girlfriends love Jet-Set's shoes so much that they don't care if they make their feet hurt. Most of the shoes are so trendy that they won't make it past a season, but during that particular six-month period, you will certainly feel *très à la mode*.

7 rue de Sèvres, 6e; tel.: 45.48.68.01;
Métro: Sèvres-Babylone or St.-Sulpice
85 rue de Passy, 16e; tel.: 42.88.21.59;
Métro: La Muette
open Monday–Saturday 10 A.M.–7 P.M.

Mac Douglas

This 44-year-old company is the crème de la crème of Paris leather outfitters, and every other Parisian dreams to have one of their coats or jackets in his or her wardrobe. Buttery soft leather and suede of the finest quality is fashioned into rather timeless styles: elegant ¾-length coats, French rocker *blousons*, and sporty "weekend" jackets are their forte. These items, along with their pants, skirts, and bags, sell at investment-like prices—but the craftsmanship and styles are such that you'll have them forever. Prices at their boutique in New York tend to run about 25% higher. Selection at the rue de Sèvres boutique is the best in all of Paris, the help is extremely friendly, and their sales are fantastic!

9 rue de Sèvres, 6e; tel.: 45.48.14.09;
Métro: Sèvres-Babylone or St.-Sulpice
20 rue Pierre-Lescot, 1er; tel.: 42.36.15.48;
Métro: Etienne-Marcel
27 rue de Passy, 16e; tel.: 42.88.96.02; Métro: Passy
open Monday–Saturday 10 A.M.—7 P.M.

Chantelivre

It's never too soon to start teaching your child a few key words in French, and Chantelivre will provide you with the most extensive and creative selection of books, records, posters, and games for children of all ages.

13 rue de Sèvres, 6e; tel. 45.48.87.90;
Métro: Sèvres-Babylone
open Monday 1–7 P.M.; Tuesday–Saturday 10 A.M.–7 P.M.

Christofle

17 rue de Sèvres, 6e; see Right Bank description p. 72

Guerlain

29 rue de Sèvres, 6e; see Right Bank description p. 89

Dorothée Bis

33 rue de Sèvres, 6e; see Place des Victoires/Les Halles description p. 177

Le Bon Marché

corner of rue du Sèvres and rue du Bac, 7e; see Department Stores p. 306

· # Rue du Dragon ·

Revillon

The Revillon legend began in the 1700s when the *frères* Revillon set out for the Hudson River region and western Canada in search of some of the most exquisite varieties of fur pelts: sable, ermine, beaver, and Canadian stone-marten. Over 200 years later, the house of Revillon is still one of the world's greatest outposts for fashionable furs and leather clothing.

In the U.S., Saks Fifth Avenue has an exclusive on this Parisian luxury label, but you'll find that the prices are in fact a good 20% higher. (With the détaxe figure it's a 35% difference, less the 10% you have to pay at customs, so you can count on about a 25% savings here.) Price savings at their sales are even more interesting. The styles shown in Paris are of course much more *parisien* than what is sold stateside; young and sporty, inside-out rabbit and lamb are the trend in Paris these days.

If you're not in the market for a fur or even a leather skirt, you can always content yourself with one of Revillon's animalesque silk or wool scarves ($175 for the silk scarves) or a bottle of one of their fragrances: Detchma and Turbulences for women, or French Line for men.

44 rue du Dragon, 6e; tel.: 42.22.38.91;
Métro: St.-Sulpice
40 rue de la Boétie, 8e; tel.: 45.61.98.98;
Métro: Miromesnil or St.-Phillippe-du-Roule
open Monday–Saturday 10 A.M.–6:30 P.M.

Furla

The last time I came here, in the span of three minutes I heard at least four different women asking each other if the bags in the window were made of real crocodile. Furla's crocodile bags are in fact fake but never before has crocodile been so splendidly imitated. Bottle-green, topaz, grape, and basic black pressed cowhide has been stylishly fashioned into women's handbags and belts in shapes ranging from the classic Kelly bag to a more sophisticated clutch. To most people, this Italian designer is synonymous with faux crocodile, but each collection also develops another fantasy-like look such as paisley-print cloth bags or sturdy leather-trimmed canvas traveling bags. Furla's prices are quite reasonable overall and here in they run about 25% lower than New York.

40 rue du Dragon, 6e; tel.: 40.49.06.44;
Métro: St.-Sulpice
open Monday–Saturday 11 A.M.–7 P.M.

San Francisco Muffin Co.

It took an enterprising young American woman to open up Paris's first muffin shop and now, after cookies and ice cream, the French are finally wallowing in our favorite treats. Stop in here for a quick snack in the form of a honey-colored muffin, a chocolaty brownie, or a cool and refreshing frozen yogurt!

35 rue du Dragon, 6e; tel.: 45.48.45.55;
Métro: St.-Sulpice
open Monday–Saturday 9 A.M.–7:30 P.M.

Aka

The sparce, yet warm, decor of this boutique provides a theatrical setting for this young Japanese designer's shoes for men and women. Leather and suede shoes and boots, in rich hues of brown, khaki, rust, and blood red are artistically trimmed with fur, silver, and pom-poms to create styles that are both soft and modern. Flats and eccentric-looking pointed-toe shapes give way to a partly classic, partly high-fashion look. Expensive.

23 rue du Dragon, 6e; tel.: 45.48.01.07;
Métro: St.-Sulpice
open Tuesday–Friday 10 A.M.–1 P.M. and 2–7 P.M.;
Saturday 11 A.M.–1 P.M. and 2–7 P.M.

Church

England's famous classic men's shoes sell here at prices considerably more interesting than those found in the U.S.

Prices average about $290 as opposed to $350 stateside.
Sorry, no sales.

4 rue du Dragon, 6e; tel.: 45.44.50.47;
Métro: St.-Germain-des-Prés
open Monday–Saturday 10:30 A.M.–6:30 P.M. (closed
Monday and Thursday 1–2:15 P.M.)
42 rue Vivienne, 2e; tel.: 42.36.22.92; Métro: Bourse
open Tuesday–Saturday 10:15 A.M.–1:30 P.M. and
2:30–6:15 P.M.

Rue des Saints-Pères

Cassegrain

81 rue des Saints-Pères, 6e; see Right Bank
description p. 81

Maud Frizon

Anyone who has ever tried to look like a fashion plate
has invested in a pair of Maud Frizon's superstylish, handmade shoes. The selection here is astounding and is in-
dicative of the wide realms of this French designer's
imagination: mink-trimmed booties, leopard-skin Wed-
gies, lace-up ankle boots, and Eiffel Tower–emblazoned
pumps are some of the more eccentric models shown next
to more low-keyed examples of Maud Frizon chic. Shoes
average $235–350 a pair and the saleswomen are particu-
larly friendly for a boutique with such a high-fashion
image.

Maud Frizon Club (a lower-priced line of women's
shoes—most of which are not handmade) and men's
shoes are found next door. Another Maud Frizon boutique, Miss Maud (for juniors), is located at rue de Grenelle. Her accessories shop is around the corner at 79 rue
des Saints-Pères.

81 and 83 rue des Saints-Pères, 6e; tel.: 42.22.06.93;
Métro: Sèvres-Babylone
open Monday–Saturday 10 A.M.–7 P.M.

Au Sauvignon

It may appear like an ordinary café, but if you look around you'll notice that this is one of the liveliest *bistrot à vin* in Paris. During the warm months, this popular wine bar more than doubles its crowd size, making it a fun place for peoplewatching. Sit down and sip a glass of Puligny Montrachet and watch the world go by. Delicious smoked ham, rillettes, paté, and cantal sandwiches, served on Poilâne bread, make for a light, tasty lunch at any hour.
80 rue des Saints-Pères, 7e, tel.: 45.48.49.02;
Métro: Sèvres-Babylone
open Monday–Saturday 8:30 A.M.–11 P.M.

Xavier Danaud

Xavier Danaud's modern-looking women's shoes are actually made by Charles Jourdan. Known for their wide range of colors and sturdy-looking, squared-off heels, these shoes may be best classified as trend-setters. Karl Lagerfeld's elegant collection of gold-initialed, black satin and suede shoes is sold here as well.
78 rue des Saints-Pères, 6e; tel.: 45.48.57.40;
Métro: Sèvres-Babylone
open Monday–Saturday 10 A.M.–7 P.M.

Carel

78 rue des Saints-Pères, 7e; see rue du Four description p. 137

Angelo Tarlazzi

74 rue des Saints-Pères, 7e; see Right Bank description p. 60

Sabbia Rosa

Sabbia Rosa is Paris's queen of luxurious lingerie. Madame Rosa fashions satin and silk into beautiful little frivolities that live up to everything you've ever expected out of French lingerie. If you can't find what you're looking for in the shop's *prêt-à-porter* collection, then you may special order a custom-made item in your own favorite color and style (takes about 10 days). The prices are steep, but the models are so classic and of such fine quality you'll have them forever.

71-73 rue des Saints-Pères, 6e; tel.: 45.48.88.37;
Métro: St.-Sulpice
open Monday–Saturday 10 A.M.–7 P.M.

Yohji Yamamoto

69 rue des Saints-Pères, 7e; see place des Victoires/
Les Halles description p. 176

Gianni Versace

67 rue des Saints-Pères, 7e; see Right Bank
description p. 68

Camille Unglik

Very high-fashioned women's shoes known for their excellent quality and comfort. Each collection offers a wide variety of pretty colors in predominantly tapered styles.

66 rue des Saints-Pères, 7e; tel.: 45.48.55.24;
Métro: St.-Sulpice
open Monday 11 A.M.–7 P.M.; Tuesday–Saturday
10 A.M.–7 P.M.
21 rue Pavé, 4e; tel.: 42.78.55.38;
Métro: St.-Paul
open Tuesday–Saturday 11 A.M.–1:15 P.M. and 2–7
P.M.

· # Rue de Grenelle ·

Inscriptions Rykiel

Having first tested her wings with the baby Rykiel collections in 1987, Sonia's daughter, Nathalie, has now taken over the rue de Grenelle sanctuary and has launched her own line, Inscriptions Rykiel. The look is young and basic, with jeans, T-shirts and jackets making up the backbone

of Nathalie's collections. The Rykiel children's fashions
have remained just next door.

4 rue de Grenelle, 7e; tel.: 49.54.60.00
8 rue de Grenelle, 7e (children's); tel.: 49.54.60.00;
Métro: St.-Sulpice
open Monday–Saturday 10 A.M.–7 P.M.

Prada

There are actually two Prada boutiques at this address.
The first one shows their elegant collection of women's
shoes, designed in Milan and fashioned in the finest of
Italian leathers. The second boutique shows travel bags,
handbags for both day- and eveningwear, and accessories
in both classic and more fanciful styles. Chanel-like
quilted bags in satin and leather are paired up against
more sporty nylon totes. The bad news is that the prices
are not too much better than in the U.S., but if you take
advantage of the *détaxe* or happen to make it to one of
their January or July sales, you can make out well enough.

5 rue de Grenelle, 6e; tel.: 45.48.53.14;
Métro: St.-Sulpice
open Monday–Saturday 10:30 A.M.–7 P.M.

Emilia

A large and lovely boutique filled with many moderately
priced, stylish bags, belts, and shoes by Emilia, a French
manufacturer located in Paris. The people who work in
the boutique are very accommodating and it is sometimes
possible to have a particular item brought in for you, in
another color or style, if it is not available in the store.
Don't hesitate to ask.

11 rue de Grenelle, 6e; tel.: 42.22.37.67;
Métro: St.-Sulpice
open Monday–Saturday 10 A.M.–7 P.M.

Stéphane Kélian

One of the top names in high-fashion shoe styling, Stéphane Kélian's trademark is his finely woven (*tresse*)
shoes in the form of pumps, sandals, and loafers. More
avant-garde fashions include pointy-toed boots, suede
booties, and coin-emblazoned sandals. The prices, which
are lower than those practiced stateside, are honest for
the caliber of design and quality.

A large selection of Kélian's men's shoes, including those that he created for Claude Montana and Jean-Paul Gaultier, may be found at all 3 of the following boutiques.
13 bis rue de Grenelle, 7e; tel.: 42.22.93.03;
Métro: St.-Sulpice
6 place des Victoires, 1er; tel.: 42.61.60.74;
Métro: Etienne-Marcel
open Monday–Saturday 10:30 A.M.–7 P.M.
36 rue de Sévigné, 3e; tel.: 42.77.82.00;
Métro: Saint-Paul
open Monday–Saturday 10:30 A.M.–12:15 P.M. and 1:15–7 P.M.; Sunday 2–7 P.M.

Charles Kammer

A few years ago Charles Kammer was one of the first to come out with the whimsical-looking, suede elfish shoes that are still going strong today. Overall his shoes are very stylish, and if they're not embroidered with a baroque sort of design or ornamented with a pilgrim-like buckle, they're very high heeled or laced up like a turn-of-the-century *bootine*! Prices here are comparable to those *chez* Stéphane Kélian.
14 rue de Grenelle, 7e; tel.: 42.22.91.19;
Métro: St.-Sulpice
4 place des Victoires, 1er; tel.: 42.36.31.84;
Métro: Palais Royal
open Monday–Saturday 10 A.M.–7 P.M.
6 rue des Rosiers, 4e; tel.: 48.04.04.68;
Métro: Saint-Paul
open Sunday and Monday 2–7:30 P.M.; Tuesday–Saturday 11 A.M.–7:30 P.M.

Chacok

The radiating lines carved in the granite floor resemble a sundial, and the grey light of Paris suddenly becomes more luminous when reflected off the pink-sand–colored walls and turquoise display racks. Such is the feeling of sunshine *chez* Chacok. And the same cheerfulness emanates from the bright reds, yellows, blues, and violets of their women's clothing.

Although they don't yet have a boutique in the States, their comfortable knit ensembles are found in some of the most exclusive U.S. shops, but here they're sold at much more reasonable prices.

The force of Madame Chacok's clothing is in their comfort, design, and versatility. Each season she introduces another ethnic-like theme that can be mixed and matched with at least three other items in the shop as well as with clothing from previous years' collections. This explains their devoted following. Many a Parisian returns each year to complement articles that she already owns. Other strong points include surprising blends of colors, such as blue and brown, the use of soft wool and linen jerseys, and always the presence of a more sober-looking, solid-color skirt or dress.

18 rue de Grenelle, 7e; tel.: 42.22.69.99;
Métro: St.-Sulpice
open Monday–Saturday 10 A.M.–7 P.M.
Palais des Congrès; 2 place de la Porte-Maillot,
17e; tel.: 46.40.22.21
Métro: Porte-Maillot
open Monday–Saturday 10:30 A.M.–7:30 P.M.

Miss Maud

A more youthful, less expensive version of Maud Frizon's high-fashion shoes. The average price per pair is about $175, which explains why there are almost as many moms buying them as teens.

21 rue de Grenelle, 7e; tel.: 45.48.64.44;
Métro: Sèvres-Babylone
open Monday–Saturday 10 A.M.–1 P.M. and 2–7 P.M.
90 rue du Faubourg–Saint-Honoré, 8e;
tel.: 42.65.27.96; Métro: Miromesnil
open Monday–Saturday 10:30 A.M.–1 P.M.
and 2–7 P.M.

Upla

These casual-looking bags have made a furor in Paris since the mid-1980s, and you're likely to spot every third French woman toting one. Their campy design is based on traditional French fishing and hunting bags, closely resembling our Coach and Dooney & Burke bags. The addition, however, of a few flashy tomato reds, emerald greens, and violets to the more conventional browns and blacks gives these bags a more cosmopolitan air. The leather, canvas, and plastified canvas Upla bags (all trimmed in leather) come in shapes ranging from small pouches to

large camera bags. Leather-bag prices are comparable with
those of Coach and Dooney & Burke as well.
22 rue de Grenelle, 7e; tel.: 45.44.24.81;
Métro: Sèvres-Babylone
97 rue de Longchamp, 16e; tel.: 47.27.41.23;
Métro: Pompe
open Monday–Friday 10:30 A.M.–1:30 P.M. and 2:30–
7 P.M.; Saturday 10:30 A.M.–7 P.M.
17 rue des Halles, 1er; tel.: 40.26.49.96;
Métro: Châtelet
open Monday–Saturday 10:30 A.M.–7 P.M.

Haga

This old-world kind of shop provides a refreshing change
from the numerous fashion boutiques that line the rue de
Grenelle. Feast your eyes on probably the most extensive
collection of wooden-spiraled, Victorian candlesticks that
Paris has to offer as well as some decorative fish-eye
mirrors, silver frames, heavy wool paisley throws, and
antique canes. Their prices are par for the neighborhood—*très cher*.
22 rue de Grenelle, 7e; tel.: 42.22.82.40;
Métro: Sèvres-Babylone
open Monday–Saturday 10:30 A.M.–12:45 P.M. and
2:15–7 P.M.

Princesse Tam-Tam

The boutique of the moment for cute, "teenagerish" lingerie. Most of the skimpy bra and panty sets and boyish
pajamas are made of 100% cotton. All of their themes are
fun and spunky: candy-stripes, blue and white gingham,
little black cats, and sweatshirt-grey trimmed with white
lace and pink ribbons! Big girls buy here, too.
23 rue de Grenelle, 7e; tel.: 45.49.28.73;
Métro: Sèvres-Babylone
open Monday–Saturday 10:30 A.M.–1 P.M. and 2–7
P.M.

Odile Lançon

A young *créatrice* on the rise, Odile Lançon is more concerned with individual style than with imposing trendy
panoplies on her clients. It's not surprising to learn that

she once worked for Max Mara and then later launched her own collection with the help of another Italian company—two connections that have surely reinforced her use of quality fabrics and refined colors. Hard to find stateside.

24 rue de Grenelle, 7e; tel.: 45.44.56.99;
Métro: Sèvres-Babylone
open Monday–Saturday 10 A.M.–7 P.M.

Anita Oggioni

30 rue de Grenelle, 7e; see Right Bank description
p. 41

Claude Montana

Rigorous lines, clean precise cuts, and unornamented styles are the trademark of Paris's most modern designer, Claude Montana. The Montana woman dresses with simple elegance, exuding a pure, unconfused look—not unlike that of a 90s version of the Greek goddess. The mostly solid colors are never overbearing, creating a feeling of subtle femininity.

31 rue de Grenelle, 7e; tel.: 45.49.13.02;
Métro: Bac
3 rue des Petits-Champs, 1er;
tel.: 40.20.02.14;
Métro: Bourse
open Monday–Saturday 10:15 A.M.–1 P.M. and 2–7 P.M.

Tokio Kumagaï

The wacky styles have toned down a bit since this Japanese designer's death a few years ago, but the men's, and especially the women's, shoe styles still remain innovative and trendy. The look these days is focused on every imaginable type of closing: zips, ties, snaps, and elastic puckered, woven, stretched and even fashioned into embroidery-like designs. Price tags of $175–215 are cut in half during sale time. A somewhat limited selection of offbeat women's ready-to-wear is also on view.

32 rue de Grenelle, 7e; tel.: 45.44.23.11;
Métro: Sèvres-Babylone
52 rue Croix-des-Petits-Champs, 1er;

tel.: 42.36.08.01;
Métro: Palais Royal
open Monday–Friday 10 A.M.–7 P.M.; Saturday 11
A.M.–7 P.M.

Barbara Bui

35 rue de Grenelle, 7e; see Place des Victoires/Les
Halles description p. 181

Krizia

35 rue de Grenelle, 7e; see Right Bank description
p. 65

Charles Jourdan

39 rue de Grenelle, 7e; see Right Bank description
p. 68

Cerruti 1881

You don't truly appreciate Nino Cerruti's women's fashions until you actually start touching some of the clothing
inside his stores. The quality here is superior to that of
the neighboring boutiques, and if you're a sucker for but-
tery-soft wool and creamy leather, you'll love the stately
designed womenswear that bears the famous Cerruti label. The look here is as classy and clean as the Cerruti
menswear, and the designer, in fact, employs the same
finely tuned tailoring for his elegant women's fashions,
whether it be for a suit, a coat, or a dress. The colors are
a blend of subtle earth tones. Needless to say, you won't
find such an assemblage of Cerruti fashions anywhere but
in this part of the world.
42 rue de Grenelle, 7e; tel.: 42.22.92.28; Métro: Bac
15 place de la Madeleine, 8e; tel.: 47.42.10.78;
Métro: Madeleine
17 av Victor Hugo, 16e; tel.: 45.01.66.12
Métro: Etoile or Victor-Hugo
open Monday–Saturday 10:15 A.M.–7 P.M.

Dalloyau

It's hard to resist the mouth-watering pastries and finger
sandwiches that you see in the window *chez* Dalloyau.

Stop in and treat yourself to a little snack from one of Paris's most famous bakers and chocolate makers since 1802. They are probably best known for their *macarons*—light and fluffy, cream-filled cookie-like meringues that come in a variety of flavors: chocolate, coffee, vanilla, strawberry, pistachio, raspberry, and more!
63 rue de Grenelle, 7e; tel.: 45.49.95.30;
Métro: rue de Bac
open daily 9 A.M.–8 P.M.

Il Pour L'Homme

68 rue de Grenelle, 7e; see Right Bank description
p. 84

The General Store

"Come on, you've got to be kidding." "No, I wouldn't kid you." That's about how the conversation starts off when I tell visitors that fine American gourmet-food products such as Velveeta cheese, Cheerios, and Campbell's baked beans are indeed imported into France and on sale at The General Store. If you're only in Paris for a short while, you probably can live without your favorite American goodies, but if you extend your stay (let's say a couple of weeks), this store is apt to represent a small source of survival for you. How many buttery croissants can one eat! In any event, if you're in the area, you should stop in because it's fun to see how charming an American food shop can look in the heart of one of Paris's most prestigious neighborhoods. The French (at least half of their clientele) find it very chic to come here for pancake mix, Tex-Mex fixings, kosher pickles, and a few of their fresh-baked cookies!
82 rue de Grenelle, 7e; tel.: 45.48.63.16;
Métro: rue du Bac
open Monday–Saturday 10 A.M.–7:15 P.M.

·   **Boulevard Raspail**   ·

Olivier Strelli

This boutique is ideal for fashion-conscious men who don't dare stray too far from the classics. The force of this Belgian designer is revealed in his strong, ample cuts and his use of rich vibrant colors. A classic trench is cut large for a fuller, more modern look, and structural-looking jackets are shown in grass green, crimson, and midnight blue. The warm welcome plus the dressing rooms all the way in the back of the boutique provide a comfortable atmosphere for trying on their generous selection of clothing.

7 bd Raspail, 7e; tel.: 45.44.77.17; Métro: rue du Bac
open Monday–Saturday 10 A.M.–7 P.M.
52 rue Etienne-Marcel, 2e; tel.: 45.08.01.90;
Métro: Etienne-Marcel
open Monday 2–7 P.M.; Tuesday–Saturday 10:30
A.M.–12:30 P.M. and 2–7 P.M.

Kenzo

16 bd Raspail, 7e (women's); See Place des
Victoires/Les Halles description p. 171
17 bd Raspail, 7e (men's); see Place des Victoires/
Les Halles description, p. 170

L'Artisan Parfumeur

This is one of the shops I suggest to my clients whenever they mention buying fragrances in Paris. Unlike other big-name perfumes that are found in every store and duty-free shop from New York to Tokyo, these delightful *eaux de toilette* still connote a sense of exclusivity to the buyer (and receiver)—a very satisfying sentiment to be had with any purchase.

Most of the women's and men's fragrances at L'Artisan Parfumeur are natural, and all are composed with one idea in mind: recreating scents that are linked to memories. Thus Symphonie de Rose, a peppery sort of fragrance made up of three different types of roses, may recall images of Grandma's old-fashioned rose garden in the month of June. Other themes include essences that were popular at the Palace of Versailles or during the French Revolution—so distinct that you'll feel as though you had been there!

Other exquisite items include boxes of their own special potpourri, glittery costume jewelry, and *boules d'ambre*—sculpted terra-cotta balls filled with aromatic vegetable ambergris.

24 bd Raspail, 7e; tel.: 42.22.23.32;
Métro: rue du Bac
open 10:30 A.M.–7 P.M.
22 rue Vignon, 9e; tel.: 42.66.32.66;
Métro: Madeleine
open Monday–Saturday 10:30 A.M.–2:30 P.M. and 3–
7 P.M.

■ Rue du Bac ■

Le Bon Marché

Corner of rue du Bac and rue du Sèvres, 7e; see Department Stores p. 306

La Mine d'Argent

Sterling silver and silverplate coffee and tea services, hand mirrors, frames, serving dishes, flatware, and teething rings glisten in this reputable boutique that sells mostly antique silver items for the home and table. English is spoken and don't be afraid to bargain—just don't tell them I told you so.
108 rue du Bac, 7e; tel.: 45.48.70.68;
Métro: Sèvres-Babylone or rue du Bac
open Monday 10:30 A.M.–7 P.M.

Venini

A large, modern store filled with stunning Venetian glassware, artistically hand-blown into nearly 100 different contemporary shapes and colors. Don't miss the downstairs.
97 rue du Bac, 7e; tel.: 45.48.95.39;
Métro: Sèvres-Babylone or rue du Bac
open Monday 2–7 P.M.; Tuesday–Saturday 11 A.M.–7
P.M.

Dîners en Ville

If you only have time to visit one tabletop shop in Paris, I suggest you come here. A festival of autumn colors warms you as you enter this boutique. Its cozy decor and cordial welcome make you feel as though you had just entered a beautiful Parisian home.

Countess Blandine de Mandat Grancey was one of the first in Paris to set the trend of mixing the old with the new—a fashion that has since become a way of life for most Parisian hostesses. Antique crystal and silver is set off against modern reproductions of old dishes, flatware, and glassware in order to present a look that is both thoroughly charming and affordable. A marriage of forms and colors is created on the many different tables that are dressed with antique English "table rugs," paisley tablecloths, and Martine Nourissat's brightly colored, 100% cotton Alsatian prints, which are currently the rage in France ($145–250).

Be sure to take the winding staircase up to the golden-colored rooms filled with decorative *trompe l'oeil* plates, over 50 different teacups and teapots, and at least 100 fanciful earthenware bowls, pitchers, and soup terrines in the form of cabbages, rabbits, apples, and more!
89 rue du Bac, 7e; tel.: 42.22.78.33;
Métro: rue du Bac
open Tuesday–Saturday 11 A.M.–7 P.M.

Ryst-Dupeyron

Eighteenth-century wooden beams and pearl-grey floor mosaics announce tradition, and you quickly realize that this is not your ordinary liquor store. Connoisseurs and amateurs alike will be thrilled with the extensive selection of Bordeaux wines, Portuguese ports, and Scotch whiskies that fill this elegant shop. The main attraction, however, is Monsieur Ryst's own brand of armagnac: a brandy similar to cognac, differing mainly in its distillation and in its provenance of grapes and oak barrels. (Armagnac's grapes and barrels come from the Armagnac region of France, whereas cognac's come from Cognac.)

Hundreds of handsome pear-shaped bottles containing various types of this golden liquid, and dating as far back as 1893, line the left-hand side wall. Celebrating an anniversary or birthday with a particular *millésimé* (good year) is an excellent gift idea, and the shop will personalize any of their bottles with the name and date of your choice. The director of the boutique, Madame de Saluces, a woman as charming as the shop itself, will allow you to taste a number of their armagnacs and liquors as well as advise you on the best years and optimal drinking conditions for the various chateaux wines.

Other tempting items include liquor-soaked fruits, armagnac-filled chocolates, foie gras, gift packages of armagnac, demicrystal glasses, and wooden boxes.

Ryst-Dupeyron has just opened a boutique in Japan and who knows, maybe someday will do the same in the U.S.
79 rue du Bac, 7e; tel.: 45.48.80.93;
Métro: rue du Bac
open Monday–Saturday 10 A.M.–12:30 P.M. and 1:30– 7 P.M.

Etamine

Whether you are in search of subtle-colored fabrics, sponge-painted wallpapers or just a few extra frivolities for your home, Etamine is Paris's latest hot spot for interior decorating ideas. The look is decidedly *nouveau* Santa Fe—an appropriate backdrop for the boutique's selection of wrought iron candlesticks, teepee-inspired table throws and Hilton McConnico's (Daum) cactus-topped decanters. Most of the prices on these un-French looking goods are quite steep—and aside from the handsome collection of high quality bed linens on the main floor, you'll probably be most impressed with Etamine's delicious display of wallpaper and fabrics on the lower level. You may either order here directly (takes 1–3 weeks), or just look around and then order from Coolman at a 20% discount (see Coup de Foudre p. 293).
63 rue du Bac, 7e; tel.: 42.22.03.16;
Métro: Bac
open Monday—Saturday 9:30 A.M.–6:30 P.M.

Missoni

All of Missoni's marvelous Italian knits, silks, and linens for men and women embellish this spacious boutique. It's no surprise that many Americans figure among their clientele because their Paris prices, which aren't much higher than those in Italy, tend to run about 30% less than those in the U.S.
43 rue du Bac, 7e; tel.: 45.48.38.02;
Métro: rue du Bac
open Monday–Saturday 10 A.M.–7 P.M.

Laure Japy

If Diners en Ville is a festival of autumn colors, then Laure Japy is in full summertime bloom. Over 20 tables draped in bold-colored tablecloths (some especially created for the boutique by Martine Nourissat) are set with Laure Japy's own hand-painted (mostly with sponges) china from Limoges. The boutique's equally colorful flatware and clear glassware, edged with a thread of color, co-ordinate magnificently with their stunning dishes. Numerous gift ideas such as vases, planters, lamps, and candlesticks are also shown in the same spectrum of rainbow colors. Their reasonable prices become even more interesting when you learn that Laure Japy's arts of the table sell for twice as much in New York at Bergdorf's and Barney's.

34 rue du Bac, 7e; tel.: 42.86.96.97;
Métro: rue du Bac
open Monday–Saturday 10:30 A.M.–7 P.M.

Christian Constant

Chocaholics beware! Even the most conditioned of us chocolate mongers can O.D. on Christian Constant's superrich *chocolat chaud* (hot chocolate so thick that your spoon practically stands up on its own). If you're not interested in this heavenly drink, then you may simply have a cup of tea, best accompanied with one of their chocolaty pastries, while relaxing a bit in this all-white, modern decor.

26 rue du Bac, 7e; tel.: 42.96.53.53;
Métro: rue du Bac
37 rue d'Assas, 6e; tel.: 45.48.45.51;
Métro: Rennes
open daily 8 A.M.–8 P.M.

·   **Rue Paul-Louis-Courier**   ·

Concertea

An unassuming *salon de thé*, perfect for a quick and
simple lunch or afternoon tea. Specialties include
homemade quiches, salads, cakes, and pies. Lyrical
music, white garden chairs, and flowery tablecloths
form a peaceful setting away from the hustle-bustle
of Paris streets.
*3 rue Paul-Louis-Courier, 7e; tel.: 45.49.27.59;
Métro: rue du Bac
open Monday 11:30 A.M.–3:30 P.M.; Tuesday–
Saturday 11:30 A.M.–7 P.M.*

Place des Victoires and Les Halles
·   (The Cutting Edge of Fashion)   ·

Once the Left Bank gained a strong foothold in the Paris
shopping world, the place des Victoires and Les Halles
were the next areas of Paris to take over as fashion hubs.
The number of boutiques that have opened up in these
two shopping districts has grown at a relentless pace
along with the widespread development of the entire
area.

Unlike Les Halles, the glorious 19th-century place des
Victoires area escaped virtually every form of physical
transformation. The changes that have taken place here
have occurred within the walls of these magnificent buildings rather than outside. Nearly two decades ago, the first
two high-fashion boutiques to set up shop here were Victoire and Kenzo; since then each year has marked the
opening of one more important fashion showcase, including 1990's most recent addition: Esprit (of California
fame).

Fashion-hungry shoppers soon made this area their
stomping ground and little by little the rather uninterest-
ing (and ugly) rue Etienne-Marcel witnessed the arrival

of some of the fashion world's hottest new designers. A mini-empire was founded by the Japanese designers who decided to make Paris their second (or even first) home. Soon every other person on the street was wearing black and Parisians started talking about the *branché* (plugged-in) types and then later the *chébran* (*branché* inverted—meaning that they were even more plugged in). New Wave had arrived, and all of the punks and the New Wave types descended upon rue Etienne-Marcel and Les Halles as if it was their haven.

The Les Halles area underwent the most drastic upheavals of all of the transformations that the French capital has experienced. (Baron Haussmann's major changes to the Opéra area were peanuts next to these.) After harboring Paris's major wholesale food market for hundreds of years, Les Halles became a hole in the ground in the 70s, which later developed into France's largest shopping mall in the early 80s. Now over 200 stores, fast foods, restaurants, and cinemas make up the Forum des Halles, the mammoth underground complex that has been the source of great controversy and change within the entire neighborhood of Les Halles. The various kitchen-supply stores clustered in Les Halles are the last vestiges of this bustling area that Zola once called "the belly of Paris." The major food markets have since been displaced outside of the capital at Rungis near Orly airport.

I won't hide the fact that the Forum des Halles is not my cup of tea. We have enough of shopping malls in America, beautiful or otherwise, that are more than capable of filling all of our conspicuous-consumption needs under one roof. If you love malls, fine. Take a look around, but just don't expect to find the same sort of charm that fills so many of the quaint little boutiques of Paris.

What is probably France's (and maybe even Europe's) biggest subway and commuter-train (RER) interchange is located underneath the Forum. This of course means that the Forum has become a real hangout for suburbanites and drifters, making it one of the most dangerous stations in Paris and also one of the most confusing. When possible, I will suggest other Métro stations from which to choose.

The area around Les Halles, however, is equally as animated without so much clutter or riffraff. The street culture is certainly the most varied and demonstrative that

Paris has to offer, and the eclectic mix of shops are among the first to reflect the latest trends. You can sit for hours in the cafés watching the world go by or wander about and take in the many different forms of street entertainment that is free for the watching: mimes, rock music, clowns, and fire eaters. *Au Père Tranquille* at rue Pierre-Lescot (rue Coquillière) and *Café Costes* (sit and drink Perrier on one of Philippe Stark's ultramodern metal chairs) at rue Berger are two of the most popular spots for peoplewatching. Open 24 hours a day, the recently renovated *Au Pied de Cochon* is somewhat of a landmark and also one of the most famous restaurants in Paris for onion soup au gratin; sit out on the terrace during the summer months and feast over a big, beautiful seafood platter. If you feel like going American, you'll discover the greatest concentration of American bars and restaurants in Les Halles; my all-time favorite is *Joe Allen* on rue Pierre-Lescot.

If you're all shopped out and need a bit of cultural stimulation, try popping into the St. Eustache church (near the rue du Jour), where, if you're lucky enough, you'll hear one of the most sonorous pipe organs in Paris. Or you may head off in the other direction toward the Marais, passing by the red lights of the rue St.-Denis, and arriving at the Georges Pompidou Center, Paris's museum of contemporary art. The area surrounding the museum is called Beaubourg, and if you sit for a while in the bordering *Café Beaubourg,* you will feel like you are right smack in the middle of everything that is new and happening in the City of Lights.

Promenade Place des Victoires/Les Halles

The promenade starts out quietly at the home-decor shops on the rue des Petits-Champs and ends in an explosive burst of energy in the heart of Les Halles. I suggest you walk down the rue des Petits-Champs toward the place des Victoires and the rue Etienne-Marcel, stopping off onto the side streets as you go along. Parts of this promenade may easily be combined with two of the passages on the Passages tour: the Galerie Vivienne and the Galerie Véro-Dodat. The closest Métro stop for the beginning of the tour is Pyramides.

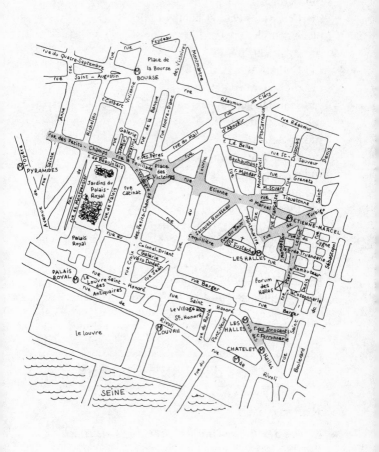

STREETS:

▪ Rue des Petits-Champs ▪

Patrick Frey

47 rue des Petits-Champs, 1er; see Left Bank description p. 110

Gérard Danton

Mixed in among an assortment of blue and white Chinese ginger jars and urns are Gérard Danton's hand-painted porcelain creations in the form of bulbous lamps, vases, candlesticks, and jars. A multitude of vibrant colors reign: strawberry, golden yellow, burnt orange, and shamrock green—most are solids, others are two-toned, such as a midnight-blue planter peppered with a jet-black glaze.

I feel, however, that the main attraction is their square, satiny cotton tablecloths ($215) that come in about six different polychromatic patterns, each one more colorful than the others. These *trompe l'oeil* designs create a marbleized effect, giving the impression that they have been sponge-painted onto the tablecloths; each one evokes elements of decor not characteristically represented on table tops: luxurious gold-fringed emerald curtains (called the Traviata), Renaissance-inspired cornices, and even a grouping of oriental vases on a lemon-yellow background.
39 rue des Petits-Champs, 1er; tel.: 45.55.21.11;
Métro: Pyramides
open Monday–Friday 10 A.M.–7 P.M.; Saturday 10:30 A.M.–1 P.M. and 2:30–7 P.M.

Malicorne

Although lesser known to Americans than Gien, Malicorne is another name synonymous with *faïence*. In fact, the region of Malicorne (about 100 miles southwest of Paris) has been known for its *faïence* since the Gallo-Roman period, but it's just within recent years that this company has emerged as one of today's fashionable home accessories designers.

The *faïence* that is featured in this shop is light and airy. Designs inspired from the most famous ceramic capitals of Europe such as Delft, Copenhagen, Nevers, Rouen, and Moustiers have created a diversity of styles and shapes that reflect a notion of old-world charm. The hallmark of the Malicorne *faïence* is feminine-like cutwork which trims many a plate, bowl, or dish, adding to the delicacy of their hand painted motifs.

Prices here are considerably higher than at Gien, yet the *faïence* is noticeably more refined. Their extensive collection is complemented with a vivid selection of Martine Nourrisat's country French tablecloths from Alsace.
36 rue des Petits-Champs, 1er; tel.: 40.15.93.66;
Métro: Pyramides
open Tuesday–Friday 10:30 A.M.–6:30 P.M.; Monday noon–6:30 P.M. (April 1–end of Sept.); Saturday 1–6 P.M. (Oct. 1–end of March)

Willi's Wine Bar

If you feel like rubbing elbows with Paris's upwardly mobile types from the neighboring financial district and with glamour girls from the nearby fashion boutiques, drop in here, the French capital's most sophisticated wine bar. The ambiance is as glossy as the clientele, making it a perfect place to stop for a bite to eat or a glass of wine when out on a chic promenade.
13 rue des Petits-Champs, 1er; tel.: 42.61.05.09; Métro: Bourse
open Monday–Friday 11 A.M.–10 P.M.

Jean-Charles de Castelbajac

5 rue des Petits-Champs, 1er; see Right Bank description p. 97

Claude Montana

3 rue des Petits-Champs, 1er; see Left Bank description p. 155

▪ ## Rue de la Vrillère ▪

Chatmotomatic

Two display windows bearing jolly-togged child-sized mannequins are locked into a revolving door, which is filled with thousands of cat's-eye marbles, engulfing at least half of the facade of this tiny children's clothing shop. If it sounds a little crazy—it is, and so are the clothes. The dreamy decor continues inside as you find yourself standing on a floor laid in more jewel-like marbles—a stagy decor worthy of the theatrical collection of Chatmotomatic clothing for kids aged 3 months to 12 years. A fake-fur stole on a sporty *blouson,* bright-colored polka dots on velvet jodhpurs, or a tweedy knicker set with its coordinating purple beret are some of the playful styles featured in this enchanting boutique. Prices are very

high, but here's the most innovative children's clothing that Paris has to offer. Don't miss it because Chatmotomatic is almost impossible to find stateside.
8 rue de la Vrillère, 1er; tel.: 49.27.94.10;
Métro: Palais-Royal
open Tuesday–Saturday 11 A.M.–7 P.M.

·   ## Rue Catinat   ·

Adolfo Dominguez

Except for the name you'd never know that this designer is Spanish. There's not a trace of flamenco-like garb in Adolfo Dominguez's sophisticated fashions for men and women. Here the look is understated and serene. His neoclassic cuts in the finest linens, silks, and wools reflect a more Hellenistic influence in his search for designs that are both quietly elegant and practical. The women's clothing is softly draped in a totally refined way without sacrificing an inch of comfort. The men's clothing is more structural and austere, emphasizing his belief that less is more. All of the fashions are shown in a palette of warm vegetable tones, mostly solids with only a smattering of understated prints. Moderate to expensively priced.
2 rue Catinat, 1er; tel.: 47.03.40.28;
Métro: Palais-Royal
open Monday 2–7 P.M.; Tuesday–Saturday 10 A.M.–7 P.M.

·   ## Rue Croix—des-Petits-Champs   ·

Tokio Kumagaï

52 rue Croix–des-Petits-Champs, 1er; see Left Bank description p. 156

Robert Clergerie

46 rue Croix–des-Petits-Champs, 1er; see Left Bank description p. 139

- ## Place des Victoires -

Miki House

1 place des Victoires, 1er; see Left Bank description p. 125

Kenzo

After having studied at a prestigious fashion school in Tokyo, followed by a short stint designing for a major Japanese department store, Kenzo Takada set out for Paris in the early 60s to lay the foundation for a fashion career that has since gained mammouth proportions. Now France's leading designer from the land of the rising sun, Kenzo has received worldwide recognition within the past 20 years for his rich and vibrant fashions that conjure up images of faraway lands and storybook characters. Enchanting motifs, such as bold flowers and paisleys, and whimsical themes based on folkloric costumes from all corners of the earth are fashioned into clothing that is as timeless as it is up-to-date. The men's fashions are less fantasy-like but equally colorful and well proportioned.

The Kenzo empire in Paris consists of five big and beautiful stores, each similarly decorated with rosy-colored walls, mosaic floors, and blond wooden display cases—the effect is as fresh as Kenzo's creations. Don't expect, however, to find the same selection of merchandise in each of these boutiques. Kenzo Place des Victoires is the only store that shows the entire Kenzo Paris collection, Kenzo's better (and most expensive) line of women's fashions. Enjoy the cheery ambiance. Although the prices may seem high, they are still better than in the U.S.

3 place des Victoires, 1er (Kenzo Paris women's, some men's; children's behind the boutique under the passageway); tel.: 40.39.72.03;
Métro: Etienne-Marcel or Palais-Royal
60 and 62 rue de Rennes, 6e; (some Kenzo Paris, some men's, mostly Kenzo City, Jungle and Jeans—see p. 131); tel.: 45.44.27.88;
Métro: St.-Sulpice
16 bd Raspail, 7e (parts of all of the women's lines, children's, and items for the home); tel.: 42.22.09.38
17 bd Raspail, 7e (men's); tel.: 45.49.33.75;

Métro for both boutiques is Bac.
18 av George V, 8e (parts of all of the women's
lines, men's and items for the home);
tel.: 47.23.33.49;
Métro: Alma-Marceau
open Monday 11 A.M.–7 P.M.; Tuesday–Saturday 10
A.M.–7 P.M.

Charles Kammer

4 place des Victoires, 1er; see Left Bank description
p. 152

Chevignon

5 place des Victoires, 1er; see Left Bank description
p. 138

Cacharel

The name Cacharel is most widely associated with the darling little Liberty of London prints that they have been using for years in their fresh and breezy collection of dresses, skirts, and men's and women's shirts. After having died down for a few years, this sugary look is back in full swing and is particularly present in their wide assortment of flowered and paisley shirts from *La Chemiserie*. Their large stock of stylish separates are also very well made, but considerably less fanciful.

This attractive boutique on the place des Victoires features only women's fashions. The main store at 34 rue Tronchet, 8e (near the big department stores) shows their moderately priced men's, women's and children's collections at prices that are slightly more interesting than those in the U.S.

5 place des Victoires, 1er; tel.: 42.33.29.88;
Métro: Palais-Royal or Etienne-Marcel
open Monday–Saturday 10:15 A.M.–7 P.M.

Stéphane Kélian

6 place des Victoires, 1er; see Left Bank description
p. 152

Thierry Mugler

10 place des Victoires, 1er; see Right Bank description p. 39

Victoire

If someone told you (your husband, for example) that you could only go to one women's clothing store in all of Paris, I would suggest that you pick this one. Victoire is *the* Paris showcase for up-to-the minute elegant womenswear from many of Europe's hottest (or soon to be hot) designer labels. Flicking through the racks you're apt to turn up creations by Thierry Mugler, Christian Lacroix, Claude Montana, and Romeo Gigli. Madame Chassagnac, the driving force behind this 20-year-old anchor of the place des Victoires, has a keen eye for upcoming fashion trends. Victoire is responsible for having launched the beloved king of buttons and bows, Patrick Kelly (whom we now all truly miss), and is currently one of the few boutiques in Paris to show creations from up-and-coming Belgian designers Anvers and Dries van Notin. More classic styles from Georges Rech and Victoire's own label complete their tasteful collection of fashions intended for women who refuse to lose their own identity when wearing designer clothing.

10 and 12 place des Victoires, 2e; tel.: 42.61.68.71;
Métro: Palais-Royal or Etienne-Marcel
open Monday–Saturday 9:30 A.M.–7 P.M.
38 rue François 1er, 8e; tel.: 47.23.89.81;
Métro: Franklin-Roosevelt
1 rue Madame, 6e; tel.: 45.44.28.14;
Métro: St.-Sulpice
16 rue de Passy, 16e; tel.: 42.88.20.84;
Métro: Passy or Muette
open Monday–Saturday 10 A.M.–7 P.M.

Blanc Bleu

14, pl des Victoires, 2e; see Left Bank description p. 137

Artic

If you came here a few years ago when this shop featured knitwear by Pôles, you'll notice a few changes have taken place since then. Now they show sexy synthetic fashions by French clothing manufacturer Plein Sud. Joan Collins recently bought here, which helps you to situate them at number 9 on a seductive scale of 1 to 10. Their form-fitted, slinky dresses, T-shirts, and suits will make you look like either an overstuffed sausage or a femme fatale. Your curves definitely have to fall in the right places, because their stretchy lycra/cotton and poly/nylon blends won't tell a lie. As Yves, the owner of the boutique, intimated, "They make great nightclub clothes." As long as they keep on showing Plein Sud's hot and sultry creations, you won't find any chilly clothes at Artic.

place des Victoires (2 rue Vide Gousset), 2e;
tel.: 42.36.75.02; Métro: Palais-Royal or Etienne-Marcel
open Monday–Saturday 10 A.M.*–7* P.M.

Enrico Coveri

If you're ever in the market for a sequined dress, you're almost sure to find one here. A few glitzy dresses and a vibrant selection of knitwear make regular appearances in this Italian designer's collections. Most of Enrico Coveri's fashions are made in France and all are touched with a quintessential note of humor or romance.

place des Victoires (2 rue Vide Gousset), 2e;
tel.: 42.36.86.23; Métro: Palais-Royal or Etienne-Marcel
open Monday 2–6:30 P.M.*; Tuesday–Saturday 10* A.M.*–6:30* P.M.

Rue d'Aboukir

Marlboro Classics

As you would expect, the look is rugged and manly in this menswear boutique. You may be surprised, however, to learn that these handsome fashions are actually very high quality and authentic versions of the clothing that you have seen on the backs of the Marlboro men in this cigarette company's ads. Philip Morris is of course behind this label, as well as the 23 other Marlboro Classics boutiques dispersed throughout Europe. Oddly enough these fashions have not made it stateside for reasons far too complicated for me to get into here.

All of the clothing is made by an Italian manufacturer, which explains the unparalleled quality and glove-like fit of their leather coats and jackets. Their reputation has been built on their full-length riding coats in both leather ($1850) and waterproof broadcloth ($410), which has cinema people such as Steven Spielberg snatching them up in droves. Another biggy is their stoned-washed leather jackets, lined in quilted wool, and fastened with buttons made out of horn. Their collections of jeans, shirts and, sweaters have also been designed for urban cowboys. In case you're wondering, they only smoke Marlboros in this shop.

9 rue d'Aboukir, 2e; tel.: 42.36.00.19;
Métro: Palais-Royal or Etienne-Marcel
50 rue St.-Didier, 16e; tel.: 45.53.03.48;
Métro: Victor-Hugo
open Tuesday–Saturday 10:30 A.M.–7:30 P.M.

Absorba

Absorba is a French manufacturer of traditional children's clothing (ages 0–8 years). Their styles are honest and rather basic, yet supposedly quite French because the collection found here and in the major department stores throughout France differs from those shown in the U.S. Their solid reputation is based on an excellent price/quality relationship, and their biggest sellers are their baby outfits, which are not only adorable but easy to care for, too. Absorba also carries Yves Saint Laurent's refined creations for children from zero to three years. The YSL all-white pantsuits are perfect for little boys who know how to stay clean in their Sunday best.

3 rue d'Aboukir, 2e; tel.: 40.13.90.75;
Métro: Palais-Royal or Etienne-Marcel
open Monday–Friday 10 A.M.–7 P.M.; Saturday 11 A.M.–6:30 P.M.

Formes

7 rue d'Aboukir, 2e; see Left Bank description p. 127

Rue Etienne-Marcel

Junko Shimada

The minimalist decor of this boutique sets a more distant tone from the heartwarming Santa Fe–inspired setting of Junko Shimada's Left Bank boutique. Nevertheless, once you take a look at the clothes, you realize that Junko Shimada is clearly the most westernized of all the Japanese designers located on this street. Her women's clothes are always refined and often sexy, consisting mainly of modern cuts on traditional fabrics. Unlike the Rive Gauche boutique, the clothes here are *très femme* and some are even femme fatale. Glittery gold leather is molded into a skintight *bustier* dress and jacket, and the sheerest of cotton blouses is teamed up with wide flowing navy pants. Junko Shimada's clothing is both sexy and classy—a totally modern look for today's fashion-conscious woman. Sophisticated prices, too.

54 rue Etienne-Marcel, 2e; tel.: 42.36.36.97;
Métro: Etienne-Marcel
34 rue des Saints-Pères, 7e; tel.: 42.22.58.55;
Métro: St.-Germain-des-Près
open Monday 2–7 P.M.; Tuesday–Friday 10 A.M.–7
P.M.; Saturday 11 A.M.–7 P.M.

Olivier Strelli

52 rue Etienne-Marcel, 2e; see Left Bank
description p. 123

En Attendant les Barbares

Waiting for the Barbarians—an ideal name for this funked-out boutique that sells some of the hippest home-decor items that Paris has to offer (at prices that are in tune with the 90s as well). Colorful mosaic tables, terracotta Greek-god candleholders, curly wrought-iron chairs and candlesticks as well as luminous candy-colored candlesticks ($185) by Migeon and Migeon (of costume-jewelry fame) are just some of the baroque and primitive-styled goodies in store for you in this fascinating showplace.

50 rue Etienne-Marcel, 2e; tel.: 42.33.37.87;
Métro: Etienne-Marcel
open Monday–Saturday 10:30 A.M.–7 P.M.

Lina's Sandwich

Paris had to wait years before a place such as this opened. Now we Parisians no longer have to flee to New York in search of deli sandwiches. Well OK, Lina's sandwiches can't quite compare to a big fat pastrami on rye from the Lower East Side, but they do help to fill a hungry shopper's stomach without your having to sit down to a lengthy one-and-a-half-hour lunch in a smoke-filled café!

50 rue Etienne-Marcel, 1er; tel.: 42.33.78.03;
Métro: Etienne-Marcel
open Monday–Friday 9:30 A.M.–5 P.M.; Saturday 10:30 A.M.–6 P.M.

Chevignon

49 rue Etienne-Marcel, 1er; see Left Bank description p. 137

Yohji Yamamoto

Yohji Yamamoto is widely viewed more as an artist than as a fashion designer. The Georges Pompidou Center even asked West German film director Wim Wenders to make a movie about him, *Notes on Clothes and Cities*, that takes place in his two favorite urban centers, Tokyo and Paris.

The stark, black-on-white minimalist decor of his boutiques evokes his firm conviction that beauty lies in the simplicity of things. His men's and women's clothing reflect the same basic principles, remaining void of any excess ornamentation. This leading Japanese designer's true strengths lie in his asymmetric cuts, which make the simplest of suits feel like a second skin. And of course your basic black reigns in a variety of shirts, jackets, dresses and pants—intended to be mixed together in the purest of avant-garde fashions.

Prices are steep, but art isn't cheap these days either.

47 rue Etienne-Marcel, 1er; tel.: 45.08.82.45 (men's)
25 rue du Louvre, 1er; tel.: 42.21.42.93 (women's)
Métro for both boutiques is Etienne-Marcel.
open Monday 11:30 A.M.–7 P.M.; Tuesday–Saturday
10:30 A.M.–7 P.M.
69 rue des Saints-Pères, 6e (men's and women's);
tel.: 45.48.22.56;
Métro: St.-Sulpice
open Monday–Saturday 11 A.M.–7 P.M.

Equipment

Shirts, only shirts, neatly line the shelves of this small shop. A note of fantasy adorns each one of these stylish shirts, making them either totally casual or festive depending on how and where you want to wear them. Stripes, checks, paisleys, polka dots, and embroidered designs create a fun, easy look that zips up any outfit. Most of the shirts, which come in cotton, rayon, silk, and chiffon, are cut large, and some may be worn by both men and women. Prices range between $105 and $200.
46 rue Etienne-Marcel, 2e; tel.: 40.26.17.84;
Métro: Etienne-Marcel
open Monday 1:30–7 P.M.; Tuesday–Saturday 10:30
A.M.–7 P.M.

Dorothée Bis

Jacqueline Jacobson is the designer behind Dorothée Bis, and the look is just as young and fun today as in the early 60s, when she launched her first collection. Well-cut knits are the hallmark of this label, whose main focus is on ready-to-wear for active women.

The 80s and 90s have provided a new realm of materials that have only enhanced the Dorothée Bis fashions. Stretchy knit lurex and a whole new line of body-hugging jerseys, molded into skimpy dresses and long, oversized sweaters, work sensationally with a style that is both sexy and free-spirited. The colors are often as daring as the fashions, always with the presence of a sparkling flash of silver, gold, or bronze. Their evening collection is shown downstairs along with a more subdued selection of tailored suits.

The menswear, which is considerably more offbeat, is upstairs toward the back of the boutique. The men's

sweaters may be worn more easily than their funky jackets. The Left Bank boutique does not show any of the
men's clothing.
46 rue Etienne-Marcel, 2e; tel.: 42.21.04.00;
Métro: Etienne-Marcel
open Monday–Saturday 10:30 A.M.–7:30 P.M.
33 rue de Sèvres, 6e; tel.: 42.22.00.45;
Métro: Sèvres-Babylone

Jean-Louis Imbert

This family-run business from Marseilles, in existence for
a number of years, spiffed-up their collection of leather
bags and shoes when Madame Imbert came on the scene.
Now their styles are modern and sophisticated, without
having sacrificed the practical side of a functional bag or
a comfortable pair of shoes.

Each season sees the arrival of two different lines of
bags: one that is more basic, emphasizing the purity of
geometric forms; another that is more fashion-oriented,
developing a swingy theme with the added ornamentation of bells, fringe, or coins. Some of their evening bags,
however, in the shape of colorful satin flowers and fans
(about $120), have become classics, and Parisians are still
coming back for more.
44 rue Etienne-Marcel, 2e; tel.: 42.33.36.04;
Métro: Etienne-Marcel
open Monday–Saturday 10 A.M.–7 P.M.

Gas

The designer and manufacturer of the exotic costume
jewelry sold here is none other than Monsieur Gas. The
sponge-painted peach walls and earthy-colored tile floor
not only furnish a warm backdrop for the ethnic-looking
creations sold in this shop, but also afford a refreshing
change from all of the chilly-looking boutiques in the
neighborhood.

Monsieur Gas draws his inspiration from Africa, the
Orient, and Santa Fe. Gold- and silver-dipped rings,
enameled charms, and gem-encrusted trinkets dangle
from jingle-jangle earrings, necklaces, and bracelets in the
most beguiling ways. A more barbaric form of this exotica
is revealed in a necklace made of rawhide and silver-
wrapped rock crystal. Prices are comparable with the

other fashionable costume-jewelry pieces sold in Paris—
earrings average about $80.
44 rue Etienne-Marcel, 2e; tel.: 45.08.49.46;
Métro: Etienne-Marcel
open Monday–Saturday 10 A.M.–7 P.M.

Comme des Garçons

Japanese designer Rei Kawakubo deliberately avoids virtually every traditional form of fashion elements. Her creations may easily be considered the most outrageous and
avant-garde of all of the Japanese designers who have set
up shop in Paris. A distinct rebellious attitude is apparent
in her knobby-kneed models who march down the runway in asymmetrically cut baggy dresses; and so one begins to understand why the designer chose the name
"Comme des Garçons," meaning like the boys.

It didn't take long, however, for this style to take off
like a rocket, and soon every third *branché* in Les Halles
was sporting the look that rejected the idea of women
being dressed like sex objects. Bloomers, smocks and,
flat black rounded-toed shoes were suddenly every-
where. The funny thing, however, is that even the most
conventional types have fallen for a few of the fashions
from this designer's exquisitely made collections. A crisp
white man-tailored shirt, a polyurethane white skirt, or a
fluorescent-colored boyish jacket might just be the thing
that you can't live without.

The Comme des Garçons Homme Plus fashions for men
follow through with the same antifashion philosophy and
are of course just as high-priced.
42 rue Etienne-Marcel, 2e (women's);
tel.: 42.33.05.21
40 rue Etienne-Marcel, 2e (men's); tel.: 42.36.91.54
Métro for both stores is Etienne-Marcel.
open Monday–Saturday 11 A.M.–7 P.M.

Bold

A search for the exceptional is the driving force behind
these very bold-looking Italian bags, shoes, belts, agendas,
and luggage. Primarily in black leather and imitation
leather, these goods are as solid as they look; each is
guaranteed waterproof, scratchproof, and basically in-
destructible. Chrome-plated nickel forms hinge-like zips,

snaps, and buckles that are used to fasten their multisized bags closed. A similar chrome-plated ID card, complete with your own personal data, is sent to you about three weeks later; it is up to you to rivet the card onto your bag or on the bottom of your tractor-soled shoes with the instrument they give you at the moment of your purchase! Not to be missed. Prices are comparable with other well-made designer-type bags in Paris.

39 rue Etienne-Marcel, 1er; tel.: 42.36.36.29;
Métro: Etienne-Marcel
open Tuesday–Saturday 10:30 A.M.–1 P.M.
and 2–7 P.M.

Marithé & François Girbaud

Funky music blares, and a greyish-blue light is cast throughout the three levels of this loft-like space. Greyish blue is of course the color of stoned washed denim, the very thing that made Marithé and François Girbaud famous in the 70s. Many of you may already know that denim originated in the French town of Nimes (de Nîmes), and although jeans are considered inherently American, denim has come full circle with the countless innovations of the French label Girbaud. Credited with having started the trend of bell-bottom jeans, baggies, and cargo pockets, the Girbaud design team continues to invent, seeking inspiration from today's street culture and exotic lands. The overall look has expanded considerably to include leather jackets, sweaters, and T-shirts.

Many of the men's and women's fashions shown in this store (called "Halles Capone") are different from those sold under licensing agreements in the U.S. Although these prices may seem higher, they are actually less than the "Halles Capone" lines sold stateside (the selection is better, too).

38 rue Etienne-Marcel, 2e; tel.: 42.33.54.69;
Métro: Etienne-Marcel
open Monday–Saturday 10:30 A.M.–7:30 P.M.

A. Simon

I love this kitchen-supply store for the strangest reasons—not for their infinite selection of cooking accessories and tableware—but for all of the very ordinary items that they sell wholesale to Paris cafés. You may find

some of the most typically French gift ideas in this store at prices that won't blow your budget. All of the dishes, demitasse cups, wine pitchers, condiment sets, crockery, and those oh-so kitsch signs that read *crudités, camembert assiette, quiche, saucisson,* and *oeuf sur le plat*—the same ones that you find in every neighborhood café in France—are sold here. These intrinsically French everyday items become real novelties when you're back home in your apartment in midtown Manhattan!
36 rue Etienne-Marcel, 2e; tel.: 42.33.71.65;
Métro: Etienne-Marcel
open Monday–Saturday 8:30 A.M.–6:30 P.M.

Interface

New Wave eyeglasses to wear with the New Wave clothing that is sold on this street.
26 rue Etienne-Marcel, 2e; tel.: 42.33.60.33;
Métro: Etienne-Marcel
open Monday 2–7:30 P.M.; Tuesday–Saturday 10:30 A.M.–7:30 P.M.

Barbara Bui

Barbara Bui, a Eurasian New Wave designer, is a lady on the rise. She now has two boutiques in Paris, exports throughout the world, and has received growing recognition from the French fashion press. The Barbara Bui look is soft, serene, and poetic. Fine-quality fabrics in muted colors are cut into long, fluid forms and draped into toga-like styles.
23 rue Etienne-Marcel, 1er; tel.: 40.26.43.65;
Métro: Etienne-Marcel
35 rue de Grenelle, 7e; tel.: 45.44.85.14; Métro: Bac
open Monday–Saturday 10:30 A.M.–7 P.M.

Claude Barthelemy

This is probably the best address on the street for attractive, stylish clothes that are traditional enough that you don't have to be an artist to wear them. Now that's not nice. It's just that the women's clothing here is easy to wear, and you don't have to worry about looking too avant-garde when you walk out the door in the morning.

The Claude Barthelemy label emphasizes the chichi way

of dressing, providing everything but stodgy fashions. Some people call their look young, but if sporting a pair of stylish wool culottes is only for the mature, then I never want to be mature. Their strongpoint undoubtedly lies in their knits and wool pants and skirts, often trimmed with a fashionable fringe or an embroidered appliqué. Prices are comparable with those of the other designers in the neighborhood—*Cher.*

10 rue Etienne-Marcel, 2e; tel.: 42.33.14.30;
Métro: Etienne-Marcel
open Monday–Saturday 10 A.M.–7 P.M.

Rue du Louvre

Ventilo

One of the best things about this immense store, which contains four floors of French-made American-like fashions for men and women, is their tearoom that occupies half of the top floor. The white-walled space is as bright and airy as the rest of the store, and even on the greyest of Paris days, light streams in through the tall windows that look out onto the rue du Louvre. The food is as fresh and crisp as the pure white linens that skirt the tables. Homemade specialties include salmon tartare, Frenchified chicken pie, goat-cheese salad, and other light luncheon suggestions. The dessert selection is even more impressive. Gooey treats such as fruit-topped cheesecake, caramel almond meringue swirl, and *charlotte aux poires* are savored with small sips of Sancerre wine and tea from Mariage Frères.

27 bis rue du Louvre, 2e; tel.: 42.33.18.67;
Métro: Etienne-Marcel
open Monday noon–7 P.M.; Tuesday–Saturday 10:30 A.M.–7 P.M.

• ## Rue Jean-Jacques—Rousseau •

Kashiyama

*80 rue Jean-Jacques–Rousseau, 1er; see Left Bank
description p. 104*

• ## Rue Tiquetonne •

Marie Mercié

"My hats are always based on a story," exclaims red-
haired, effervescent Marie Mercié. And so they are,
whether it be one of New Guinean natives or modern-day
Cinderellas, each of these young designer's creations
looks as though it came from a different place and time,
which is of course why there is one for everybody's tastes
and, most of all, why they are so charming. The notion of
humor and simple beauty is present in them all. Bee-stung
sunflowers, plastic fruits, and even nests filled with robin's
eggs crown a few of them, while others extract their wit
and grace merely from the artist's choice of color and
form. Prices start at $50 and go on up to $850 for certain
custom-made bridal pieces. Marie Mercié's enchanting
creations are sold at selected stores outside of France
for close to 40% more. Some Casablanca-ish men's hats
are also on sale here. Don't miss it—even if it's just to
take a look around.
*56 rue Tiquetonne, 2e tel.: 40.26.60.68;
Métro: Etienne-Marcel
open Monday–Saturday 11 A.M.–7 P.M.*

• ## Rue du Jour •

Pom d'Api

*13 rue du Jour, 1er; see Left Bank description p.
135*

Diapositive

Another one of the women's-clothing manufacturers from the Sentier that seems to have mushroomed overnight. Diapositive now has three shops in Paris and sales are growing worldwide. And it's no wonder. Their styles are so young and fresh that I've even spotted a number of middle-aged women snatching up their fashions. (There's no age barrier in France.)

Body-hugging creations have been the backbone of their most recent collections and everything from sweatshirts to T-shirt dresses seem to have an elasticized bounce to them. Brightly colored Monet-print silk blouses pull up the slack for those who aren't quite ready to show every ripple and bump to the outside world. Diapositive's fashions sell in the same reasonably-priced bracket as those of Naf Naf and Kookaï.

12 rue du Jour, 1er; tel.: 42.21.34.41;
Métro: Etienne-Marcel
open Monday–Saturday 10:30 A.M.–7 P.M.
18 rue de la Grande-Truanderie, 1er;
tel.: 42.33.97.09;
Métro: Etienne-Marcel
96 rue de Longchamp, 16e; tel.: 47.04.52.82;
Métro: Pompe
open Monday 2–7 P.M.; Tuesday–Saturday
10 A.M.–7 P.M.

Naf Naf

Naf Naf was the Sentier's (Paris's garment district's) biggest success story of the 80s. It all started in 1983 when their flowery jumpsuits started to pop up in the trendiest boutiques and orders poured in from all over the world. (Naf Naf had cleverly printed their name and telephone number on each of the clothes.) Their fun casualwear now forms the base of many a French teenager's wardrobe and even moms and dads are spotted toting their overstuffed *blousons* and gaily colored print shirts. Prices are much better than what you pay at home.

10 rue du Jour, 1er; tel.: 42.21.36.47 (age 14 and up);
Métro: Les Halles
open Monday, Tuesday, Thursday, Friday 10:30 A.M.–
7:00 P.M.; Wednesday and Saturday 10:30 A.M.–
7:30 P.M.
5 rue des Canettes, 6e; tel.: 43.54.75.25 (adult's and
children's);

Métro: Mabillon
open Monday–Saturday 10 A.M.–7:30 P.M.
100 rue de Longchamp, 16e; tel.: 47.27.91.53 (adult's
and children's);
Métro: Pompe
open Monday–Saturday 10 A.M.–7 P.M.
55 rue de Passy, 16e; tel.: 42.88.47.56 (adult's);
Métro: Muette
open Monday 12:30–7 P.M.; Tuesday–Saturday 10:15
A.M.–7 P.M.

Un Après-Midi de Chien

10 rue du Jour, 1er; see Left Bank description p. 138

La Droguerie

They have everything you need in this shop to stimulate
your creative instincts: rows and rows of yarn in glossy
silk, nubby cotton, and fluffy angora; jar after jar of candy-
colored beads and buttons in every imaginable shape and
size; and strands of sparkling gold chains, silken cord,
and irridescent threads—all in a marvelous panorama of
colors. It's enough to make you want to go home and start
knitting, making jewelry, or just sewing on those missing
buttons!
9 rue du Jour, 1er; tel.: 45.08.93.27;
Métro: Les Halles
open Monday 2–6:45 P.M.; Tuesday–Saturday 10:30
A.M.–6:45 P.M.

Accessoire

8 rue du Jour, 1er; see Left Bank description p. 139

Junior Gaultier

Jean-Paul Gaultier has immortalized the streets of Paris
in this boutique that features not only his revolutionary
versions of street fashion, but also the famous elements
that punctuate the French capital's urban landscape: lamp-
lights, muse-encircled fountains, and *colonnes Morris*
(six-foot–tall cyclindrical display cases used to announce
upcoming shows)—all in Paris's classic forest green. Here
the emphasis is more on the decorative purpose of these

"street accessories" than on their function; even the dressing-room doors come from the public toilets found in the Métro. You can't get more Parisian than that!

The men's and women's fashions are not just for juniors either, but for anyone interested in more affordable Gaultier creations. The look is dynamic, sensual, and modern. Partly worn out clothes in stretch or heavy cotton are takeoffs on garb typically worn by boxers, divers, joggers, and army men (as in the case of the camouflage series). The clothes are easier to wear than you think!

7 rue du Jour, 1er; tel.: 40.28.01.91;
Métro: Les Halles
open Monday–Friday 10 A.M.–7 P.M.; Saturday 11 A.M.–7 P.M.

Agnès B.

Agnès de Fleurieu, the creative talent behind Agnès B., opened her first small shop on the rue du Jour in the mid-1970s. Now the street looks more like the Agnès B. kingdom, with four separate boutiques featuring fashions for women, men, teenage girls, and children.

The success of Agnès B. is largely due to the timelessness of their fashions. Nothing is so trendy that you have to get rid of it with the onslaught of the next season. This form of low-keyed elegance is of course inherently French. Agnès B. has made it possible for everyone— French or not—to carry off this look. The clothes here may best be described as more stylish versions of BCBG (French preppy); simple cuts in soft jerseys give way to a tasteful way of dressing that is never too flashy or too boring.

The Agnès B. creations are so unpretentious that it's often hard to tell whether it's Agnès B. or not, without looking at the label (which is sometimes no fun, especially since they're not cheap, either). If you do, however, want to bring home one of her signature fashions, take a look at her little crayola-colored sweatshirts that snap closed with a long series of mother-of-pearlish buttons ($80). If you are a small size, don't miss the ones at Lolita (for teens); the color selection is not as spectacular, but they are priced about $15 less.

6 rue du Jour, 1er (women's); tel.: 45.08.56.56
4 rue du Jour, 1er (children's); tel.: 40.39.96.88
3 rue du Jour, 1er (men's); tel.: 42.33.34.13

3 rue du Jour, 1er (teenage girl's); tel.: 45.08.49.89
The Métro station for all of the above boutiques is
Les Halles.
22 rue St.-Sulpice, 6e (men's); tel.: 40.51.70.69;
Métro: St.-Sulpice
open Monday noon–7 P.M.; Tuesday–Saturday 10:30
A.M.–7 P.M.

Claudie Pierlot

4 rue du Jour, 1er; see Left Bank description p. 128

•   Rue Coquillière   •

Dehillerin

Since 1820 professional cooks have outfitted themselves at this Alladin's cave of traditional cookware and kitchen utensils. The dimly lit decor in this dusty store probably hasn't changed much within the past hundred years, either. As you stand there looking at the rows of amply stocked shelves and at the hundreds of goods hanging from the ceiling, you can almost feel the authenticity oozing out from within the very walls of this shop.

Every inch of Dehillerin is covered with kitchen equipment for both professional and amateur use. Their pots and pans come in a stupendous variety of sizes (some so big you could sit inside of them), shapes, and materials: stainless steel, cast iron (such as Le Creuset), and copper. (Dehillerin will even repair and retin your old ones.) Other typically French, and inexpensively priced, items include wooden butter molds, *madeleine* tins, *terrine* molds, and those marvelous aluminum seafood platters and pedestals found at every *brasserie* in France.

18 rue Coquillière, 1er; tel.: 42.36.53.13;
Métro: Les Halles
open Monday–Saturday 8 A.M.–12:30 P.M.
and 2–6 P.M.

Tous les Caleçons

The word *caleçon* refers to underpants, boxer shorts, and long johns. Since the mid-1980s, this word has been tossed around a lot in France and has come to refer to just about any type of clingy undergarment. These clingy undergarments, however, were never really intended to go underneath anything at all, but to be worn by themselves in the most athletic of fashions.

Tous les Caleçons has their own line of reasonably priced men's and women's cotton stretch tank tops, T-shirts, dresses, and bicycle pants. These basic fashion pieces work well with casual, dynamic wardrobes and for men and women who are not afraid to bare their bods. Slightly more conservative creations by APC and Michel Klein round out the selection of fashions that are housed on the two floors of this loft-like space. Those of you who were *habitués* of Tous les Caleçons in New York should keep in mind that that boutique has since closed.

34 rue Coquillière, 1er; tel.: 40.26.36.84;
Métro: Les Halles
open Monday–Saturday 11 A.M.–7 P.M.
11 rue du Pré-aux-Clercs, 7e (women's only);
tel.: 45.44.32.07;
Métro: St.-Germain-des-Prés
open Monday–Saturday 10:30 A.M.–7 P.M.

▪ Rue de Turbigo ▪

Duthilleul & Minart

After you've purchased everything you need at Dehillerin to become a true French chef, stop in here for the clothing that will enable you to look the part. Uniforms for everyone from café waiter to maître d'hôtel are sold here to both professionals and the general public. Sporting a soufflé-like *toque* (chef's hat), a pastry-maker's heavy cotton jacket, or a *tour de cou* (the white dish-towel–like scarf that French cooks wear around their neck) will help friends to take your culinary talents seriously at your next stateside dinner party. *Bleus de travail*, the royal-blue work clothes worn by laborers throughout France, are also sold here, and if you dress them up with a wide belt and some showy jewelry, they could be a hot addition to your wardrobe back home. *Pourquoi pas?*

14 rue de Turbigo, 1er; tel.: 42.33.44.36;
Métro: Etienne-Marcel
open Monday–Saturday 9 A.M.–7 P.M.

Scooter

Whenever any of my clients ask for gift ideas for their teenage daughters, if their tastes are anything but classic, I bring them here. To the beat of loud rap music, you are instantly bedazzled by the far-out selection of costume jewelry sold at Scooter. Cases of African and Oriental-inspired earrings, rhinestone-studded bangles, and punkish bracelets (that look as though you'd hurt yourself if you ever fell down wearing them) make up just a small part of their trendy trinkets that have been the rage of many a young *parisienne.* Scooter was one of the first boutiques in Paris to show such an extensive selection of spunky jewelry at prices that have people coming back for more.

The display racks as well as the salesgirls sizzle with a collection of Mademoiselle Zaza (made expressly for the boutique) ready-to-wear that is just as electrically charged as their jewelry. Skirts and dresses are short and skimpy in a pizazz of fun colors. Unconstructed nylon travel bags, in a variety of sizes, look as though they have been designed for a quick weekend getaway!

10 rue de Turbigo, 1er; tel.: 45.08.89.31;
Métro: Etienne-Marcel
open Monday 2–7 P.M.; Tuesday–Saturday
10 A.M.–7 P.M.

Courrèges

7 rue de Turbigo, 1er; see Discount Shopping p. 296

Elizabeth de Senneville

Elizabeth de Senneville's computer-designed knits and separates represent the fashion world's most visual interpretations of high technology. Fascinated with computers, video, and graphic design, Elizabeth de Senneville continues to explore and apply different high tech principles to the design and creation of her modern fashions. Computer-printout prints, angular cuts, and bright vibrant colors are just a few of the by-products of this designer's passion with today's technology. This boutique features moderately priced fashions for both women and children.

7 rue de Turbigo, 1er; tel.: 42.33.90.83;
Métro: Etienne-Marcel

The following boutiques only sell children's clothing:
38 place du Marché–St.-Honoré, 1er; tel.:
42.60.08.10;
Métro: Tuileries
55 rue Bonaparte, 6e; tel.: 46.33.57.90;
Métro: St.-Germain-des-Prés or St.-Sulpice
open Monday–Saturday 10:30 A.M.–7 P.M.

Chevignon

5 rue de Turbigo, 1er; see Left Bank description
p. 137

• # Rue Mondétour •

Free Lance

22 rue Mondétour, 1er; see Left Bank description
p. 135

Maria-Pia Varnier

Maria-Pia Varnier started the carpetbagger's trend in the mid-1980s, and what was once a fad has turned into a classic item. These velvety and voluminous handbags, decorated with brilliant flowers or wide-eyed Scottish terriers, have since become somewhat of a trademark for this young designer.

New and amusing themes, with influences from around the world, are constantly being developed. There are woolen Tyrolian-inspired knapsacks, western cowhide shoulder bags, Victorian-like needlepoint totes, and Indian-inspired suede pouches that jingle with coins. These original designs and unusual fabrics have transformed functional and classically shaped bags into unique and moderately priced fashion accessories. Leather and suede ballet slippers, in coordinating colors and designs, complement each season's collection of bags.

22 rue Mondétour, 1er; tel.: 42.33.34.59;
Métro: Etienne-Marcel
open Monday–Saturday 11 A.M.–7 P.M.

Rue Pierre-Lescot

Mac Douglas

20 rue Pierre-Lescot, 1er; see Left Bank description p. 144

Fil à Fil

11 rue Pierre-Lescot, 1er; see Left Bank description p. 126

Geneviève Lethu

1 rue Pierre-Lescot, 1er; see Left Bank description p. 131

Boutique Paris-Musées

Most of the Paris museum shops are found at the museums. This shop, however, is located at the entrance of the Forum des Halles, and the only major exhibition that may be viewed here is in the street. The shop sells a variety of gifty items at prices that won't have you going home penniless (or rather francless). Artsy articles include cardboard models of Paris's famous monuments ($12), books, postcards, jewelry, porcelain plates signed by Jean Cocteau, and T-shirts defining the meaning of Dada.

Bigger and more bountiful museum shops are located at the Louvre, the Pompidou Center, the Musée d'Orsay, and the Musée des Arts Decoratifs. Here you may pick up an endless variety of gift ideas including posters, books, and a few scarves.

1 rue Pierre-Lescot, 1er; tel.: 40.26.56.65;
Métro: Les Halles
open Monday 2–7 P.M.; Tuesday–Saturday
10 A.M.–7 P.M.

Go Sport

1 rue Pierre-Lescot, 1er (Forum des Halles); see More Big Stores description p. 307

Rue de la Grande-Truanderie

Diapositive

18 rue de la Grande-Truanderie, 1er; see Rue du Jour description p. 184

Rue des Halles

Chipie

22 rue des Halles, 1er (adult clothing); see Left Bank description p. 124

Upla

17 rue des Halles, 1er; see Left Bank description p. 152

Rue St.-Opportune

Chipie

5 rue St.-Opportune, 1er (shoes); see Left Bank description p. 124

Rue de la Ferronnerie

Chipie

31 rue de la Ferronnerie, 1er (children); see Left Bank description p. 124

Rue des Innocents

Arche

Moderately priced, rainbow-colored shoes and boots for men and women in smooth leather and suede are the trademark of this shoe manufacturer. Their styles are sleek and modern without a hint of ornamentation. If you like comfortable, rubber-soled walking shoes, don't miss Arche.

9 rue des Innocents, 1er; tel.: 45.08.19.96;
Métro: Châtelet
21 rue du Dragon, 6e; tel.: 42.22.54.75;
Métro: St.-Sulpice
open Monday 2–7 P.M.; Tuesday–Saturday
10:30 A.M.–7 P.M.

Passages (Paris's 19th-century Shopping Malls)

It was a romantic era and Paris's *grands boulevards* were in full swing. Balzac, Zola, and Alexandre Dumas held court in local cafés while crowds packed the nearby theaters and dancehalls. Money flowed freely during these pre–Industrial Revolution days and now that shop merchants had acquired a more respectable stature, commercial expansion was imminent.

The early part of the nineteenth century experienced a building boom and gave birth to a new type of architectural development—the covered passage—throughout most of the big European cities and America. Also known as arcades or galleries, these passages, which usually cut through or alongside buildings, provided shortcuts the length of city blocks. Glass roofs, hand-carved woodwork, and tile floors typified most of the thoroughfares that became precious commercial space for shopowners.

In Paris, the increasingly important *haute bourgeoisie* could stroll through the brightly lit passages—away from the already congested streets of Paris and free from rain, mud, and dust. In these protected passageways, boutique storefronts shimmered with a variety of goods displaying everything from walking sticks to freshly baked bread.

Nearly all of Paris's passages are located on the Right Bank, north of the rue St.-Honoré. The chic part of town throughout most of the nineteenth century, it proved to be the ideal neighborhood for setting up luxury boutiques. Proximity to a theater, a ballroom, or later a train station was also part of the criteria for choosing the correct location for a passage.

The popularity of the *grands boulevards* grew and Paris's earliest department stores (*grands magasins*) were established here toward the end of the nineteenth century. The success of these *grands magasins* led to the demise of the passages and, as time went on, the luxury boutiques were forced to move out. Craftspeople and more specialized boutiques, such as stamp collectors, that were sure of a loyal following moved into these beautiful places. As time went on, the upkeep of the passages proved too burdensome and many of them fell to near ruin. Fortunately, renewed interest in their future has restored some of them to their original splendor, and the hollow echo of footsteps on tile floors can once again be heard resounding from within.

Promenade Passages

This walk will help you discover six very different passages across three Paris *arrondissements*: the 1st, the 2nd, and the 9th. Allow yourself a few hours to explore them at a leisurely pace. Each passage has its own unique personality, depending largely on the sort of renovations it has experienced in recent years, as well as the types of boutiques found there. The suggested Métro stop for the start of the tour is rue Montmartre; Métro stops for each passage have been indicated in case you want to choose another starting point.

Passage Jouffroy

12 bd Montmartre, 9e;
Métro: Montmartre or Richelieu-Drouot
This is the most colorful of the passages on the walk. Here you see a variety of contrasts representative of the slow transition from a once chic shopping arcade to a run-down, neon-lit, mishmash of boutiques and now to an eclectic mix of shops on the rise. One of the busiest of the passages, the Passage Jouffroy attracts many different types of people: Those coming from the nearby *grand boulevards*, or the neighboring Musée Grevin (Paris's wax museum) or even those who make a special trip just to browse through the varied assortment of shops.

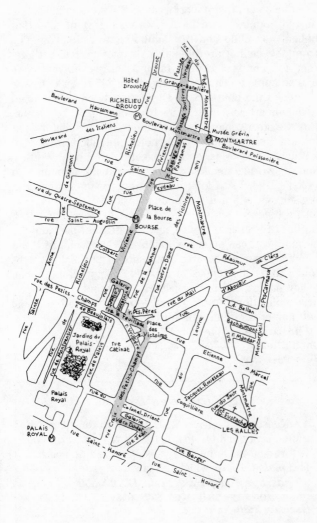

Pain d'Epice

Pain d'épice means gingerbread, one of French childrens' best-loved snacks, and I'm sure Pain d'Epice, the store, must be one of their favorites as well! The shop looks like an old country store loaded with the sort of toys that delight any child and that adults enjoy giving. Hanging from the ceiling are all kinds of marionettes: a three-foot–tall pirate, a winged fairy, a starry-eyed magician, and an apple-green frog ranging from $45 to $930. In one corner of the boutique, you'll find lovely porcelain-faced dolls whose glass-eyed gazes beg you to be taken home. But the strongpoint of this boutique is its miniatures; at least a hundred little cubbyholes are filled with mini kitchen accessories, straw baskets, dolls' baby bottles, and the world's smallest games (chess, backgammon, and poker). Be sure to look in the glass case near the cash register where you'll find mini, mini foods for the table— all no bigger than a quarter: cheese platters, *baguettes*, bottles of French red wine, and a plateful of peel-and-eat shrimp! You can spend as much as $50 on one of these minute, ceramic treasures that's sure to give just the right touch to a mini replica of a Louis-Philippe dining table. (They have them, too!) Upstairs you'll find a pastel-colored collection of soft, huggable dolls, stuffed animals, and numerous other gifts for baby.
29 passage Jouffroy, 9e; tel.: 47.70.82.65
open Monday 12:30–7 P.M.; Tuesday–Saturday
10 A.M.–7 P.M.

La Tour des Délices

I suggest you stop here on the way out for a Turkish coffee or a *thé à la menthe* (green tea) to warm you before you move on. They also serve exotic pastries and *plats du jour* which are fair.
30 passage Jouffroy, 9e; tel.: 47.70.88.50
open Monday–Saturday 8:30 A.M.–7:30 P.M.;
Sunday 2:30–7:30 P.M.

Galerie 34

You feel as though you had just stepped back in time once you enter the cozy, red-velvet interior of this small shop

entirely devoted to antique canes. If you don't already have a cane collection, this boutique will inspire you to start one because you have probably never seen such a vast variety of canes. There are five-foot–tall wooden theater canes, glass and Baccarat crystal canes, and an array of sculpted knobs in almost every imaginable material: ivory, wood, stone, ceramic, porcelain, silver, and brass.
34 passage Jouffroy, 9e; tel.: 47.70.89.65
open Tuesday–Saturday 11:30 A.M.–6:30 P.M. or by appointment.

Pain d'Epice

Their boutique for *la maison* is as yummy as the Pain d'Epice toy store. They have almost everything a girl needs to pamper herself at particularly interesting prices: luxurious soaps, bath oils, and lotions—all wrapped up in very tempting gift packages. Oversized ceramic coffee and hot-chocolate cups are some of the more Frenchie items, perfect for long, leisurely Sunday mornings at home. Don't miss the exquisite heart-shaped dried-flower arrangements on the wall; prices range between $35 and $95.
35 passage Jouffroy, 9e; tel.: 47.70.51.12
open Monday 12:30–7 P.M.; Tuesday–Saturday 10 A.M.–7 P.M.

Thomas Boog

This newcomer is evocative of the types of quality boutiques that are changing the face of the Passage Jouffroy. The card says *objets de curiosité*, but the decorative items found inside can easily be envisioned in one's home. Artist and shop owner Thomas Boog ferrets out antique boxes and covers them with a sculptural arrangement of seashells, coral, and even a few crab shells. Most of these creations follow very subtle color themes such as sandy pink, smoky salmon, or creamy mother-of-pearl. More dramatic tones encompass his *passementerie*-covered boxes. (*Passementerie* refers to the regal-looking, gold-threaded silk cords and tassels used for attaching curtains, found throughout Europe.) These small boxes are Victorian in feeling, and the warm reds, lush browns, and classic greens conjure up images of rich, wood-paneled interiors.

Prices start at about $580 for the boxes and go up to $2,350 for a spectacular shell-encrusted wall mirror.
36 passage Jouffroy, 9e; tel.: 47.70.98.10
open Monday–Saturday 1–7 P.M.

Le Bonheur des Dames

Another charming boutique to help you beautify yourself and your home. If you have not found what you were looking for at Pain d'Epice then you probably won't find it here, either, because these two boutiques are strikingly similar. They do, however, have a nice selection of decorative planters although this is not the sort of thing that you would want to cart stateside.
39 passage Jouffroy, 9e; tel.: 47.70.99.11
open Tuesday–Friday 10 A.M.–7 P.M.; Monday and Saturday 10:30 A.M.–7 P.M.

La Boîte à Joujoux

Even though this is the type of boutique that you're apt to find at home, it is fun to see what the French are selling in terms of gags, jokes, and tricks. Sure, you'll come across plastic dog do (as if Paris doesn't have enough of the real thing), hot pepper gum, and buzzer handshake rings, but you might also discover a rubber mask of France's President Mitterand, a singing sausage, a revolutionary peasant's costume, or other French contributions to the world of fun.
41 passage Jouffroy, 9e; tel.: 48.24.58.37
open Monday–Saturday 10 A.M.–7 P.M.

Cinédoc

Just looking in the window tells you that this shop is a must for serious cinema aficionados—I once counted 14 different books on Marilyn Monroe! Their selection of photos, posters, books, and magazines covers the world of cinema from A to Z, which is exactly how their files of international movie stars are listed. Unlimited unusual gift ideas—why not bring home a poster for your teenager that announces the film *Desperately Seeking Susan* in Italian?
45 passage Jouffroy, 9e; tel.: 48.24.71.36
open Monday–Friday 10 A.M.–7 P.M.; Saturday 10 A.M.–1 P.M. and 2–7 P.M.

Le Grenier à Livres

You practically trip across this bookstore whose clutter of new and second-hand books spills out into the passageway. Breathe in that old-world charm and you just might come up with a copy of Victor Hugo's *Les Misérables*.
*50 passage Jouffroy, 9e; tel.: 48.24.98.89
open Monday–Friday 9 A.M.–6:45 P.M.*

·   Passage Verdeau   ·

---

6 rue de la Grange-Batelière, 9e; Métro: Montmartre or Richelieu-Drouot. Once you have come to the end of the Passage Jouffroy, cross the street and you will arrive at the entrance to the Passage Verdeau. This passage is not as lively as the Passage Jouffroy, but there are more and more attractive boutiques opening up every year.

Le Bonheur des Dames

This continuation of the Passage Jouffroy boutique is more devoted to the home than to personal items. Toward the back of the boutique are rows and rows of pantry-like shelves filled with a wide variety of ceramic teapots and water or juice pitchers in all different sizes and shapes: a fat pink piggy, a timid little black cat, a jolly-looking butler, a motherly baker, and, of course, apples, pumpkins, and pears—to name a few. Needlepoint, cross-stitch, and embroidery kits line another wall, and you can also buy some of the samplers, already made and framed at reasonable prices.
*8 passage Verdeau, 9e; tel.: 45.23.06.11
open Monday–Saturday 10 A.M.–7 P.M.*

Photo Verdeau

Looking at some of the marvelous antique cameras in this shop reminds you that photography did indeed begin in France over 150 years ago. Most of the cameras shown are now collector's items and make beautiful *objets d'art*, such as an old wooden *appareil de photo* that dates back to 1884.

14 passage Verdeau, 9e; tel.: 47.70.51.91
open Tuesday–Friday 9 A.M.–1 P.M. *and 2–7* P.M.

La France Ancienne

Paris is loaded with little shops such as this one that specialize in antique books, posters, magazines, and postcards. It is always fun to discover just one more! Some of the old postcards are so beautiful that they could easily be framed and hung on the wall.
26 passage Verdeau, 9e; tel.: 45.23.09.54
open Tuesday–Friday 11 A.M.–7 P.M.*; first Saturday of the month 2–7* P.M.

• # Rue Montmartre •

C. Mendès

65 rue Montmartre, 2e; see Discount Shopping p. 297

• # Passage des Panoramas •

Once you have visited the Passage Verdeau, trace your steps back out through the Passage Jouffroy to the boulevard Montmartre where we started the tour. Cross the street (with great caution) and enter the Passage des Panoramas. Paris's oldest passageway, dating back to 1800, it's probably the most interesting passage from a historical point of view. The shopping is more lackluster than it once was when Jean-Marie Farina (now Roget-Gallet) peddled his special blend of *eau de cologne*, and Marquis sold their chocolates to some of the most famous and wealthy people of Paris. The *trompe l'oeil* panoramas, Paris's first gaslights, and the Turkish embassy are long gone, but despite the neon lights and seedy restaurants, the original charm still remains. Stroll through and breathe in a bit of the nostalgic past as you stumble upon boutique after boutique of old stamps and the backstage entrance to the Theatre des Variétés.
11 bd Montmartre, 2e; Métro: Montmartre or Richelieu-Drouot

Stern

Engravers since 1840, Stern occupies the most beautiful as well as the oldest boutique in the Passage des Panoramas. Sober, dark-wood paneling evokes a staid, traditional reputation, which is necessary when your client index reads like the guest list to an emperor's coronation. All of the engraving is still carried out by hand. Aside from executing embassy-reception invitations, calling cards, and letterheads, Stern's true forte lies in illustrating one's family tree.

47 passage des Panoramas, 2e; tel.: 45.08.86.45
open Monday–Friday 9:30 A.M.–12:30 P.M.
and 1:30–5:30 P.M.

· # Galerie Vivienne ·

Built in 1823 on what once were the stables of the Duc d'Orléans, the galerie Vivienne is a superb example of neoclassic architecture. The galerie is now restored to its original splendor and has become a very fashionable place to shop. In fact, the boutiques that you find here are the most chic of all of those on this promenade. Enter the Galerie at 6 rue Vivienne.

6 rue Vivienne, 2e; Métro: Bourse

Moholy-Nagy

Purity of design is second nature to André Moholy (his grandfather started the Bauhaus School in Chicago), a Frenchman who has become Paris's most recent *chouchou* (sweetheart) shirt designer. Moholy-Nagy's shirts embrace a blissful blend of classic cuts and sophisticated styling—a look that may be dressed up or down in the most elegant ways. The quality of these cotton and linen shirts is excellent; the women's are presented in the purest of whites, the men's in vibrant screamy colors in addition to a few basic *blancs*. Prices range between $145 and $200—considerably less than their New York price. Moholy-Nagy's shirts are also sold for considerably more at other selected stores around town.

2 galerie Vivienne, 2e; tel.: 40.15.05.33;
Métro: Bourse

open Saturday noon–7 P.M.
Monday–Friday 11 A.M.–2:30 P.M. and 3–7 P.M.

Jean-Paul Gaultier

The first time I entered this boutique, I walked about 10 steps past the door and suddenly found myself standing on a glass-covered television monitor playing a video from Gaultier's last fashion show. Masked male models stalked the runway in what seemed to be Batman-inspired attire while photographers frantically clicked away and journalists applauded loudly. Gaultier has conquered the media through his bizarre clothes and zany fashion shows. It's worth a trip to this boutique just to take a look at its innovative decor.

Gaultier, a French designer, opened his first boutique in Milan with the backing of a Japanese group, Kashiyama, whose stores are responsible for launching many young designers. The neobaroque decor in the galerie Vivienne boutique is patterned after other boutiques that Gaultier designed himself. To many, this is one of the most outrageous boutiques in Paris. Aside from the series of monitors set into the floor, there is also a giant video screen above the door that bends and twists like a provocative one-eyed monster (a beast that made the cover of *INTERVIEW* magazine a few years ago). The floor was designed to look as though it survived the centuries—Gaultier even flew in an Italian mason to recreate mosaics like the ones unearthed in Pompeii. The two curved, plaster staircases that lead up to the men's department are patterned after the original 19th-century one that you see to the left as you pass through the door.

Now for the clothes. Gaultier is the trendsetter of avantgarde fashion and was showing far-out, futuristic-looking collections before they even came into fashion. The Gaultier team is still trying to remain ahead of the times. Pascal, the director of the boutique, declared that "a lot of the crazy clothes that Gaultier did a few years ago are now beginning to look pretty normal to us."

At first glance, it's hard to believe that Gaultier spent years designing for Jean Patou and Pierre Cardin, yet if you look closer, it is clear that his cuts are classic, but the unique way in which they are assembled is not. A very tailored jacket is given an inventive twist with a patchwork of different shades of stretchy spandex; another looks as though it has been turned inside out because the seam stitching is shown on the outside.

Gaultier's prices are more tuned in to the 21st century, too, but if you want to wear what the future will bring—it just may be worth it.

6 rue Vivienne, 2e; tel.: 42.86.05.05
open Monday–Friday 10 A.M.–7 P.M.; Saturday
11 A.M.–7 P.M.

Si Tu Veux

This is a quaint little shop brimming with a ton of inexpensive toys for children. I fell in love with their costumes that are perfect for make-believe time; *robe de rêve* creates a taffeta-clad princess; *coccinelle* gives life to a black velvet polka-dotted ladybug; and *l'ours* produces a fuzzy, brown bear. There is also a wide selection of hats to complete their assortment of *deguisements* such as a bee bonnet with feelers, a feather-tipped pirate's hat and a pom-pom–studded clown's cap. The ready-made outfits cost between $50 and $60 ($25–$35 for the kits). Rows of tables hold many different types of trinkets that children have fun collecting: miniature plastic pastries, fruit for playing grocer, fake French money, and many different sizes of irridescent *billes* (marbles) that a friend of mine confessed to use in the bottom of her glass flower vases!

The boutique at 62 galerie Vivienne has a nice collection of teddy bears and near-extinction paper dolls. Take a look at their cardboard-backed posters depicting the making of milk, bread, and cheese in France; you just might find them better suited for your country kitchen than for your child's bedroom.

68 galerie Vivienne, 2e; tel.: 42.60.59.97
open Monday–Saturday 11 A.M.–7 P.M.
62 galerie Vivienne, 2e; tel.: 42.60.29.97
open Tuesday–Saturday 11 A.M.–7 P.M.

Ixi:z

The name is Greek to me, but the designer is in fact a Japanese man who creates comfortable casualwear for men (although some of the sweaters are so yummy that women buy them, too). The quality of clothing is excellent—all 100% wools and cottons, which come in an array of luscious colors. Squash, berry, and mauve shirts and sweaters are enticingly displayed so that you spot them from far away in the gallery. Prices are moderate to expensive.

48-50 galerie Vivienne, 2e; tel.: 42.97.49.03
open Monday 1–7 P.M.; Tuesday–Friday 10:30 A.M.–
7 P.M.; Saturday 11 A.M.–7 P.M.

Librairie D.F. Jousseaume

Having been here since 1826, when Galerie Vivienne first opened, this bookstore has of course changed hands a few times, but the current shop has been in the same family for the past four generations. All types of books, both old and new, may be found along the oak woodwork and windowpanes that form the walls of this shop once almost entirely devoted to a clientele of *haut luxe*.

45-46-47 galerie Vivienne, 2e; tel.: 42.96.06.24
open Monday–Saturday 11:30 A.M.–7 P.M.

Yuki Torii

Move away the French; here come the Japanese! You can tell that the designer is a woman because most of the clothes have been conceived with a beguiling touch. A form-fitted dark suit is dressed up with black fringe; a casual cardigan becomes instantly irresistible with the addition of a few inlaid ribbons; another is jazzed up with some intricate embroidery. This is the kind of boutique where you could really flash for something, but be careful—the prices are a bit steep.

38-40 galerie Vivienne, 2e; tel.: 42.96.64.66
open Monday–Saturday 10 A.M.–7 P.M.

Casa Lopez

Casa Lopez's 100% wool, needlepoint rugs have taken the French decorating world by storm. More than 10 different sizes, at least 90 assorted colors, and nearly 20 miscellaneous designs in both figurative and abstract patterns make up their collection of rugs ($815–1750), which work well with both modern and classic decors. Their needlepoint kits for making pillows, pin cushions, and small tapestries have also helped to bring this venerable art form back into fashion. The pillow kits are priced at $115; or you'll pay $175 for the finished product. Designs include blue and white Chinese vases, Victorian-inspired flowers, and even an adorable little brown dog—one that you could allow on your couch!

39 galerie Vivienne, 2e; tel.: 42.60.46.85
open Monday–Saturday 9:30 A.M.–7 P.M.
27 bd Raspail, 7e; tel.: 45.48.30.97
58 av Paul-Doumer, 16e; tel.: 45.03.42.75
open Tuesday–Saturday 10 A.M.—1 P.M. and
2–6:30 P.M.

A Priori Thé

This is one of the most popular tea salons of the moment, frequented by a lot of people from the fashion world and a fair amount of *branchés* from the nearby place des Victoires and Les Halles areas. The three Americans who started A Priori Thé enhanced the light, airy feeling of the galerie by adding large, comfortable wicker chairs that pour out into the passageway. Relax and enjoy a nice, hot pot of Darjeeling with one of their famous brownies. They also serve delicious lunches and brunches.

35 galerie Vivienne, 2e; tel.: 42.97.48.75
open Monday–Saturday noon–6:30 P.M.;
Sunday 1–6 P.M.

Emilio Robba

Realistic and imaginary-looking artificial flowers, fashioned out of cotton, silk, and velvet, as well as lamps and vases, liberally swathed in strips of colorful fabrics, are all part of the artistic visions of French decorator Emilio Robba. Much of Monsieur Robba's inspiration is drawn from plants and flowers. Before creating his tremendously successful collection of decorative items for interiors, he worked as a florist, which enabled him to develop his sense of composition in forms and colors.

Having aligned himself with a Japanese partner, there are now more than 30 Emilio Robba boutiques throughout Japan, and plans are in full swing for some developments stateside.

29 galerie Vivienne, 2e; tel.: 42.61.71.43
open Tuesday–Saturday 10:30–11:30 A.M. *and noon–*
6:30 P.M.
392 rue Saint-Honoré, 1er; tel.: 49.27.97.70;
Métro: Madeleine or Concorde
open Monday–Saturday 10 A.M.–*7* P.M.

Catherine Vernoux

Here the greeting is warm and friendly—from both the owner and her cat. Take a peek at the many coordinated knits, designed by Catherine Vernoux, at moderate prices.
26 galerie Vivienne, 2e; tel.: 42.61.31.60
open Monday–Friday 10:30 A.M.–*7* P.M.; *Saturday*
11 A.M.–*7* P.M.

Wolff & Descourtis

This place is a real find although you would never know it from the outside. They specialize in couture fabrics—most of which are the same that the big names use for their own creations but are unavailable to the public. Yet the best part of this shop is that you can find great prices on those sensationally soft, 100% wool challis scarves that you see all of the French women wearing (if you happen to visit Paris between October and March). Most of them sell for about $93, depending on the print, whereas elsewhere you will find them for about $150 and up. You can buy the scarves for even less at Wolff & Descourtis if you pay by the meter and fray them yourself. Also don't miss their wool and cashmere capes that are made *sur place* for about $290.
18 galerie Vivienne, 2e; tel.: 42.61.80.84
open Monday–Friday 11 A.M.–*12:30* P.M. *and*
2–7 P.M.

•   **Rue de la Basque**   •

Lucien Legrand & Fils

Although you can see the back end of this boutique from the galerie Vivienne, the main entrance is around the corner at 1 rue de la Banque where you will discover a beautiful old *epicerie* (food store) that is now best known for its selection of fine wines and alcohols. The first time I walked into this shop there was no one there. It wasn't until I had walked almost all the way to the rear of the store that I heard voices and found the shopkeeper in the back room with a French couple discussing the merits of a particular Bordeaux wine that they were in the midst of tasting. Right then and there I felt reassured and knew that I would be steered in the right direction in choosing the proper wine to accompany my evening's *blanquette de veau*. The boutique is filled from bottle-cork–covered ceiling to tile floor with an extensive choice of wines as well as many different kinds of pâtés, jams, coffees, teas, candies, and even chilled champagne (a rarity in Paris)!

1 rue de la Banque, 2e; tel.: 42.60.07.12
open Tuesday–Friday 8:30 A.M.–7:30 P.M.; Saturday 8:30 A.M.—1 P.M. and 3–7 P.M.
Dépôt des Grandes Margues
15 rue de la Banque, 2e; see Discount Shopping p. 296

Galerie Colbert

Just next door to the galerie Vivienne is the galerie Colbert which houses the Bibliothèque Nationale (public library). It has been magnificently restored after having been closed to the public for a few years. The elegant rotunda, stately arcades, and *trompe-l'oeil* marble columns remind us of a time when the passages were among the most majestic places in all of Paris.

6 rue des Petits-Champs, 2e; Métro: Bourse

Le Grand Colbert

In a resplendent decor gleaming with polished brass, mahogany, and sumptuous wall panels painted with garlands of olive leaves and branches (typical of the neoclassic style) is located one of Paris's most recently opened *brasseries*, Le Grand Colbert. You can almost feel yourself go back nearly two centuries in time as you feast upon fresh oysters, sole meunière, and crème brulée. At lunchtime the restaurant is a popular place for nearby financial whizzes to meet and strike up new deals; in the evening it fills up late

with the local theater crowd. Le Grand Colbert is a delightful address for a long, leisurely lunch, but if this doesn't fit into your promenade you may stop in either for a café crème and fresh croissants in the morning or mull over your purchases with an afternoon cup of tea. There are two entrances to this handsome establishment: one in the galerie Colbert, the other on rue Vivienne. *Bon appetit!*
2 rue Vivienne, 2e; tel.: 42.86.87.88
métro: Bourse
open daily from 8 A.M.–1 A.M.

Rue Croix-des-Petits-Champs

La Chaise Longue

As you walk down the rue Croix–des-Petits-Champs toward the galerie Véro-Dodat, you will come across this tantalizing boutique which features a variety of fun gift ideas for those who have everything. Aside from a lot of little gadgets (such as the noise-sensitive "rockin' flowers" that made such a big hit in the States), they also show some typically French items; stainless-steel demitasse cups, mod plaster sculptures of France's famed cartoon character Tin Tin, amusing T-shirts with famous French cinema quotes splashed across the front, and reproductions of French deco items from the 30s and 50s.
30 rue Croix–des-Petits-Champs, 1er; tel.: 42.96.32.14
20 rue des Francs-Bourgeois, 3e; tel.: 48.04.36.37;
open Monday–Saturday 11 A.M.–7 P.M.
Métro: St.-Paul
8 rue Princesse, 6e; tel.: 43.29.62.39;
Métro: Mabillon
open Monday and Tuesday 11 A.M.–7 P.M.;
Wednesday–Saturday 11 A.M.–8 P.M. and 9 P.M.–1 A.M.

Galerie Véro-Dodat

Somber woodwork and bronze window frames give a jewel-like quality to this narrow passageway that was created in 1826 by two *charcutiers* (cold cuts, sausage, and pâté salesmen). It is in remarkable condition considering that this ancient thoroughfare has not undergone much renovation over the years. The serenity of the galerie Véro-Dodat contributes to the privileged feeling that the visitor experiences when strolling through this fine example of architecture from the Restoration period.

2 rue du Bouloi, 1er; Métro: Palais-Royal or Louvre

Robert Capia

Once I visited this boutique with a group of American women and by the time all eight of us had entered, we were standing single file the whole length of the shop, so narrow is the space. Monsieur Capia's boutique is actually fairly large, but it is overrun with all sorts of *objets de curiosités*, antique dolls' body parts, movie actresses' couture dresses from the 30s and 40s (I even spotted one from Saks Fifth Avenue), and of course the real *raison d'être*, about 600 antique dolls—most of which are stored away, thank goodness!

Monsieur Capia is as interesting as the goods he sells and his shop has occupied the passage Véro-Dodat longer than anyone else's. People come from all over the world to have their dolls repaired in his atelier—not to mention the movie folk who occasionally stop by for an unusual prop or two. One movie director recently dropped in looking for an *absinthe* spoon (designed for a now outlawed alcohol that proved fatal to many at the end of the past century) to be used in a film—Monsieur Capia came up with 70 of them!

Antique dolls by Steiner, Bru, Thuillier, and Jumeau are here in great force as well as a few fascinating *automates* (mechanical dolls). True collectors should be sure to price them wisely. Monsieur Capia informed me that prices are sometimes better in the U.S. since so many of these dolls were bought up by Americans during the 60s.

24-26 galerie Véro-Dodat, 1er; tel.: 42.36.25.94
open Monday–Saturday 10 A.M.–Noon and
2–6:30 P.M.

Il Bisonte

When Wanny di Filippo, the creator of Il Bisonte, caught a glimpse of the galerie Véro-Dodat he knew that this was where he had to set up his first Paris boutique. It's no surprise that he fell in love with this setting because his very first boutique was started in a similar passageway in Florence, Italy. For more on Il Bisonte, see Left Bank description p. 141.

7-9 galerie Véro-Dodat, 1er; tel.: 45.08.92.45
open Tuesday–Saturday 10:30 A.M.–1:30 P.M. and
2:30–7 P.M.

▪ Rue Jean-Jacques–Rousseau ▪

Alexis Lahellek

Just across the street from the galerie Véro-Dodat is Alexis Lahellek's showplace for his half-primitive/half-baroque creations. This designer's imaginative genius is demonstrated in a variety of forms including jewelry, furniture, and decorative arts as wide and varied as vases and coocoo clocks! The range of ideas and merchandise is endless. As one of the salespersons said, "Anything goes!"

14-16 rue Jean-Jacques–Rousseau, 1er;
tel.: 42.33.40.33; Métro: Palais-Royal
open Monday–Friday 11 A.M.–7 P.M.; Saturday
2–7 P.M.

▪ Palais Royal ▪

Although not officially considered a passage, the arcades at Palais Royal were precursors to the nearby galleries constructed a short time later. Originally made of wood, these arcades were built in 1786 (a few years before the revolution) so that newly installed merchants could generate a few extra funds for the aristocratic family of Orléans (the occupants of the palace at the time). Even though the passageways within the Palais Royal are not as shop-laden as they once were, the area and its surrounding gardens do provide a picturesque landscape for strolling, browsing, and accomplishing a little shopping.

Aside from a hodgepodge of shops specializing in old and new civilian and military medals, there are a few other boutiques that have great drawing power for gen-trified Parisians. The Count Jean de Rohan-Chabot's bou-tique, *La Vie de Château*, features choice table accessories for discerning antique connoisseurs. The shop *Didier Ludot*, also presents neatly arranged treasures from days gone by in the shape of used Hermès bags, Chanel suits, and Pierre Cardin minis.

Other Passages

Nineteen different Paris passages remain today, most of which are experiencing some sort of rebirth—partly due to the rising prices of retail space throughout the French capital. The six mentioned in this promenade are considered to be the most attractive; others have not quite survived more than a century of dilapidation. Keep your eyes out whenever you are near the *grands boulevards*, since you may just discover another passageway that will tickle your fancy.

Serious (or even not-so-serious) artists may want to visit the *Passage Choiseul*, 36 rue des Petits-Champs, 2e (near galerie Vivienne), which houses *Lavrut*, one of Paris's most celebrated suppliers of graphic, technical, and fine-art materials. Thousands of brightly colored pencils, hundreds of paint brushes in every imaginable shape and size, French and Dutch oil paints, and even a box with 525 different kinds of pastels answer to both amateurs' and professionals' every whim.

If you like poking around the Sentier, Paris's garment district, then stop into the passage du Caire, 2 place du Caire, 2e, which has been taken over almost entirely by wholesalers. Most of these *prêt-à-porter* boutiques claim not to sell retail, but if you push the right doors and use a savvy approach, you may get lucky.

• The Marais (The *Quartier* of Contrasts) •

The old-world charm of the Marais promises a refreshing contrast with the frenetic pace that you experience in other parts of the French capital. A labyrinth of small and narrow streets intimates a time when this area resembled a peaceful 17th-century village.

This is a neighborhood to explore by foot. A walking tour of the Marais not only provides you with the possibility of countless hours of treasure hunting, but also enables you to catch a glimpse of some of the nearly 100 *hôtels particuliers* (private mansions) that have made this *quartier* one of the most historic neighborhoods of Paris. The Marais was the fashionable place to live during the 17th century and these mansions attest to the elegance and grandeur of that era. In the 18th century these magnificent homes fell out of glory; small industries moved in, setting up heavy machinery in the *salons* that once housed Paris's aristocratic elite. Years of destruction and impoverishment followed until 1962 when France's then Minister of Culture, André Malraux, called for the renovation of this depressed area. Now most of the mansions have been fully restored and converted into office space, luxury apartments, and a few museums—a complete turnabout that has made the Marais one of the priciest and most fashionable places to live in Paris.

The fashion world caught on fast, too, as the whole neighborhood began to change. In the early 80s, designers on the rise, such as Lolita Lempicka and Popy Moreni, started buying up old run-down shops and converting them into alluring fashion showcases. More boutiques followed with the idea that an off-the-beaten-path location would provide a more intriguing address for their clientele. This movement spurred a whole new trend, that has made the Marais Paris's latest fashion hub.

Now trendy fashion boutiques sit in perfect harmony alongside quaint little curiosity shops that have existed for years. It is this intermingling of the old with the new that creates the beguiling charm of the neighborhood. You can spend hours wandering in and out of dusty old shops or embarking on the most exciting shopping spree in some of the hottest shops that the city has to offer. The Marais is the only area in Paris where many of the shops remain open on Sundays. Stroll about at a leisurely pace, and be sure to stop for a succulent pastry in one of the numerous tea salons that populate the Marais. You will certainly feel like you are miles away from the corner mall.

The place des Vosges, symmetrically surrounded by rosy-pink brick townhouses once intended for the king and queen, is the highlight of a visit to the Marais. Built in 1605 by Henri IV, the place des Vosges is Paris's oldest square and, in my opinion, the most beautiful. The shopping on the place, however, is somewhat sparce; the greatest concentration of shops is found on the rue des Francs-Bourgeois, the main thoroughfare of the Marais, which leads into the place des Vosges.

The **Musée Carnavalet** (the museum of the city of Paris) and the **Picasso Museum**, both housed in *hôtels particuliers*, are not to be missed. A visit to a museum combined with exploring a diverse selection of boutiques is an ideal way to spend a culturally diversified day in the French capital.

Toward the rue des Rosiers and the rue du Roi-de-Sicile, you will discover the area of Paris that has been the Jewish quarter since the 13th century. Breathe in all of the delightful aromas of this colorful area of Paris. Synagogues appear among Jewish bakeries, delicatessens, Turkish baths, and Greek cafés—more unexpected contrasts of the wonderful Marais district of Paris!

Promenade Marais

Start at the rue Pavée (Métro: St.-Paul) and work your way into the heart of the Marais, toward the rue des Francs-Bourgeois, stopping off at the boutiques on the side streets as you go along. From the rue des Francs-Bourgeois, head east toward the place des Vosges; from there, head back in the opposite direction toward the rue de Sévigné, cross over rue du Parc-Royal and rue la Perle, and head down the rue Vieille-du-Temple. You may either cut off to the rue du Bourg-Tibourg and the rue de Moussy or head straight toward the Seine and pick up rue du Pont–Louis-Philippe, Paris's paper-shop street. Here you are at equal distances from two Métro stops: St.-Paul and Hôtel de Ville.

STREETS:

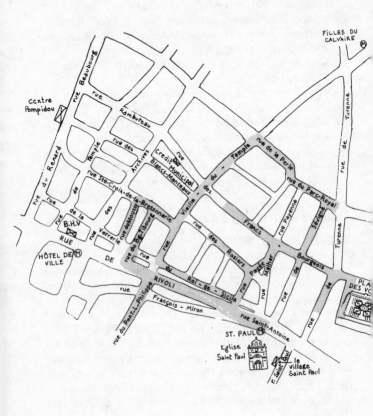

Rue du Roi-de-Sicile

Il pour l'Homme

13 rue du Roi de Sicile, 4e; see Right Bank description p. 84

Jules des Prés

46 rue du Roi-de-Sicile, 4e; see Left Bank description p. 141

Rue des Rosiers

Alain Mikli

A name synonomous with avant garde eyewear, the Alain Mikli boutique is a must for sophisticated trendsetters in search of eye-catching specs. Prices here run less than in Mikli's New York branch, and yes, eye prescriptions are international.

1 rue des Rosiers, 4e; tel.: 42.71.01.56;
Métro: St.-Paul
Open Monday 2–7 P.M.; Tuesday–Saturday 11 A.M.–7 P.M.

Le Loir dans la Théière

The decor in this popular tearoom is as unpretentious as their delicious assortment of homemade quiches, *terrines*, pies, and cakes. An odd selection of oversized chairs and round wobbly tables (local garage-sale–type furnishings) provide a laid-back set-

ting for those interested in a quick, tasty bite at an
honest price.
*3 rue des Rosiers, 4e; tel.: 42.72.90.61;
Métro: St.-Paul
open Monday–Saturday noon–7 P.M.; Sunday
11 A.M.–7 P.M.*

Lolita Bis

*3 bis rue des Rosiers, 4e; see Lolita Lempicka
description p. 217*

Chevignon

*4 rue des Rosiers, 4e; see Left Bank description
p. 137*

Apparence

Apparence designs and manufactures fake fur coats and
bags in a wide variety of amusing styles and colors. The
biggest problem you'll have here is choosing the right one
for you!

The look is stripped way down in the summer with
their collection of slinky bathing suits and wraps. They
also have a good representation of costume jewelry from
a few of Paris's most fashionable manufacturers as well
as some trendy ready-to-wear from lesser-known labels.
Don't miss the smaller Apparence shop at 5 rue des Rosiers which specializes in accessories and loungewear by
Paris's bow and tassle queen, Chantal Thomass.
*5 bis rue des Rosiers, 4e tel.: 42.77.88.95
Métro: St.-Paul
open Monday–Saturday 11 A.M.–7 P.M.; Sunday
noon–7 P.M.*

Charles Kammer

*6 rue des Rosiers, 4e; see Left Bank description
p. 151*

Olivier Chanan

If you're looking for the ultimate in Parisian chic, why not
buy a hat from one of Paris's hottest millinery designers,

Olivier Chanan? Whether it be a picture hat, a pillbox, a toque, or a bow on a barrette, Monsieur Chanan enlivens these timeless forms with just the right touch of fashionable detail and good taste. Plan to spend plenty of time trying on the countless creations in order to find the right one that fits your face as well as your personality. Custommade hats require a month's wait. Prices aren't cheap ($200–300), but there is little chance that your hat will go out of style.

6 rue des Rosiers, 4e; tel.: 42.77.15.87;
Métro: St.-Paul
Open Monday–Saturday 11 A.M.–7 P.M.

Jo Goldenberg

Paris's most famous delicatessen chockfull of pastrami, bagels, challah bread, and other kosher delights. Their terrace is one of the few places in the Marais where you can eat outside in the summertime.
7 rue des Rosiers, 4e; tel.: 42.77.67.74;
Métro: St.-Paul
open daily (except during Jewish holidays)
9 A.M.– 2 A.M.

Rue Pavée

Lolita Lempicka

Lolita Lempicka was one of the first fashion designers to set up shop in the Marais in 1984 and her business has grown as rapidly as the neighborhood itself. After many years designing for Cacharel, Lolita Lempicka tasted her own success when she launched her first collection in 1983. Since then, over 200 shops from New York to Tokyo have selected her sweet, yet sophisticated, fashions to sell to their own clients.

The Lempicka look is feminine and classic with a coquettish touch of fantasy that distinguishes it from the rest. She is most known for her tailored suits, whose precise and well-adjusted cut has earned her much acclaim from today's working women. Playful trimmings of lace and cut-work embroidery are often used to take the seriousness out of more traditional styles.

Lolita Bis, a less-expensive line cut in lower-quality materials, is intended for the refined, yet daring, teens of today, but older women buy it too.

13 bis rue Pavée, 4e; tel.: 42.74.50.48;
Métro: St.-Paul
Open Tuesday–Saturday 10:30 A.M.–7 P.M.

Aïch A

Their bags are as original as their name. Smooth and satiny leather has been crafted into shapes that remind you of your high-school geometry class: parallelograms, trapezoids, and isosceles triangles. Sometimes two different geometric shapes, in the same or different colors of leather, are used together to create a more interesting effect. The styles and colors of these reasonably priced bags ($160–290) are intended to be timeless, and depending on the sort of life-style you lead, they may very well be!

19 rue Pavée, 4e; tel.: 42.77.62.65;
Métro: St.-Paul
open Monday 2–7 P.M.; Tuesday–Saturday 11 A.M.–7 P.M.

Camille Unglik

21 rue Pavée, 4e; see Left Bank description p. 149

▪ Rue Mahler ▪

Paule Ka

Paule Ka was enamored with the glamour and elegance of Brigitte Bardot, Grace Kelly, Audrey Hepburn, and Jackie Kennedy in the 60s. His women's clothes for the 90s are a reinterpretation of many of the elements of style from that era. Form-fitted suits button all the way up to a neat little collar in a very pristine manner. Sexy strapless dresses, cut in classic velvets and taffetas, cast an elegant air.

The desert-sand–colored walls and soft lighting create a peaceful ambiance in this boutique, allowing the clothes to speak for themselves. Bloomingdale's and Barneys have already started to show some of Paule Ka's suits, but here you'll find the whole collection at better prices. A name to watch out for.

20 rue Mahler, 4e; tel.: 40.29.96.03;
Métro: St.-Paul
open Tuesday–Saturday 11 A.M.–7 P.M.

· Rue des Francs-Bourgeois *·*

A l'Image du Grenier sur l'Eau

You could spend hours in this quaint shop flicking through their wide and sundry collection of antique postcards. Hundreds of boxes filled with thousands of postcards, arranged according to subject and theme, line one wall of the boutique—and there's a lot more in stock!

What's the big deal about postcards? "They are one of the world's most valuable forms of documentation," says owner and collector Yves di Maria. "Every monument, city, and region has been photographed and put on a postcard at one time or another," he adds. So this is where you can find a turn-of-the-century shot of the Champs-Elysées, the Spanish Steps or Mother Russia. This is how photographs became accessible to the public—postcards started using photos when the newspapers were still limited to illustrations.

Most of the boutique's clientele is made up of true collectors. However, it is a great place to find a unique gift idea. Most of the cards cost $1.50–30, although the rarer the image, the higher the price; one of the more unusual postcards—a Frenchman taking a nap on the banks of the Seine, by the famous early-1900s photographer, Adjet—is priced at $260!

Antique prints, posters, and books complement their extensive selection of postcards.

45 rue des Francs-Bourgeois, 4e; tel.: 42.71.02.31;
Métro: Rambuteau or St-Paul
open Monday–Friday 10 A.M.–6:30 P.M.; Saturday 2–6 P.M.

Les Enfants Gâtés

This tea salon looks like a less shabby version of Le Loir dans la Théière. They also serve a fine assortment of homemade salads, quiches, cakes, and pies in a casual environment. If you're alone or don't feel like talking with the person you are with, you can seek refuge in their eclectic selection of magazines and comic books available for your enjoyment.

43 rue des Francs-Bourgeois, 4e; tel.:
42.77.07.63; Métro: Rambuteau or St.-Paul
open daily noon–7 P.M.

Marais Plus

Yet another homelike *salon de thé* to ease you through your day of shopping in the Marais. Standard fare still includes fresh salads and home-baked goodies, with the atmosphere of a serene, Harvard Square–like café. The tearoom is adjacent to a lovely little shop that sells books, maps, postcards (contemporary), and inexpensive gift ideas.

20 rue des Francs-Bourgeois, 3e; tel.:
48.87.01.40;
Métro: St.-Paul
open Monday–Saturday 9 A.M.–midnight;
Sunday 9 A.M.–7 P.M.

Inna Kobja

Folkloric and Oriental prints fashioned into classic styles create an innovative look for this designer's womenswear. New to the Paris fashion scene, Inna Kobja draws inspiration from her travels to foreign lands for her exotic-looking creations that are young and reasonably priced.

A straight skirt in gold-threaded Thai silk is shown with a brightly colored oversized sweater; woven cotton Guatemalan print pants are paired up with a tailored linen jacket. The combinations are surprising—dressy fabrics are used in sportswear and saris are converted into skirts—but the result is fun and easy to wear.

23 rue des Francs-Bourgeois, 4e; tel.: 42.77.41.20;
Métro: St.-Paul
open daily 11 A.M.–7 P.M.

Le Garage

Enter into this converted *boulangerie/pâtisserie* to find
Paris's most outrageous collection of men's and women's
shirts. These are weekend shirts to wear when you feel
like having fun with your wardrobe. They come in several
bright and screamy colors or the purest of blacks and
whites—all either beaded, embroidered, rhinestoned, or
splashed with loud bursts of flowers in full bloom. The
shirts are made of cotton, rayon, and silk and are cut
large. Average price is $100. You'll run into them in other
shops around town, but here they have the biggest selection. The men's shirts (which women wear, too) are upstairs, and the women's are downstairs along with an
equally hip collection of ready-to-wear.
23 rue des Francs-Bourgeois, 4e; tel.: 48.04.73.72;
Métro: St.-Paul
open Sunday and Monday 2–7 P.M.; Tuesday–
Saturday 11 A.M.–7 P.M.
40 rue du Four, 6e; (shirts only) tel.: 45.44.97.70;
Métro: St.-Sulpice
open Monday–Saturday 10:30 A.M.–7 P.M.

Jean-Pierre de Castro

As soon as you push open the door, you're almost
knocked over with a heavy, pungent smell of tarnished
silver and silver in the midst of being polished. The odor
only adds to the charm and authenticity of the boutique,
which is considered to be one of Paris's best shops for
buying antique silver and silverplate items.

Much of what is sold here comes from hotels that have
gone out of business, estates, and old cruiseships such
as *Le Normandie*. A huge table in the center of the boutique is covered with mixed patterns of flatware that are
sold by the kilo; the walls are lined from top to bottom
with shelves that contain hundreds of reasonably priced
gift ideas, including silver teapots, frames, platters, champagne buckets, and more out-of-the-ordinary items such
as silver egg cups, wine tasters, and toastholders (which
you can also use for your mail!).

17 rue des Francs-Bourgeois, 4e; tel.: 42.72.04.00;
Métro: St.-Paul
open Monday 2–7 P.M.; Tuesday–Sunday 11 A.M.–
7 P.M.

Et Vous

15 rue des Francs-Bourgeois, 4e; see Left Bank
description p. 130

Autour du Monde

Autour du Monde is the Frenchified version of Banana Republic, which of course means slightly more stylish safari wear at higher prices. The boutique was started up a few years ago by Serge Bensimon of Bensimon Surplus fame (French army wear), who has since opened at least six shops in France, two in Japan, and several others throughout the world (excluding the U.S.).
12 rue des Francs-Bourgeois, 3e; tel.: 42.77.16.18;
Métro: St.-Paul
open Monday–Saturday 11 A.M.–7 P.M.; Sunday
noon–7 P.M.
54 rue de Seine, 6e; tel.: 43.54.64.47;
Métro: Mabillon

Les Bourgeoises

Flowered prints and faded walls create a cozy setting in this tiny restaurant that serves oriental specialties in addition to traditional French fare. Stop in for a hearty plate of beef curry accompanied with a bottle of Brouilly before you take in the second half of your Marais promenade.
12 rue des Francs-Bourgeois, 3e;
tel.: 42.72.48.30; Métro: St.-Paul
open Monday 8–10:30 P.M.; Tuesday–Saturday
12:30–2 P.M. and 8–10:30 P.M.

Fugit Amor

This closet-sized boutique glistens with a goldmine of creations from Paris's most exciting costume-jewelry designers of the moment. Philippe, the owner of the boutique and a designer himself, has all the right connections in obtaining much-in-demand treasures from Paris's most persnickety designers (they don't sell to just anybody)—all at lower than normal prices.

   The look is avant-garde in the most modern of materials: magically luminous resin, featherweight metal, and brightly colored plastics have been molded and sculpted into countless different unconventional shapes—such a realm of creation that you know you've come across a real find!

11 rue des Francs-Bourgeois, 4e; tel.: 42.74.52.37; Métro: St.-Paul
Open Sunday 2–7 P.M.; Monday–Saturday noon–7 P.M.

Imex

Walk through the doorway at no. 8, cross the courtyard and you'll discover this manufacturer's store and showroom which houses year-round their extensive collection of reasonably priced, imitation furs. The styles are both classic and trendy; 1990's biggie was a fake-fur duffle coat shown in several mod colors. More traditional styles—such as a trench coat in conventional grey, brown, or olive green, lined in fake rabbit or bear—are also effective in keeping you warm and dry without taking a critter's life.

8 rue des Francs-Bourgeois, 3e; tel.: 48.87.14.76; Métro: St.-Paul
open Monday–Saturday 10 A.M.–7 P.M.

Blanc Bleu

8 rue des Francs-Bourgeois, 4e; see Left Bank description p. 136

Casa Costanza

These men's and women's shoes are made in Italy and designed by an Italian, but so far you can only find them in this handsome boutique here in the Marais. Their stylish selection of shoes comes in colors as earthy as the burnt-orange–colored, sponge-painted frescoes on the walls of this boutique. The shoes are moderately priced at about $110 for a pair of pumps.

7 rue des Francs-Bourgeois, 4e; tel.: 42.76.01.99; Métro: St.-Paul
open Sunday and Monday 2–7 P.M.; Tuesday–Saturday 10 A.M.–7 P.M.

Catimini Babymini

My mother found this children's (0–12 years) clothing store just after it first opened several years ago when she was here visiting me. The outfits she bought for my nieces were so adorable that I had to trot on over to check out the rest of what they had to offer. I've been in love with Catimini Babymini ever since, and if you like fun and innovative children's clothing, you will be, too.

Their styles and prints are creatively designed in a rainbow of colors. The look is loose, modern, and comfortable: a baggy baby outfit is dotted with bunches of pink and red radishes; a little girl's skirt and jacket are invaded with wide-grinned purple crocodiles; and a basic yellow slicker is jazzed up with a big colorful race car. The quality is excellent, and the only drawback is that the prices are steep.

6 rue des Francs-Bourgeois, 3e; tel.: 42.72.72.66;
Métro: St.-Paul
open Sunday 2–7 P.M.; Monday 11 A.M.–7 P.M.;
Tuesday–Saturday 10 A.M.–7 P.M.
57 av Franklin-Roosevelt, 8e; tel.: 42.25.08.27;
Métro: Franklin-Roosevelt

Chevignon Trading Post

Another American-heritage store that is remarkably similar to neighboring Autour du Monde Home—which of course proves that the French have gone head over heels for the American look. First there was the invasion of the blue jean; then American eateries, offering everything from hamburgers to Tex-Mex, started to spring up in all of the fashionable neighborhoods; now the Parisians want to have their interiors looking like a farmhouse in the dead of Kansas! Painted signs that read "God bless this home," wooden decoys, Shaker boxes, jumbo-sized American mailboxes, and homespun patchwork quilts are just a few of the items that the French have discovered they can't live without!

6 rue des Francs-Bourgeois, 3e; tel.: 48.87.12.99;
Métro: St.-Paul
open Sunday and Monday 2–7 P.M.; Tuesday–
Saturday 11 A.M.–7 P.M.

Carnavalette

This is my favorite Paris shop for prints, books, and news-papers from yesteryear. The ambiance is warm and cozy, mostly because the people who work at Carnavalette are friendly and serviceable. Although most of their 19th- and early-20th-century prints are neatly classified according to subject and theme, the people here are so passionate about what they sell that they often come up with helpful suggestions that you may have overlooked.

This is how I found out about Sem, France's great car-icaturist during La Belle Epoque (early 1900s), whose orig-inal lithographs line a couple of their walls just above eye level. Sem followed the rich and famous to Deauville, Monte Carlo, and then back to Paris, in order to capture in his own satirical way the pomp and opulence of that era. Sem's lithographs are a bit high, but if you look in the folders, you'll discover many inexpensively priced prints and postcards.

2 rue des Francs-Bourgeois, 3e; tel.: 42.72.91.92;
Métro: St.-Paul
open Sunday 11 A.M.–5:30 P.M.; Monday–Saturday
10:30 A.M.–6:30 P.M.

• Rue de Turenne •

l'Arlequin

This is *the* best Paris address for finding 19th-century French crystal and glassware in the most exquisite and diverse patterns. A lot of the French come here to replace glasses from their family heritage that have been lost or broken over the years.

Rows and rows of tiny shelves fill this boutique from top to bottom. The crystal is on the left-hand side wall, the glassware is on the right. Baccarat and Saint-Louis are here in great force, and I can't think of a more romantic gift from Paris than a matching pair of champagne flutes from the First Empire (the oldest period represented in the shop). If you're in the market for coupes, your choice is more limited, because contrary to what you may think, they didn't surface until the late-19th century, long after the flutes; most of the coupes from that era were engraved.

These glasses—along with hand-painted glass vases, carafes, and candy dishes—are sold here for far less than in America. I found out from one of my clients (a true collector) that his antique dealer in Toronto buys from l'Arlequin and marks the items up at least five times above their boutique price.

19 rue de Turenne, 4e; tel.: 42.78.77.00;
Métro: St.-Paul
open Tuesday–Saturday 2:30–6:30 P.M.

• Place des Vosges •

Ma Bourgogne

No trip to the Marais (especially the first one) is complete without stopping in this often busy café—not necessarily for the food, but for the view of the magnificent place des Vosges, Paris's most stately square. Rain or shine, you may sit at one of the tables underneath the centuries-old arcades and order up *un plat du jour, un café noir,* or a chilled glass of Beaujolais.

19 place des Vosges, 4e; tel.: 42.78.44.64;
Métro: St.-Paul
open Tuesday–Sunday 8 A.M.–1 A.M.

Popy Moreni

After having spent a number of years designing womenswear for various designers including Nino Cerruti, Popy Moreni was among the first to take the plunge and set up her own boutique in the Marais. She is Italian inside and out, which explains the *commedia dell'arte* side to all of her creations. Popy Moreni feels that the street is the theater and her clothes serve as the decor. Hence her sophisticated fashions are bought by the most eccentric of women, and she is most known for her glittery collection of eveningwear.

13 place des Vosges, 4e; tel.: 42.77.09.96;
Métro: St.-Paul
open Monday 11 A.M.–7 P.M.; Tuesday–Saturday
10 A.M.–7 P.M.

Issey Miyake

Japanese designer Issey Miyake is one of the most recent
arrivals at the place des Vosges, and his captivating showplace is as artistically designed as the clothing sold here.
The minimalist decor may at first put you off, but once
you enter the world of Issey Miyake, you will never go
back. His use of traditional and nontraditional fabrics in
his interpretations of classic Japanese costumes creates
a look that is both striking and timeless.

The choice of fashions shown here is sometimes different from what you will find in New York. The prices,
however, run about the same as in the U.S.—very high.

The Miyake Permanente collection (more timeless ver-
sions of the designer's creations) is shown at 201 bd. St.-
Germain; the Plantation collection (menswear) is at 33 bd
Raspail.

3 place des Vosges, 4e; tel.: 48.87.01.86;
Métro: St.-Paul
open Monday–Saturday 10 A.M.–12:30 P.M. and 1:30–
7 P.M.

Fanny Liautard

Just a few steps away from the Victor Hugo museum on
the resplendent place des Vosges, Fanny Liautard showcases silky creations as luxurious as the place itself.
Quickly becoming one of Paris's most talked-about addresses for quality lingerie, Fanny Liautard features classically styled ready-to-wear and custom-made frivolities.
In addition to the lingerie, the boutique also presents its
own feminine collection of terry robes, mohair bed jackets
(for wearing over negligés), and even a sugar-and-spice
selection of blush-colored blouses and snow-white wedding dresses.

2 place des Vosges, 4e; tel.: 42.77.73.44;
Métro: St.-Paul
open Tuesday–Saturday 10 A.M.–7 P.M.

Rue de Sévigné

Meubles Peints

Monsieur Jean-Pierre Besenval ferrets out 18th- and 19th-
century Alsatian armoires that have fallen to ruin and

restores them, inside and out, to their original splendor. Each armoire is stripped, treated, and painted according to artisanal methods in the tiny workshop behind this boutique. All of the egg-tempera paintings are bright, colorful, and highly decorative. Most of the images are folkloric paintings of fruits and flowers from the eastern part of France; others bear Renaissance-inspired landscapes in the *trompe l'oeil* technique.

A good number of foreigners figure among Monsieur Besenval's clientele. The shop will gladly handle all shipping arrangements and provide the necessary papers for customs. Even after these additional expenses, the prices for these hand-painted cupboards remain far more interesting than if you were to buy them in the U.S.

32 rue de Sévigné, 4e; tel.: 42.77.54.60;
Métro: St.-Paul
open every day except Monday noon–7 P.M.

Stéphane Kélian

36 rue de Sévigné, 3; see Left Bank description
p. 150

La Maison des Bonbons

It smells like spun sugar inside this boutique—and it's no wonder because almost every inch of the place is covered with thick glass jars and different-sized packages chock full of colorful sugar-coated sweets. You've just entered Paris's most delightful penny-candy store! Of course, nothing costs a penny anymore (especially in France), but this shop is loaded with all of the nostalgic treats that were a part of every French person's childhood.

La Maison des Bonbons provides an attractive and highly tempting assortment of typically French gift ideas, most of which are packaged in pretty little metal boxes, decorated *à l'ancienne*—perfect for travel. French favorites include pierrot gourmand suckers, almond-paste animals, silver-wrapped chocolate sardines, almond nougat, gingerbread, and cookies from the provinces!

46 rue de Sévigné, 3e; tel.: 48.87.88.62;
Métro: St.-Paul
open Monday–Friday 10 A.M.–7 P.M.; Saturday and Sunday 2:30–7 P.M.

Romeo Gigli

Italian designer Romeo Gigli opened up his first Parisian boutique in early 1990 in the wake of a series of triumphant reviews from the French fashion press. Here a stark, loft-like decor creates an art-gallery–like setting for fashions that are anything but sparse. Your eye quickly focuses on the designer's theatrical creations rather than on the space itself. Gossamer fabrics scintillate with touches of silver and gold in romantic styles fit for modern-day princesses. And you almost have to be of royal lineage to buy these fantasy-like fashions, so high are the prices. If you do, however, fall in love with a glossy transparent blouse, chances are it will never go out of fashion and, in any event, who can pass up a piece of Italian baroque anyway?

Romeo Gigli also features a menswear line that offers more masculine interpretations of 90s romanticism. Jackets in rich blood reds and dramatic blacks bring to mind the kind of soft-spoken, dark-haired men one encounters in the Mediterranean.

46 rue de Sévigné, 3e; tel.: 42.71.08.40;
Métro: St.-Paul
open Monday 3–7 P.M.; Tuesday–Saturday 10:30
A.M.–7 P.M.

Rue du Parc-Royal

Zandoli

Whenever one of my clients asks me for belts, one of the first places I think of is Zandoli. They always have a sizable selection of fashionable belts in a wide color assortment, and if you don't find exactly what you're looking for here, they can have one made up for you (takes about a week). Zandoli is a French manufacturer that started exporting their attractive accessories to the east (Japan and Australia) before they opened up this handsome boutique a few years ago. Belt qualities range from pigskin to supple lambskin, fetching prices between $60 and $160.

Other important fashion accessories include Jean-Paul Gaultier's heavy metal trinkets, gobby baroque-inspired costume jewelry, and a tasteful collection of bags.

2 rue du Parc-Royal, 3e; tel.: 42.71.90.39;
Métro: St.-Paul
open daily 10:30 A.M.–7 P.M.

· ## Rue Vieille-du-Temple ·

Artisflora

Located not far from the ***Picasso Museum*** in the Hôtel
de la Tour du Pin, a 17th-century *hôtel particulier* characteristic of the Marais, is this boutique specializing in
handmade reproductions of antique tapestries. If I hadn't
already told you they were copies, you would probably
think that they were the real thing; *hélas* no, most of the
real ones are hanging in the ***Musée de Cluny***, Paris's
fortress of Medieval treasures.

Nevertheless, these tapestries are made outside of Paris
by a very intricate silkscreening process on canvas. Poetic
images from the Middle Ages, regal 17th-century hunting
scenes, and festive scenes from the late 18th century are
reproduced with great precision in two different patinas:
one that keeps the vivacity of the many colors alive, another that washes them out so that they actually look
hundreds of years old. The result is highly convincing
and it's exciting to imagine one of France's most famous
museum tapestries back in the States in your own home.
Prices run $550–1,750 and the works can easily be rolled
up for travel. Sometimes they have a bin filled with
semi–worn-out tapestries—not only are these less expensive, but I find them to be even more authentic-looking.

In the same wooden-beam setting of this historical monument, they also sell reproductions of Art Nouveau tile
panels that have been painted with lusty-looking women
and spindly flowers. Very pretty but tough to lug home.
75 rue Vieille-du-Temple, 3e; tel.: 48.87.76.18;
Métro: St.-Paul
open Monday–Saturday 9 A.M.–6 P.M.

La Calinière

If you're in the market for antique lamps or lighting fixtures, but don't have time to hit the flea markets, you may
want to have a look around at La Calinière. This anti-

quated boutique offers a charming collection of knickknacks and *objects* from days gone by, which makes it
interesting just to browse around even if you're not looking to buy. Their forte is a great and varied collection of
every imaginable type of illumination from the Art Nouveau and Art Deco periods, all of which can easily be
wired to plug in stateside.
68 rue Vieille-du-Temple, 3e; tel.: 42.77.40.46;
Métro: St.-Paul
open Monday–Saturday 11 A.M.–6 P.M.; Sunday 3–
6 P.M.

Casta Diva

A shrill of high-pitched soprano and sharp tenor notes
rings out into the street as you push open the door of this
red-carpeted shop that specializes in opera and ballet
music. If you're a true opera buff, you'll particularly enjoy
this boutique because some of the recordings that may
be unearthed here are not available in the U.S. Besides
selling over six different versions of Maria Callas singing
La Traviata, they also claim to have a fair amount of old
live recordings that have never made it off the Continent.
Casta Diva also sells a few rare gems made by very small
French and Italian music companies that don't export
abroad.
58 rue Vieille-du-Temple, 3e; tel.: 42.72.63.49;
Métro: St.-Paul
open daily 11 A.M.–7:30 P.M.

Accessoire

36 rue Vieille-du-Temple, 4e; see Left Bank
description p. 139

A la Bonne Renommée

Late-19th-century dark-wood floors, paneling, and showcases create a warm and handsome setting for the lux-
uriously rich patchworks sold in this shop. This is exactly
the sort of boutique that most visitors yearn to stumble
upon during a typically Parisian shopping excursion, but
relatively few actually do.
    Patchwork takes on a different meaning here from the
one we are familar with back home in America. The as-

sortment of ready-to-wear and accessories sold in this
shop is made up of rather Slavic-looking patchworks com
posed of the finest jacquards, satins, velvets, paisleys
flower prints, and, most of all, the most extraordinary
ribbons that the town of Lyon has to offer. The strongpoin
of these folkloric designs lies in their unusual mixture o
materials, textures, and colors as well as the finishing of
of each creation with a fanciful touch of tassle or fringe

Many of the shapes used in the women's apparel an
bags are as heartwarming as the patchworks. Ample cu
jackets, shirts, and vests, soft and floppy drawstring
pouches, and Gothic-shaped handbags conjure up image
of Eastern European lands. Belts, change purses, eyeglass
cases, and pins make up some of the more traditiona
items that are both affordable and easy to bring home a
gifts.

Amble on downstairs to take a look at their collection
of home-decoration items. Tablecloths, pillows, quilts
and rugs are all prettily displayed in a sitting room tha
looks like it's waiting for you to move in. To this date
only a few of these home accessories may be found a
Bergdorf's in New York, where they're priced at nearly
twice as much. (The rest of their merchandise is not ex
ported.)

Before you head out, take a peek in the back of the
shop where you'll see nimble fingers working away at the
creation of all of these enchanting patchworks—one more
indication that this is truly a unique shop.

26 rue Vieille-du-Temple, 4e; tel.: 42.72.03.86;
Métro: St.-Paul or Hôtel de Ville
1 rue Jacob, 6e; tel.: 46.33.90.67;
Métro: St.-Germain-des-Prés or Mabillon
open Monday–Saturday 11 A.M.–7 P.M.

• Rue Du Bourg-Tibourg

Mariage Frères

Located on the fringes of the Beaubourg quartier is
the most unforgettable *salon de thé* of the Marais. The
neocolonial decor, rattan chairs, and white-jacketed
waiters make you feel as though you have just

stepped into one of the most elegant tearooms in East India! Here the tea is meticulously prepared and served, respecting every rule of the ritual. One may choose from 350 varieties of tea from 22 different countries. Coffee lovers beware—the menu is strictly tea-oriented, offering only fruit juice and champagne as alternatives. Delectable lunches and a scrumptuous selection of *gâteaux* from their pastry cart provide the perfect ingredients for a relaxing respite from your day in the Marais.

After a leisurely tea, enjoy browsing in the Mariage Frères boutique, where you may buy tea from the 350 handsome canisters that line the walls. Their collection of classic teapots and strainers, ranging from Chinese to Art Deco, is equally impressive. *Les frères* Mariage (Mariage brothers) started working as tea merchants in 1854.

30-32 rue du Bourg-Tibourg, 4e; tel.:
42.72.28.11; Métro: Hôtel de Ville
tearoom: open Tuesday–Sunday noon–7:30 P.M.
boutique: open daily 10 A.M.–7:30 P.M.

Rue de Moussy

Azzedine Alaïa

The only designer in Paris (if not the world) to dare to show his collections a month later than everyone else, only this tiny man from Tunisia is capable of bringing the international press and buyers back for more. The world's top models come back too, jumping at the chance to be a part of an Alaïa show and often insisting to be paid in clothes rather than cash. Celebrities, including Grace Jones and Tina Turner, swear by him; designers throughout the world have copied him.

What's the trick? Slinky body-hugging clothes in the most modern of stretchy fabrics, masterly stitched together. Alaïa started a body-conscious trend in the early 80s that gained momentum throughout the decade and so far shows no sign of letting up in the 90s. Amazingly enough, even the most curvaceous women look smashing slithering around in an Alaïa dress, proving the theory that his tight fits are designed to hold you in—rather than out!

Paris is of course the place to shop for Alaïa. Nowhere else in the world will you find such a collection of this designer's clingy fashions.

7 rue de Moussy, 4e; tel.: 40.27.85.58 or 42.72.19.19;
Métro: Hôtel-de-Ville
open Monday–Saturday 10 A.M.–7 P.M.

•   ## Rue du Pont–Louis-Philippe   •

Melodies Graphiques

Turn back the clock a few centuries as you enter this attractive boutique that features countless gift ideas covered with Florentine papers. Although invented by the bookbinder of Louis XIII during the 17th century, this art has been kept alive by the Italians over the past few hundred years. The papers found in Mélodies Graphiques have been made by hand in the Il Papiro workshop in Florence.

These marbleized papers, which come in a variety of melded colors, are made sheet by sheet in a vat filled with a mixture of water and herbs. Drops of color are sprinkled on the surface of the liquid and blended with several different tools: brushes, combs, feathers, etc. The colors become permanently fixed to the paper once the sheet is delicately placed on the prepared surface. No two sheets of paper are the same, which only adds to the charm of these exquisite creations.

Various-sized and -shaped boxes, photo albums, portfolios, blank books, stationery, and desk accessories covered with these colorful papers are attractively displayed in blond wooden bookcases that make up this pretty shop. Although the prices may appear a bit high, they're more interesting than those in the U.S.

10 rue du Pont–Louis-Philippe, 4e; tel.: 42.74.57.68;
Métro: St.-Paul
Monday 2–7 P.M.; Tuesday–Saturday 11 A.M.–7 P.M.

Papier Plus

Former art-book publisher, Laurent Tisné blends modernity with elegance in his sober collection of fine-quality stationery and paper articles. Blank notebooks, photo albums, guest registers, artists' portfolios, and more, bound in heavy canvas, have been neatly arranged in piles that form a rich temple of color within the shop.

Most of the binding is done semimanually by small firms in France which carefully select the various papers needed for different purposes: a certain paper for books destined for writing, another for drawing, etc. There is much attention paid to detail, which explains their devoted following by artists, architects, illustrators, and non-professionals from all corners of the world.

9 rue du Pont–Louis-Philippe, 4e; tel.: 42.77.70.49; Métro: St-Paul
open Monday–Saturday noon–7 P.M.

Calligrane

Calligrane, the new kid on the block, has two boutiques on the rue du Pont–Louis-Philippe. You'll find desk accessories at no. 6 and paper products at no. 4. Both stores sell design-oriented products that create a highly contemporary look—ideal for work at home or at the office.

Their black and chrome selection of desk accessories is made up of some of the most streamlined *objets* from all over Europe: fountain pens from France, desk blotters from Italy, and minicalculators, staplers, and organizers from Germany.

The other boutique specializes in equally modern-looking paper products from Fabriano, Italy. Recycled paper, handmade paper, and paper made from hay are some of the more interesting types of products sold with their 20 different colors of stationery. Don't miss their hand-folded papers that form both letter and envelope in one. Most papers are reasonably priced.

4 and 6 rue du Pont–Louis-Philippe, 4e;
tel.: 48.04.31.89 or 40.27.00.74;
Métro: St.-Paul
open Monday 2:30–7 P.M.; Tuesday–Saturday
11 A.M.–7:30 P.M.

Rue de Rivoli

A l'Olivier

If you head back toward the métro St.-Paul after your promenade in the Marais, stop in this quaint shop that sells many different types of olives, olive oil, vinegars flavored with raspberry, tarragon, and sherry plus cooking oils made from hazelnut, walnut, and palm. Their country French packages make for pretty, inexpensive gifts for culinary-enlightened friends back home.

**23 rue de Rivoli, 4e; tel.: 48.04.86.59;
Métro: St.-Paul
open Tuesday–Saturday 9:30 A.M.–1 P.M. and 2:30–
7 P.M.**

BHV

52 rue de Rivoli, 4e; see Department Stores p. 307

The Bastille (Paris's SoHo)

Since the 17th century, artisans have populated the crooked little streets and courtyards that typify the Bastille district. Artists, writers, and architects moved in over a decade ago after other areas of Paris, such as, the Left Bank, became too pricey for their uncertain means. The once middle-class neighborhood of the Bastille took on a cultural slant. Artists' lofts began to replace small industries that were becoming increasingly obsolete; avant-garde art galleries and theaters started to open up, followed by an onslaught of trendy restaurants and even trendier boutiques. All of Paris, and later the rest of the world, began to talk about the cultural explosion taking place in the Bastille. The area became gentrified and real-estate costs skyrocketed.

The opening of the new and highly controversial opera house coincided with the many celebrations held to commemorate the two-hundredth anniversary of the French Revolution. Many of these festivities were centered around the Bastille (not only the name of the area, but also the name of the prison that was seized in 1789, at the onset of the Revolution), which of course encouraged a great number of curious onlookers to flood the area.

Often likened to New York's SoHo district, the Bastille differs in that it has always been a hustle-bustle area of Paris and never had to experience the empty-warehouse syndrome that occurred in New York. Despite such on-going development, many of the artisans and small trades have managed to remain in their *ateliers*. As you explore the Bastille, walk into some of the courtyards (don't be afraid to push open a few doors as you go along) and you'll discover craftspeople carrying out *vieux métiers* (old trades) such as cabinet making, gilt work, and hand varnishing.

The furniture-making industry was once big business here. Now most of the craftspeople carry out highly specialized jobs for some of Paris's most prestigious antique dealers and flea-market merchants. Paris's reknowned furniture street, the glitzy rue du Faubourg–St.-Antoine, sells tacky living-and dining-room sets ostentatious enough to make you think that this was where Liberace did all of his shopping.

The ambiance in the Bastille becomes particularly electrified at night. Motorcyclers crowd around their slick and shiny Harley Davidsons weekend nights at the place de la Bastille or gather together at *La Rotonde* (a café on the corner of rue St.-Sabin and rue de la Roquette) for a couple of beers. Nightclubbers dance until the wee hours of the morning to the soulful sounds of reggae and salsa at the *Chapelle des Lombards* and swoon to retro tunes amid the 1930s decor at the *Balajo*. Both are located on the rue du Lappe (infamous for its high crime rate years ago) along with an equally tantalizing selection of exotic restaurants and bars.

If all of this is just a bit too much for you, try heading over to *Bofinger* (across the place de la Bastille), Paris's oldest brasserie. If you're more in the mood for walking, stroll along the banks of the Canal St.-Martin, where many a French detective story has been filmed. If you happen to be in Paris in October, you are really in luck. This is when the *Genie de la Bastille* takes place, an open house held by the local artists and art galleries that allows you to take a peek behind closed doors until midnight every day for almost a week!

The Bastille offers the most unique shopping experience of all of the Paris shopping districts. Even if you only pick up a knickknack or two, you're sure to have an exciting time in the French capital's latest hot spot.

Promenade Bastille

Start at the beginning of the rue de la Roquette at the place de la Bastille. Head down rue de la Roquette and turn left onto rue Daval and rue St.-Sabin. After you have taken in the boutiques and art galleries there, continue up the rue de la Roquette and cross over the rue Keller until you reach rue de Charonne. (Take the rue des Taillandiers if you want to check out a few retro clothing and music shops.) Head down the rue de Charonne and take a right onto the rue de Lappe, continue on this street, and you will end up where you started. The Métro stop for the Bastille tour is Bastille.

STREETS:
rue de la Roquette p. 238
rue Daval p. 241
rue St.-Sabin p. 243
rue Keller p. 243
rue de Charonne p. 244

·   **Rue de la Roquette**   ·

L'Usine

A hodgepodge of everything one needs to fill their loft: contemporary home accessories, trendy gift items, and Conran-like furniture. Kitchen musts include stainless-steel café trays, mini espresso makers, and lace-trimmed rubber gloves and aprons for looking designer-label–glamourous when scrubbing at home. L'Usine is also one of the best outposts for Moon Line, French-made bags in rubbery PVC, a material similar to the one used in wet suits. Moon Line bags are highly resistant, inexpensive ($30–75), and sporty and come in amusing shapes such as half moons and mini knapsacks.

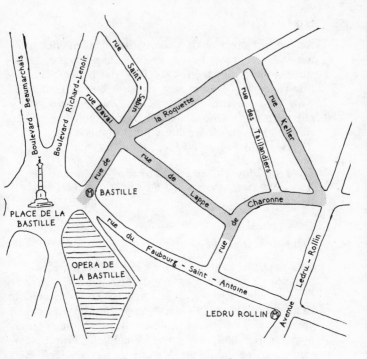

9 rue de la Roquette, 11e; tel.: 43.38.68.87;
Métro: Bastille
open Sunday 2–7:30 P.M.; Monday–Friday 10 A.M.–1
P.M. and 2–7 P.M.; Saturday 10 A.M.–6 P.M.

Pastille

If you're looking for the perfect outfit to wear out dancing
to the sizzling Balajo, you're almost sure to find it here.
Pastille sells moderately priced, modish fashions for men
and women who lead swinging nightlives—or at least like
to look as though they do even at 3 P.M. in the corner café.
The women's fashions highlight Plein Sud's (see p. 174)
skintight creations and Bill Tornade's more baroque versions of velvety chic. Bill Tornade's baseball-stripe pants
and patchwork jackets are for men who don't care to be
taken seriously. A more middle-of-the-road collection of
flowery rayon shirts may be worn by both sexes.
19 rue de la Roquette, 11e; tel.: 48.06.61.73;
Métro: Bastille
open Monday–Saturday 11 A.M.–7:30 P.M.

Salambo

Across the street at Salambo, girlish fashions flirt in an assortment of cotton-candy colors. This French manufac turer is best-known for fake furs and flouncy peplum fitted suits, which have recently turned up in a couple o. New York department stores. Their Oh! Les Filles opaqu stockings are not for the skittish; hieroglyphic-like designs run up black legs in a glittery burst of color.
38 rue de la Roquette, 11e; tel.: 47.00.06.30;
Métro: Bastille
open Monday 2–7:30 P.M.; Tuesday–Saturday 11
A.M.–7:30 P.M. (often until 8 or 8:30 P.M. during the
warm months)

Optic Bastille

This eyeglass boutique comes highly recommended by some of my most avant-garde friends. Whether you're an artist, a gallery owner, an architect, or just someone ou to modernize his or her image, Optic Bastille will provide you with one of Paris's best selections of contemporary eyewear from designers such as Alain Mikli, François Pin ton, and Robert LaRoche. A more conservative collectior of Vuarnet sunglasses is sold for those of you who are a bit less daring.
38 rue de la Roquette, 11e; tel.: 48.06.87.00;
Métro: Bastille
open Tuesday–Saturday 10 A.M.–7 P.M.

Nota Bene

Nota Bene is the best boutique in the neighborhood fo: high-fashion costume jewelry. Top designers such as Spol (creates for Chanel and Lagerfeld), Patrick Retif, an Chantal Thomass are delightfully represented in thi: bright and spacious boutique. Silk scarves from days gon by and Pixie & Cie's mini couture mannequins are also on view among the red-velvet displays and gold-en crusted mirrors that add a hint of Italian spirit to Not: Bene.
40 rue de la Roquette, 11e; tel.: 43.55.83.04;
Métro: Bastille
open Tuesday–Saturday 11 A.M.–8 P.M.

Comptoir du Desert

One more Banana Republic–inspired answer to casual dressing for urban dwellers. The most interesting part of this store is the well-stocked selection of sporty footwear for men and women. Aside from their own brand of rugged made-in-England leather shoes, they also sell a rather complete collection of Dr. Marten's unbeatably comfortable shoes. The styles aren't as big and clunky as you'd expect, and you might even go as far as to call them attractive.

72-74 rue de la Roquette, 11e; tel.: 47.00.57.80;
Métro: Bastille
open Sunday and Monday 4:30–7:30 P.M.; Tuesday–Saturday 11 A.M.–8 P.M.

• Rue Daval •

Duelle

You're apt to walk right past this boutique because it's no bigger than a shoe box—but don't, or else you'll miss the area's best selection of avant-garde costume jewelry. Here plastic and metal have been worked and molded into a variety of gobby forms. How about a mini Eiffel Tower or Mona Lisa locked in a Lucite pin for your grooviest friends back home?

21 rue Daval, 11e; tel.: 47.00.93.72;
Métro: Bastille
open Tuesday–Saturday noon–8 P.M.

Franck Joseph Bastille

Women's-clothing designer Franck Joseph Bastille is so hooked on this part of town that he decided to set up his atelier, his showroom, and his boutique in the heart of the Bastille. And as one more confirmation of his faith in Paris's most recent hot spot, he officially changed his name to Franck Joseph Bastille.

The decor in his rue Daval boutique is in tune with the overall look of much of the Bastille neighborhood: pretty shabby. If you are able to look beyond that, however, you'll discover a rich collection of easy-to-wear creations by one of the French fashion world's youngest talents. Franck

Joseph Bastille's clothes are based on simple designs cut in quality fabrics. Humor plays an important part in each of the designer's creations, whether in a subtle way with fake fur bordering a classic wool cape or more daringly with skull heads embroidered onto a basic top. His clothing has begun to show up stateside, but buy here where the prices are more interesting.
21 rue Daval, 11e; tel.: 48.07.20.10;
Métro: Bastille
open Tuesday–Saturday 1–8 P.M.

Brûlerie Daval

At first glance, you may think that I've sent you to the wrong address, but as you walk past the old car garages and workshops in the passageway at 12 rue Daval, you will discover the movie-like setting of this specialty coffee-and-tea shop on your left. Here you see the flip side of the SoHo beat that echoes throughout the area. A visit to this small shop is like a step back in time, when the streets and inner courtyards hummed with *petits commerçants* like this one.

As you push open the door, you are greeted with a robust odor of freshly roasted 100% arabica and the smile of Madame D'Amico, the owner of the shop. The dimly lit interior, void of any decoration except for tea canisters and a large accumulation of burlap bags displaying different coffee beans from Africa and Central and South America, looks as though it could have been moved here from any one of the countries marked on the bags: Mexico, Costa Rica, Guatemala, Colombia, Ethiopia, or Brazil. It's easy to see why the Brulerie Daval has become a neighborhood favorite. Madame D'Amico also sells airtight canisters, which enables you to bring her special blends of freshly ground French roast back home.
12 rue Daval, 11e; tel.: 48.05.29.46;
Métro: Bastille
open Tuesday–Saturday 10 A.M.–1 P.M. and 3–7:30 P.M.; Sunday 10 A.M.–1 P.M.

Rue St-Sabin

En d'Autres Thermes

Soft lighting, white walls, and marble flooring create an exquisite setting for the elegant furniture and *objets* sold on the two levels of this store. Michèle Segers, the owner of the boutique, has assembled a tasteful collection of Art Deco items and reproductions of famous pieces from the 30s and 40s with works from contemporary designers such as Philippe Starck. The result is stunning. If you don't spot anything that you really have to have, you'll at least walk away with some great home-decoration ideas.

The *tour de force* of this boutique is Madame Segers's ability to offer a wide variety of items at prices that range from $8 for a ceramic dish to $4,700 for an ivory-handled rosewood makeup table. Other exciting gift ideas include silver-plated reproductions of the Orient Express tea services and champagne flutes and ice cream cups used on the cruise ship, *Le Normandie*.

4 bis rue St-Sabin, 11e; tel.: 47.00.80.33;
Métro: Bastille
open Tuesday–Saturday 2–7 P.M.

Rue Keller

Bonus Beat

Groove to techno, acid, rock, rap, Latin, hip hop, and house music with the Bonus Beat crew (a Frenchman, an Italian, and a Spaniard) in this smoke-filled boutique. Most of the music sold at Bonus Beat is imported from the U.S. and Great Britain, but even though the prices are higher, you may just feel like buying here on a whim. The guys are so friendly and knowledgeable that they'll do their best to tune you into your favorite kind of rythmic vibes.

1 rue Keller, 11e; tel.: 40.21.02.88;
Métro: Ledru-Rollin
open Tuesday–Saturday 1–9 P.M.

Rue de Charonne

Pause Café

A favorite hangout for artists and for those pretending to be ones, the Pause Café offers a bona fide glimpse of local color. Savor their homemade quiche and *plats du jours*, or munch on some tasty pain Poilâne sandwiches in this laid-back setting worthy of its following.

41 rue de Charonne, 11e; tel.: 48.06.80.33;
Métro: Ledru-Rollin
Tuesday–Sunday 10 A.M.–8 P.M.

Verreglass

A marvelous kaleidoscope of colors radiates from within this small shop. Inside you discover superb pieces of glassware as old as the end of the past century and as recent as the 1960s. After many years working at the flea markets, Monsieur Breig decided to open his glass showcase in the up-and-coming neighborhood of the Bastille. His reputation has grown, and now collectors and antique dealers from all over the world call for his most select pieces of European glassware. Monsieur Breig's favorites include 50s glassware from Italy and Sweden, two countries whose reputation for excellence in design and purity of lines has always preceded them. Do take a look around. Aside from the investment-type pieces, the shop also offers a wide variety of reasonably priced gift items.

32 rue de Charonne, 11e; tel.: 48.05.78.43;
Métro: Ledru-Rollin
open Monday–Saturday 11 A.M.–7:30 P.M.

Dolce Vita

Step into what looks like the stage set of Fellini's *La Dolce Vita* as you enter this boutique specializing in antiques and curiosity objects from the 20th century. Once inside, you'll probably feel as though you're caught in a time warp, an eery sentiment that might provoke a reaction such as

"My God, that thing was worth this much! How could I ever have thrown it away!"
25 rue de Charonne, 11e; tel.: 43.38.26.31;
Métro: Ledru-Rollin
open Tuesday–Saturday 11 A.M.–1 P.M. and 2:30–7 P.M.

Chez Paul

A traditional-styled bistro with a New Wave twist. The clientele, an eclectic mix of Paris's avant-garde artists, writers, and theater people, crowds this restaurant for all of the same reasons: it is conveniently located to their nearby lofts; the help is hip and particularly friendly; the price is right; and, most of all, the food is delicious. Thick, juicy steaks and succulent *confit de canard* (duck preserved in its own fat) are served up with golden-brown fried potatoes and washed down with generous swallows of Bordeaux wine. Their escargots and homemade desserts more than satisfy the appetite as well. Best to reserve for dinner.
13 rue de Charonne, 11e; tel.: 47.00.34.57;
Métro: Bastille
open for lunch Monday–Friday, dinner Monday –Saturday

Axis

Upscale designer gadgets at upscale prices are this boutique's forte. Rug designer Laurence Dumaine displays her contemporary creations alongside Alessi tea kettles, Art Deco teapots, colorful graphic T-shirts, black and white bags by the artist Ben, and cardboard coiffes (to be worn as hats) that evoke the most current couture follies.
13 rue de Charonne, 11e; tel.: 48.06.79.10;
Métro: Bastille
open Monday–Saturday 10:30 A.M.–7:30 P.M.
18 rue Guénégaud, 6e; tel.: 43.29.66.23;
Métro: Odéon
open Monday–Saturday 10:30 A.M.–1 P.M. and 2–7:30 P.M.

· The Sixteenth (Parisian Preppy) ·

The Sixteenth is not only a Paris *arrondissement*, but a way of life. To be *seizième* (or sixteenth) is to be BCBG (bon chic, bon genre), the French equivalent of preppy. French preppies lead amazingly similar lives to their American counterparts. Like in the U.S., BCBGs are found at the heads of major corporations; BCBGs work at the Bourse (stockmarket) and hold top-level positions at the most reputable banks; and BCBG moms make sure that household activities and family obligations run like clockwork.

The differences, however, are not to be overlooked. Only the BCBGs know how to pull off a *baise-main* (kiss-hand—which is actually more of a gesture toward kissing the hand rather than a real kiss), stay in and play bridge on Saturday nights, or organize the proper *rallyes* for their daughters (soirées intended to expose young women to a potential good catch). The breeding in France is far thicker than in the U.S.—a distinction that creates a different set of rules from which to live and act, whether young or old.

All of the stately 19th- and early-20th-century buildings that line the elegant, tree-lined streets of the 16th *arrondissement* provide *de très bonnes adresses* (excellent addresses) for France's uppercrust. Although the rents here are among the highest in the capital, the 16th is one of the most residential areas in Paris. Like many other European cities, the wealthy are settled in the western part of the French capital or in the western suburbs so as not to be disturbed by pollution blown east by the prevailing westerly winds. (Factories are located to the north and east of most European metropolises.)

Not too many tourist attractions are found in the 16th, either, which makes the streets and the shopping districts less crowded and more devoted to the local clientele. If you like shopping in large stores, you may be better off going to Franck et Fils or Sephora on rue de Passy, rather than battling it out with the tourists in the major department stores on the boulevard Haussmann. Rich women from the 16th deposit their used clothing in neighboring resale shops, making the area a haven for recycled designer apparel at bargain-basement prices.

I consider the 16th to be divided into three primary shopping areas. Although they are all typically BCBG, each one reflects its own distinct personality. From L'Etoile to the first part of the avenue Victor-Hugo, a great number of big names such as Celine, Guy Laroche, and Jean-Louis Scherrer have opened up here for the ladies of the 16th who have a hard time making it over to the nearby 8th *arrondissement*. Many of the people who live in this part of town never shop elsewhere, which of course explains why the shopping here is so good. ("If they won't come to us, we'll go to them" seems to be the philosophy of the storeowners in this neighborhood.) The major fashion designers in this part of town tend to feature more classic sides of their collections than those shown on avenue Montaigne.

I call the next shopping district the Golden Triangle of the 16th, because of the triangular formation of the three shop-laden streets that make up this prestigious area: rue de la Pompe, rue Gustave-Courbet, and rue de Longchamp. The neighborhood has been Anglo-Saxonized to a max and sports an intrinsically 16th look that has taken the rest of Paris by storm.

The area around Passy is considerably more commercial. One shop owner recently complained to me that it has become abominably *nouveau riche*—an unnerving fate that has sinced forced many of the real BCBGs to move elsewhere. Nonetheless, many of the names for which Paris is famous have opened up stores in this neighborhood, and shopping here provides a refreshing change from other more congested areas of town.

You'll notice that I haven't indicated any charming tearooms to stop off in during these promenades. In the 16th, it is more widely accepted to invite friends over for tea or to go to *Ladurée*, the genteel tea parlor on rue Royale (near place de la Concorde). There are, however, numerous cafés and brasseries where you may stop for coffee or lunch. The *Brasserie Stella* on the corner of avenue Victor-Hugo and rue de la Pompe is a classic BCBG institution. High-priced *Café Mexico* on the place de Mexico serves decent food in a particularly high-gloss ambiance. Here you will recognize the true BCBGs by their Chanel suits, Hermès scarves, pearl necklaces, tweed jackets, oxford shirts, Westons, Burberry trench coats, and, nowadays, Docksiders and Ralph Lauren polo shirts. The men are often accompanied by their faithful Labradors (good for those traditional weekend hunts); the women carry well-groomed and extremely well-behaved chihuahuas in their arms.

If you do plan to spend a day in the 16th, you may want to devote part of it to shopping and the rest to viewing the extensive collection of Monet paintings and Medieval manuscripts in the ***Musée Marmottan*** (2 rue Louis-Boilly). It is not only one of the most intimate museums in Paris, but also one of the least crowded. At the ***Musée du Vin***, or Wine Museum (rue des Eaux), enjoy lunch and be sure to visit their vaulted cellars which date back to the Middle Ages. If you feel like being more of a tourist, the Eiffel Tower and the many sun-filled cafés at the place du Trocadéro are just a short distance away from all three of the marvelous shopping districts of the 16th *arrondissement*.

Promenade Victor-Hugo

Start at l'Etoile and work your way down the avenue Victor-Hugo. Most of the big-name designers are clustered together on the first block of the avenue; the rest of Victor-Hugo is less interesting. The Métro stop for the beginning of this tour is Etoile.

· ## Avenue Victor-Hugo ·

Céline

3 av Victor-Hugo, 16e; see Right Bank description p. 43

Bonnichon

For the past hundred years or so, Bonnichon has crafted fine-quality baby furniture and baby buggies for France's most pampered babies. Cradles, cribs, beds, changing tables, and rockers are attractively displayed in pretty pastels and pure white. Each set is enhanced with Bonnichon's coordinating sheets, dust ruffles, and curtains—most of which have been hand-embroidered in the sweetest of fashions.

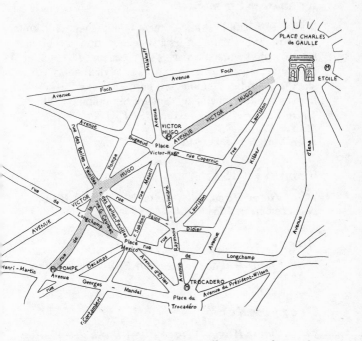

   Their traditional-styled baby strollers are also quite
grand, and in addition to their own brand, they sell England's Silver-Cross, the Rolls Royce of baby carriages.
Their selection of baby outfits is just as prim and proper.
The store will even create a custom-made trousseau for
baby from their exquisite selection of fabrics, ribbons, and
frills. Prices are high. If you aren't able to cart it home
with you, Bonnichon will take care of shipping.
*7 av Victor-Hugo, 16e; tel.: 45.01.70.17; Métro: Etoile
open Monday–Saturday 10:30 A.M.–1 P.M. and 2–
7 P.M.*

Guy Laroche

*9 av Victor-Hugo, 16e; see Right Bank description
p. 36*

Jean-Louis Scherrer

*14 av Victor-Hugo, 16e; see Right Bank description
p. 38*

Rodier Femme

Rodier is probably France's most famous name for knits. This Rodier boutique offers a wide selection of their classically styled womenswear. It's a great place to pick up a basic navy-blue cardigan or a more stylish short striped skirt. The Rodier fashions sell here for about 20–30% less than in the U.S. See also Discount Shopping p. 300
15 av Victor-Hugo, 16e; tel.: 45.01.79.88;
Métro: Etoile
open Monday–Saturday 10 A.M.–7 P.M.

Cerruti 1881

17 av Victor-Hugo, 16e (women's); see Left Bank description p. 155

Carel

20 av Victor-Hugo, 16e; see Left Bank description p. 137

Georges Rech

23 av Victor-Hugo, 16e; see Right Bank description p. 82

Fabrice Karel

39 av Victor-Hugo, 16e; see Left Bank description p. 117

Stéphane Kélian

42 av Victor-Hugo, 16e; see Left Bank description p. 150

Emanuelle Khanh

45 av Victor-Hugo, 16e; see Left Bank description p. 115

Bottega Veneta

Bottega Veneta is probably your best reason for shopping in this part of town. All of the superbly designed Bottega

Veneta bags (sorry, no shoes) are sold here at the same
prices as in Italy, which are about 25% lower with *détaxe*
than those in the U.S. The boutique is big and beautiful,
offering an extensive selection of their high-quality leather
products including women's handbags, attaché cases,
agendas, and their famous woven bags. A wide selection
of plastified canvas luggage and vibrant silk scarves and
ties round out the handsome collection of Bottega Veneta
goods sold in this luxurious store.
48 av Victor-Hugo, 16e; tel.: 45.01.70.58;
Métro: Victor-Hugo
open Monday—Saturday 10 A.M.–7 P.M.

Courrèges

50 av Victor-Hugo, 16e; see Right Bank description
p. 44

Descamps

52 av Victor-Hugo, 16e; see Left Bank description
p. 133

Lemaire

What Lemaire lacks in cigars, it makes up for in luxury
gift items from Cartier, Dunhill, Dupont, Davidoff, and
Montblanc. Lemaire claims to store a modest 10,000 cigars
in their cellars, and they have been doing so for over a
century. If you don't find the special blend that you're
after here, try looking across the street at Boutique 22 at
22 av Victor-Hugo.
59 av Victor-Hugo, 16e; tel.: 45.00.75.63;
Métro: Victor-Hugo
open Monday–Saturday 8 A.M.–8 P.M.

Petit Bateau

Petit Bateau is best known for their children's nightwear
and underwear (ages 0–16). Most of their babies' pajamas
are so adorable that you could keep your little sweet-
hearts in them all day long. Cuddly soft, 100% cotton
pajamas in the most distinguished shades of powder pink
and baby blue are trimmed with little bows on the feet
and stiff white Rembrandtesque pleated collars. The look
is very refined and indisputably BCBG.

Most of these huggable creations are downstairs. Up-stairs they show their classic collection of children's cloth-ing, much of which sports a sailor-like theme—a look that is typically Petit Bateau (little boat).
72 av Victor-Hugo, 16e; tel.: 45.00.13.95;
Métro: Victor-Hugo
81 rue de Sèvres, 6e; tel.: 45.49.48.38; Métro: Vaneau
open Monday–Saturday 10 A.M.–7 P.M.

Promenade BCBG

Start at rue de la Pompe near the Métro station Pompe. You will pass by the series of Réciproque second-hand clothing-and-accessories shops (see Discount Shopping p. 305) as you head toward the Golden Triangle. After you have covered the shops on the rue de la Pompe, head up rue Gustave-Courbet to rue de Longchamp and then back down Longchamp to where you started.

STREETS:

·   Rue de la Pompe   ·

Réciproque

123, 101 and 95 rue de la Pompe, 16e; see Discount Shopping p. 303

Creeks

Creeks is a French manufacturer of fun, casual separates for kids and teens. In addition to their collection of leather jackets, shirts, and jeans, they also sell fashions by popular casualwear outfitters Liberto, Fugitif, and Chevignon. The fashions shown in these two rue de la Pompe shops are slightly more classic than those found in their Left Bank boutiques.

129 rue de la Pompe, 16e (kids 4–16 years);
tel.: 47.27.40.22;
Métro: Pompe
open Monday 2–7 P.M.; Tuesday–Saturday 10 A.M.–
7 P.M.
155 rue de Rennes, 6e; tel.: 45.48.26.36;
Métro: St.-Placide
43 bd St.-Michel, 5e; tel.: 43.54.48.29;
Métro: Luxembourg or St.-Michel
open Monday 11 A.M.–7 P.M.; Tuesday–Saturday 10
A.M.–7 P.M.

Chipie

129 rue de la Pompe, 16e; see Left Bank description
p. 124

Renoma

Although Renoma is known for both men's and women's clothing, their menswear takes up more than three-quarters of the store. Their fashions are smart and chic, with just the right dash of style that won't raise too many eyebrows in the neighborhood. Patronized by many French showbiz people, Renoma is particularly well known for their fine-quality leather jackets and coats, and once again the men's selection is broader than that of the women's. Classic suits and stylish tuxedos are on view upstairs in the men's department.
129 rue de la Pompe, 16e; tel.: 47.27.13.79;
Métro: Pompe
open Monday–Saturday 10 A.M.–7:25 P.M.

John Demersay

As you stroll along the rue de la Pompe, your eye catches the attractively dressed mannequins in the display windows of this boutique. Inside, the shop is no disappointment. John Demersay is one of the most spacious and handsome boutiques in this part of the 16th *arrondissement*. Wooden floors, honey-colored club chairs, and neatly arranged racks of merchandise create a warm ambiance, making you feel as though you have just entered a very English sort of men's club.

The men's department, which is mainly composed of moderately priced, fine-quality classic fashions from Arthur Fox, encompasses the greater part of the store. Their elegant collection of women's clothing is located downstairs on the lower level. The men who work in this shop are not only friendly, but they also have a knack for adding just the right touch of panache to a suit or jacket. In suggesting the perfect striped shirt (you may choose from an impressive selection of stripe widths and colors), paisley tie, or silk pochette, they tie your look together with French savoir faire—the sort of assistance you find in the best menswear establishments.

133 rue de la Pompe, 16e; tel.: 45.53.05.15;
Métro: Pompe or Victor-Hugo
open Monday–Saturday 9:30 A.M.–7 P.M.

• Rue des Belles-Feuilles •

La Maison du Champagne

Monsieur Charly Delmare, enologist and champagne aficionado, is more than qualified to advise you in your choice of champagne to bring back home. Over 120 top brands are represented including rare treasures such as Clos du Mesnil de Krug '78 and tickly pink bubbles from Cristal Roederer '78 and Dom Perignon '82—all priced at $160 a bottle. Other less expensively priced, lesser-known *crus* are also available for sale. Prices tend to run less than in other liquor stores and the selection is far more imaginative.

48 rue des Belles-Feuilles, 16e; tel.: 47.27.58.23
Metro: Victor-Hugo
open Tuesday–Saturday 10 A.M.–1 P.M. *and*
3–7:30 P.M.

• Avenue Victor-Hugo •

Naj-Oleari

130 av Victor-Hugo, 16e; see Left Bank description
p. 125

Fil à Fil

140 av Victor-Hugo, 16e; see Left Bank description
p. 126

• **Rue Gustave-Courbet** •

Hervé Chapelier

Enter into the kingdom of the classic sweater. Shetland, lamb's wool, cashmere, merino, and wool from sheep in Geelong, Australia, are fashioned into the softest sweaters and scarves expressly for this boutique by the finest knitting mills north of the English Channel. Each size comes in 28 different colors and four traditional styles: turtleneck, cardigan, V-neck, and roundneck. Prices start at $65 for a rugged-looking Shetland sweater and go on up to $620 for a downy cashmere cardigan.

Their basic-looking nylon bags and knapsacks, which come in a variety of low-key colors, have also taken French preppies by storm. And like some of the finest stores in London, Hervé Chapelier sells a delightful selection of heady teas from the Orient.

13 rue Gustave-Courbet, 16e; tel.: 47.27.83.66;
Métro: Pompe or Victor-Hugo
55 bd de Courcelles, 17e; tel.: 47.54.91.27;
Métro: Courcelles
open Monday 2–7 P.M.; Tuesday–Saturday 10 A.M.–
7 P.M.

Jacadi

Renowned for their magic formula of price, quality, and style, Jacadi is one of French moms' favorite addresses for outfitting kiddies aged 3 months to 12 years. Their clothing is classic enough that it can be handed down throughout the years, and their reasonably priced selection is always fresh and neatly presented. This is one of numerous Jacadi boutiques in Paris.

7 rue Gustave-Courbet, 16e; tel.: 45.53.33.73;
Métro: Pompe
51 rue de Passy, 16e; tel.: 45.27.03.01; Métro: Muette
open Monday–Saturday 10:15 A.M.–7 P.M.

Curling

There's no doubt that the French have a knack for turning even the most classic clothing into chic, up-to-the-minute fashions. The inspiration is as British as the name of this shop, but this French manufacturer's reasonably priced interpretations of typically English styling are clearly Parisian.

In the men's boutique, the color assortment for their shirts and sweaters is anything but mundane. Electric blues and amethysts vie to be chosen over more traditional pale pinks and yellows.

The color selection and fashions have a similar zip to them in the women's boutique. Bermudas and short straight skirts are paired up with tailored jackets for a look that is both young and polished. The cuts run a bit small, however, and the sizes don't go much beyond a 10.

8 rue Gustave-Courbet, 16e; (men's); tel.: 47.27.64.75
6 rue Gustave-Courbet, 16e (women's);
tel.: 47.27.76.80
Métro for both stores is Pompe or Victor-Hugo.
open Monday 2–7:30 P.M.; Tuesday–Saturday
10 A.M.–7:30 P.M.

Annick Goutal

3 rue Gustave-Courbet, 16e; see Right Bank
description p. 87

■   **Rue de Longchamp**   ■

Bathroom Graffiti

The neon lights, rock music, and mod selection of gadgets in this shop provide an exciting contrast with the more subdued interiors of the neighboring boutiques. Much of what is sold here has been imported from America. However, they do sell some typically French products that make for fun and inexpensive gifts. Many of their goods indicate that the French don't take themselves as seriously as you think: bedroom slippers in the shape of their most prominent politicians; 70ish-looking, daisy-dappled cheese bells made out of screening; and bread knives in the form of *baguettes* (loaves of French bread) and sausages. They also feature a large selection of Coup de Coeur items (cotton slippers, pajamas, and boxer shorts in colorful whimsical motifs) and rubbery Mandarina Duck bags.

98 rue de Longchamp, 16e; tel.: 47.04.23.12;
Métro: Trocadéro
open Monday–Saturday 10 A.M.–7:30 P.M.

Alain Figaret

99 rue de Longchamp, 16e; see Right Bank
description p. 92

Naf Naf

100 rue de Longchamp, 16e; see Place des Victoires/
Les Halles description p. 184

Kookaï

106 rue de Longchamp, 16e; see Left Bank
description p. 111

Promenade Passy

Begin your tour at the end of the rue de Passy and work
your way down the street, stopping off onto some of the
side streets as you go along. The closest Métro stop for
the beginning of the tour is Muette. You may either go
back to Muette or pick up Passy at the end of the tour.

STREETS:

▪ Boulevard Emile-Augier ▪

Hemisphères

One of the main attractions of the 16th, Hemisphères specializes in chic fashions for men and women that are
particularly *bon ton*. In an elegant decor signed Andrée
Putnam, handsome sweaters made of the finest woolens

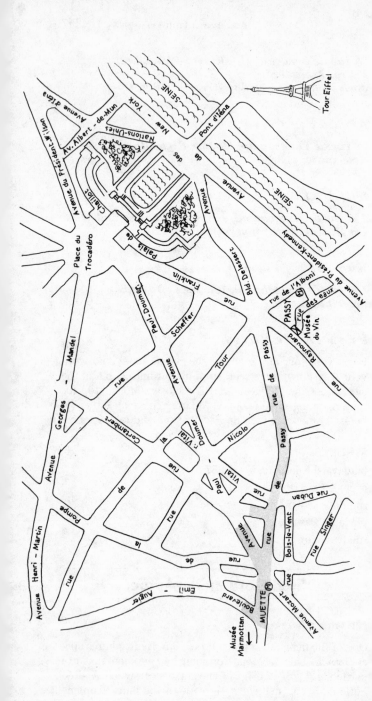

(cashmere, Geelong, and lamb's wool) form the backbone of their collection. Stylish suits round it out and print shirts bring it into the spotlight.

Hemisphères was the precursor to the current fantasy-shirt rage that has new shirt labels mushrooming all over the capital. Since the early 80s, Hemisphères has featured men's and women's shirts based on amusing interpretations of classic prints such as checks, plaids, flowers, and stripes. Some are embroidered in the folksiest of fashions; others are cut in the purest of whites. Their shirts come in silk, linen, rayon, and cotton, averaging about $150 each. Although Hemisphères has opened eight boutiques in Japan, their high-quality fashions have not yet arrived stateside.

1 bd Emile-Augier, 16e; tel.: 45.20.13.75;
Métro: Muette
22 av de la Grande-Armée, 17e; tel.: 42.67.61.86;
Métro: Argentine
open Monday–Saturday 10:30 A.M.–7 P.M.

■   **Avenue Paul-Doumer**   ■

Paralèles

96 av Paul-Doumer, 16e; see Left Bank description
of Emanuel Ungaro p. 34

Chapitre 3

For the past 25 years Bernard Ehret has designed durable sportsbags for Dunlop, Rossignol, Look, and even the U.S. Army and Navy. He later created his own brand, Jump, followed by Chapitre 3, a more fashionable version of these sporty bags. Chapitre 3 was first launched in New York with great success. Their Greenwich Village boutique has since closed, but Chapitre 3 plans to reopen soon in another part of Manhattan.

Chapitre 3's reasonably priced handbags and traveling bags are as stylish as they are solid. Most of the bags are made of nylon and PVC (a handsome vinyl) and trimmed with leather or leather and canvas. Their color assortment is as varied as their shapes; classic autumn hues, plaids and paisleys, as well as trendier violets and tomato reds play upon forms that are both traditional and up-to-date. Plans for two new lines of all leather bags, in rugged buffalo and supple calfskin, are also in the works. Prices run $100–$150 for their handbags and $170–$250 for their luggage.

86 av Paul-Doumer, 16e; tel.: 45.24.59.32;
Métro: Muette
open Monday 2–7 P.M. Tuesday–Saturday 10 A.M.–
1 P.M. and 2–7 P.M.

Souleiado

83 av Paul-Doumer, 16e; see Left Bank description
p. 118

•   # Rue de Passy   •

Christofle

95 rue de Passy, 16e; see Right Bank description
p. 72

Guerlain

93 rue de Passy, 16e; see Right Bank description
p. 89

Jet-Set

85 rue de Passy, 16e; see Left Bank description
p. 143

Caroll

85 rue de Passy, 16e; see Left Bank description
p. 134

Franck et Fils

This store reminds me of the kind of department stores I used to go to in upstate New York when I was a young girl. The decor is a bit stuck in time, but the fashions are for the most part up-to-date. Franck et Fils caters largely to the *grandes bourgeoises* (upper-middle-class ladies) of the 16th *arrondissement*. The first floor presents classic fashions from the store's own label—some are fuddy-duddy, others are more in tune with the times. The second floor features sophisticated fashions by Thierry Mugler, Chantal Thomass, and Georges Rech as well as a few other Parisian designers. The main floor showcases a mini Chanel boutique, stockings, lingerie, a small men's department, fashions for teens, and oodles and oodles of *grande dame* costume jewelry.

80 rue de Passy, 16e; tel.: 46.47.86.00;
Métro: Muette
open Monday 1:30–6:45 P.M.; Tuesday–Saturday
9:45 A.M.–6:45 P.M.

La Bagagerie

74 rue de Passy, 16e; see Right Bank description
p. 69

Chevignon

72 rue de Passy, 16e; see Left Bank description
p. 137

Burberrys

56 rue de Passy, 16e; see Left Bank description
p. 130

Naf Naf

55 rue de Passy, 16e; see Place des Victoires/Les
Halles description p. 184

Jacadi

51 rue de Passy, 16e; see Promenade BCBG
description p. 255

L'Entrepôt

The entrance to this store is small and unassuming, but if you follow the stairs up to the first floor, you will enter a huge warehouse (*entrepôt*) lined with metal shelves displaying an incredibly wide and fun range of inexpensive gift ideas. Different sections of this loft-like space are filled with cards, posters, bath products, T-shirts with French sayings on them, kitchen accessories, useless but decorative gadgets, avant-garde socks, and Jenna de Rosnay's sexy swimwear. Many of the items are American (I was thrilled the day I discovered that they sell cocktail napkins, a rarity in Paris), but if you hunt and pick you will turn up some of the latest knickknacks bearing the "made in France" label.

L'Entrepôt has devoted a corner of the store to Paris Plage, a beachy café that serves sandwiches, salads, and fresh-fruit drinks.

50 rue de Passy, 16e; tel.: 45.25.64.17;
Métro: Muette
open Monday–Thursday 10 A.M.–7:30 P.M; Friday
and Saturday 10 A.M.–7:30 P.M.

Sephora

Sephora offers a supermarket-like supply of perfumes, cosmetics, and beauty products. Many items are set up so that you may serve yourself without having to deal with the salesladies. If you are looking for a classic French gift idea, Sephora sells the complete collection of the famous Rigaud candles (found in nearly every apartment in the 16th). The most popular scent is the green-colored cypress, priced at $65—a bit steep for a candle, but bringing Parisian chic into your home is never cheap.

50 rue de Passy, 16e; tel.: 45.20.03.15; Métro: Muette
open Monday–Friday 10 A.M.–7 P.M.; Saturday
10 A.M.–7:30 P.M.

Descamps

44 rue de Passy, 16e; see Left Bank description p. 133

Mac Douglas

27 rue de Passy, 16e; see Left Bank description p. 144

Victoire

16 rue de Passy, 16e; see place des Victoires/Les Halles description p. 172

Place de Passy

Daniel Hechter

2 place de Passy, 16e; see Left Bank description p. 103

Rue Guichard

Pom d'Api

6 rue Guichard, 16e; see Left Bank description p. 135

Accessoire

9 rue Guichard, 16e; see Left Bank description p. 139

MORE
≈
SHOPPING

Antiques (Shops, Auctions, and Flea Markets)

From the flea markets at Saint-Ouen to the museum-like antique shops of the quai Voltaire, the city of Paris and its outskirts make up one of the world's prime hunting grounds for the discovery of interesting bric-a-brac and rare quality antiques. In the Promenades section of this book, I indicated numerous antique stores, which aside from being my favorites, tend to be more accessible to those who are not out to do serious antiquing but simply enjoy the thrill of unearthing something that is old, charming, and difficult to find at home. Needless to say, those addresses only scratched the surface of the Gallic capital's wealth of fascinating antique outposts. This chapter establishes a few more guidelines about the great and sometimes perilous adventure of antiquing in Paris.

Although nearly every street in Paris at least boasts a token antique shop, the most important *antiquaires* are clustered together in the city's two main shopping districts: the Right Bank and the Left Bank. The upper part of the rue du Faubourg–St.-Honoré (toward the very beginning of the St.-Honoré promenade) abounds with Paris's leading antique dealers offering museum-quality pieces at investment-level prices. Some of Paris's most prestigious art galleries are located next door to these same antique shops, which greatly facilitates shopping for those who are looking to match an old master's painting with their newly acquired Louis XV armchair. The Left Bank embodies a similar intermingling of art and antiques in its renowned shops which make up the *Carré Rive Gauche*, the square-like formation of streets, bordered to the north by the Seine and to the south by the rue de l'Université. (See Left Bank promenade map p. 103) These boutiques cast a sense of old-world charm and Château de Versailles grandeur which, to me, is even more enchanting than those of the Right Bank. During a week in May, the *Carré Rive Gauche* boutiques conduct a *portes ouvertes* (open house), allowing curious onlookers to comfortably browse in their shops well into the evening hours. During the rest of the year, warm welcomes from most of the prominent Left Bank and Right Bank dealers are reserved more for serious shoppers than for passing tourists.

Other sizable groupings of antique shops are located at the Louvre des Antiquaires, the Village Suisse, and the Village St. Paul; each touts its own distinct image and the quality of their antiques varies accordingly.

Nearly all of the important Paris antique dealers will handle shipping arrangements and customs formalities. Be sure to verify that the proper documents regarding authenticity and age have been carefully provided. Remember that if you have a certificate proving that your purchase is at least 100 years old, you will not have to pay duty on it—or French sales tax, for that matter. Find out the cost of shipping and insurance before you decide to ship home an 18th-century *armoire*, and, above all, remember that bargaining (10–25% less), even in your finer shops, is the name of the game. Last but not least, if you do purchase something of truly exceptional quality, whether at an antique shop, an auction, or at the flea markets, find out ahead of time whether or not you might have difficulty bringing it out of the country. For truly valuable pieces, the store (or even the stand at the flea markets) should provide a letter from an *expert* along with the bill of sale. This letter or *certificat* should provide a descriptive account of the nature of the piece, the approximate date in which it was made, any particular markings (such as the signature of the crafts person), etc. For more modest purchases, a much less formal certificate is sufficient. The shopowner should write up a brief description of the purchase and its approximate age. Make sure that this piece of paper includes the name of the store and its address. This simple act serves to bind the seller to his or her word, if a dealer tells you that the porcelain tea service you are contemplating buying dates back to the mid-19th century, make sure you can have that in writing.

Shops

La Cour aux Antiquaires

Located at the end of a sunny courtyard in the middle of Paris's high-fashion boutiques is this congenial gathering of some 15 fine-quality antique shops. The setting is elegant without being a bit pretentious—an excellent way to take a closer look at properly pretty French masterpieces.

54 rue du Faubourg–St.-Honoré, 8e; (See
Promenade Saint-Honoré map p. 55)
Métro: Concorde or Madeleine
open Monday 2–6:30 P.M. Tuesday–Saturday 10:30
A.M.–6:30 P.M.

Louvre des Antiquaires

Just across from the Musée du Louvre, museum-quality pieces are sold in this modern shopping-mall setting. There's no doubt that the antiques at the Louvre des Antiquaires are expensive, but they're not necessarily overpriced, because even dealers from all over the world are known to buy here. Even if you're not out to make a major purchase, it is just fun to browse through the more than 200 shops selling antiques ranging from Ming Dynasty vases to Napoleon III dining-room tables.

2 place de Palais-Royal, 1er; (See Place des
Victoires and Les Halles map p. 165)
tel.: 42.97.27.00;
Métro: Palais Royal

Village St.-Honoré

Only a few of the shops in this small complex are truly
worthy of close attention, but if you are touring the Les
Halles area, the Village St.-Honoré is just a short walk
away. While you're here, plan to have lunch or tea at **Rose
Thé**, a charming pink-walled tea salon that serves delicious quiche and cakes.
*91 rue St.-Honoré, 1er; (See Place des Victoires and
Les Halles map p. 167)*
Métro: Châtelet
open Monday–Saturday noon–7 P.M.

Village St.-Paul

Probably the most country-like and charming of all of the
Paris antique complexes, the Village St.-Paul consists of a
courtyard (surrounded by a refurbished grouping of 17th-
century townhouses) populated by antique dealers and
brocanteurs selling a great variety of antiques and second-
hand goods. My favorite boutique is **R.V. des Dames
Curieuses**, which specializes in 19th- and 20th-century
glassware and crystal, as well as a mishmash of *objets*
that fills this boutique all the way up to its 17th-century
wooden rafters!

An even greater concentration of antique shops is located on the rue St.-Paul, the street bordering the village.
(See Marais map p. 216). Stop into **Térébenthine** at 13
rue St.-Paul to see their eclectic mix of arts of the table,
paintings, and furniture from every imaginable era that
strikes the proprietor's fancy!

The Village St.-Paul shops are open every day except
Tuesday and Wednesday noon–7 P.M.; Métro: St.-Paul

Village Suisse

The Village Suisse is probably the least charming place to
go antiquing in all of Paris. I've also heard many mixed
reports about the quality of their goods. Although if you're
knowledgeable enough, you may do as well as the Paris
decorators who shop here. Some 150 antique shops fill
the two levels of buildings that make up this outdoor
shopping-center–like complex. The selection of goods is
as vast as the "village" itself and the prices, for the most
part, are up in the nosebleed range.

54 av de La Motte-Piquet, 15e; tel.: 43.06.69.90;
Métro: La Motte-Piquet
open Thursday–Monday 10:30 A.M.–7 P.M.

Auctions

Hôtel Drouot

Housed in an ungainly, modern glass-and-steel structure, the decor at the Hôtel Drouot hardly lives up to what one would expect from Paris's most reputed auction house, but the pickings inside represent the best antique buys to be had in town. Much of the bidding is done by dealers, but if you're confident enough, you can easily join in the fun, too. If you just want to go to admire some beautiful things or to take in another colorful aspect of French life, anyone can walk in off the street. If you're interested in buying, here are a few tips on how you should precede:

- Buy *La Gazette de l'Hôtel Drouot,* a weekly publication found at newsstands. It announces upcoming sales at Drouot and at other auctions in and outside of Paris. You may also pick up a catalogue on the main floor at Drouot, which will help you keep track of the numerous sales and exhibitions that go on throughout the day.
- You don't have to register to bid, but make sure you have cash with you because the house only accepts cash and French checks. You may pay the total amount in cash (francs of course). If you wish to make other arrangements, there is a bank on the main floor. Foreign currency may be exchanged at the same office. If you pay in cash, you will be able to take the piece with you when you leave. (Goods paid for with a French check are sometimes held until the check clears unless previous arrangements have been made.)
- If you don't speak French fluently, you're at a great disadvantage because the bidding goes fast enough as it is. If you don't have a French-speaking friend to accompany you to the sale, you may arrange to have one of the auctioneer's assistants bid for you.
- Be quick with your calculator in order to know exactly how much money you're talking about in dollars. Re-

member that you have to pay a 10–18% commission to the house and, if it's a large item, you'll also have to pay shipping expenses. Additional storage fees will be charged if the purchase is not shipped out right away.

- The shipping department at Drouot can make arrangements to have your purchase transported oversea (sometimes via another shipping agent).
- All of this may sound confusing to you, but it's no as complicated as you think. One more reassuring factor about buying at Drouot is that the French auctioneers run a tight ship and it's rare that something will be represented as anything more than it really is. In other words, if they claim that the item up for sale was a part of Marie-Antoinette's trousseau, it probably was!

9 rue Drouot, 9e; (See Passages map p. 195)
tel.: 48.00.20.20;
Métro: Richelieu-Drouot or
Le Peletier
open Monday–Saturday 11 A.M.–6 P.M.
exhibitions: 11 A.M.–6 P.M. day before the sale;
11 A.M.–noon the day of the sale
sales: 2–6 P.M.

Drouot Montaigne conducts the more prestigious sales of antiques and contemporary art work.
15 av Montaigne, 8e; (See Promenade Golden
Triangle map p. 32) tel.: 48.00.20.80;
Métro: Alma-Marceau

Crédit Municipal de Paris

Tucked into an elegant *hôtel particulier* in the Marais the Crédit Municipal de Paris, one of the most modern auction houses of Europe. All of the action takes place in one movie-theater–like hall where bidders sit comfortably on red velvet seats as the show unveils before them. Only a dozen or so auctions a month are conducted here, and nearly all consist of jewelry, silver, art objects, and furniture that have been pawned off by once well-to-do Parisians. The rules are similar to those at Drouot and their sales are also announced in the *Gazette*. Viewing takes place the morning of the afternoon sale.

*55 rue des Francs-Bourgeois, 4e; (See Marais map
p. 216) tel.: 42.71.25.43;
Métro: Rambuteau*

Service des Domaines

Little known to visitors to the capital (even though it's
just a few steps away from American Express), the Service
des Domaines auctions everything from Christofle dessert
spoons to unmatched sets of golf clubs. The sales are few
and far between, but there's no doubt that you can pick
up some real bargains. Almost everything that is sold here
has been confiscated in exchange for unpaid taxes, parking tickets, etc. Viewing takes place the day of the sale
between 10 and 11:30 A.M. and goods are sold strictly on
a cash-and-carry basis. Call to see what sort of sales are
taking place when you're in town or consult their monthly
review, which is sold on premises.

*15-17 rue Scribe, 9e; (See Promenade Saint-Honoré
map p. 55) tel.: 42.66.93.46;
Métro: Opéra*

The Flea Markets

Porte de Clignancourt/Saint-Ouen

Parisians like to do a lot of grumbling about the fact that
there are fewer and fewer bargains *aux puces*, but the
flea markets today are still their favorite places to go in
search of the rare, the antiquated, and the extraordinary.
Of course, chances are one in a million of paying next to
nothing for a porcelain figurine that you later discover is
worth a small fortune on the rue du Faubourg–St.-Honoré.
An excursion to the flea markets should not be made
solely with the intention of striking a deal, but more with
the idea of experiencing the most fabulous buying and
selling place of antiques in the entire world.

Prices have been driven up at Clignancourt (also called
Saint-Ouen) because antique dealers come from all corners of the earth in search of France's most treasured
antiquités. Their day is Friday, when the crack of dawn
sees the arrival of trucks, vans, and station wagons un-
loading the week's take from the provinces, producing
goods tempting enough to whet the appetite of even the

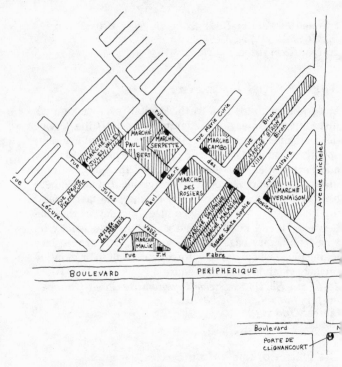

most blasé Madison Avenue antique dealer. If you have
enough gumption, you too may mingle among the collectors on Friday mornings in search of that rare find that
would cost at least four times as much back home.

If you can't quite get up the nerve to go on a Friday
(the day supposedly reserved for dealers only) Saturday
mornings aren't bad either. Start out early, stop at *Le*
Restaurant Paul-Bert (20 rue Paul-Bert) while the
croissants are still warm on the counter, and then begin
to *chine* (search) with the rest of Paris's antique buffs.

The flea markets at Clignancourt are comprised of almost 10 different markets. Each has its own personality
and each is made up of countless stalls that sell an assortment of goods in all price ranges. Don't limit yourself
to looking at the best and the most beautiful markets
because the true spirit of the *puces* lives in the shabbier
stalls that sell second-hand goods that have not yet re-
gained their polish of earlier years. As you stroll through
the endless series of alleys filled with 19th-century curiosity items, turn-of-the-century memorabilia, and rusted

metal parts, you'll have a greater sense of the feeble beginnings of this massive market, which was started over 100 years ago by Paris's most affluent ragpickers.

The *Marché Jule Vallès* is probably the most typical example of this sort of lower-end marketplace. Often the best deals are found here and it is not uncommon for Paris antique dealers to buy from Vallès, do a little fixing up, and resell the same goods at a hefty profit. Although more expensive, the *Marché Paul-Bert* is somewhat similar to Vallès with considerably more charm because of its series of open-air stalls. The ambiance is quite village-like; at lunchtime the dealers set their tables with red-and-white checked tablecloths and sit down to a crusty loaf of bread, cheese, and a healthy bottle of wine. The antiques that are sold in these two markets are for the most part *brocantes* or rather second-hand items that are of less importance and value than full-fledged antiques.

The most handsome markets at Clignancourt are *Vernaison, Biron, Cambo*, and *Serpette*. Opened in 1920, Vernaison is the granddaddy of them all and to this day continues to be the biggest and most eclectic of the Clignancourt markets. Biron and Cambo are probably the slickest, and haggling in these markets is best reserved for true pros. The *Marché Serpette*, which opened a little over 10 years ago, is the dealers' favorite stomping ground because everything here is sold in mint condition. The new kid on the block is the *Marché Malassis* (named after the field where the first traders set up their wares) where over 100 exclusive boutiques are housed in a Mediterranean-like sun castle. Plans are also under way to open yet another market, the *Marché Dauphine*, sometime in 1991.

Part of a day at the flea markets should include a stop in one of the informal restaurants that have played an important role in the history of *les puces*. Traditional meals include *moules/frites* (mussels in wine with French fries) or *boeuf gros sel* (tender pot roast) and can be found at *La Chope des Puces* (122 rue des Rosiers) or *Chez Louisette* (Marché Vernaison), where you will be serenaded by a spirited trio that will charm you with Edith Piaf and Yves Montand classics.

If you're going to the flea markets by Métro, you have to walk a good 10 to 15 minutes toward the outskirts of Paris from the Porte de Clignancourt station. Often people make the mistake of getting caught up in the **Marché Malik** (one of the first markets which used to specialize solely in *fripes* or used clothing) and become so turned off by the series of tacky clothing shops that they turn around and head back. You have to pass through part of this market to arrive at the good ones. Once you're on the rue des Rosiers (the main drag), all of the other markets are clearly marked. If you're traveling by car, you're better off coming very early in the morning because the parking space is limited.

Antiquing at the flea markets is not unlike antiquing in Paris, but here you will probably feel more comfortable with dickering down the prices. Although many of the dealers (especially at Biron and Cambo) now accept credit cards, it is best to come well-supplied in cash (preferably French francs). Cash also increases bargaining power and if you're clever enough, you may be able to drive the price down by about 25% to 35%. You have to know your limits, though, because some dealers are less flexible than others. There is no *détaxe* on items that are 100 years old or more, and if you want to ship, that can be arranged at most of the stalls. The prices can be exorbitant, however, but it may very well be worth it considering all of the money you have just saved by buying your French antique(s) in France.

Good luck and have fun!

Métro: Porte de Clignancourt
open Saturday, Sunday, and Monday 7:30 A.M.–7 P.M. ***(approximate hours)***

Porte de Vanves

The flea market at Porte de Vanves consists mainly of *brocanteurs* or second-hand items. It is much much smaller than those of Clignancourt and certainly less animated, but nonetheless can prove to be great fun for the adventuresome antique enthusiast. The first part of the market overflows with merchants selling new and cheap merchandise; you have to go at least halfway down before you find the good stuff.

Métro: Porte de Vanves
open Saturday and Sunday 9 A.M.–6:30 P.M.

Porte de Montreuil

Certainly the most exotic of all of the Paris flea markets, Porte de Montreuil is overrun with dime-store peddlers and only a few *brocantes* are on hand to sell some questionable collectibles. If you've never been to Africa, this may be the closest you will get in Paris. Not for the skittish.
Métro: Porte de Montreuil
open Saturday, Sunday and Monday 7:30 A.M.–
7 P.M. (Monday mostly new clothing)

For more antiquing, look in the local papers or check with your concierge for news about antique shows taking place during your stay. In the spring and fall, shows called *foire* or *brocante* are often held in Paris at the place de la Bastille, Piscine Deligny, and Batignolles. On the fringes of the city, shows take place periodically at Vincennes, Chatou, and Le Bourget.

Marché Dauphine

This new market will open in 1991, as indicated on the flea market map p. 274.

- # Paradise Street -

A quiet residential street for princely Parisians during the 18th century, the rue de Paradis inherited a quite different destiny when the Cristalleries de Baccarat moved in in 1831. Just a few streets away from the Gare de l'Est (the train station for the east), the rue de Paradis proved to be an ideal address for setting up the Paris showrooms of France's great crystal makers—all of whom were (and still are) located in the eastern part of France, near Alsace. Cristallerie de Saint-Louis followed Baccarat and, by the end of the 19th century, the great manufacturers of Limoges moved onto the newly budding street as well.

Today the headquarters of many of France's most important table-arts companies still reside on the street that has since become the world's most spectacular showplace for fine-quality crystal, silver, and china. Showrooms and retailers rub shoulders in an area that offers the widest selection of tableware in Paris, including Quimper *faïence* and glassware from Biot. This is the place to shop if you are looking to invest in an entire table service or even if you just want to add a couple of place settings to an existing one. The prices here are the best in Paris, because in addition to the shops' already low prices, shop owners offer reductions from 5 to 20% depending on the amount you purchase. This of course does not apply to $100 knick-knacks.

The regular retail price of crystal and silver tends to be about the same throughout most of Paris. However, I've noticed that china usually costs about 10–15% less in the smaller boutiques than in the department stores. Here are the types of savings that you can expect to encounter on the rue de Paradis as well as in numerous other Paris boutiques:

- Lalique, Daum, and Saint-Louis crystal cost 20–30% less; savings on Baccarat can be as much as 40%.
- Buying Christofle and Ercuis silverplate in France saves you 15–25%.
- Most brands of Limoges china cost about 25–35% less
- Other European brands such as Wedgewood, Rosenthal, and Villeroy & Boch run about 20% less in France

The 15% savings from *détaxe* (and a bit more) cancel out the shipping, insurance, and customs expenses that are incurred to send your merchandise home; any additional discounts that the boutique gives you only sweeten the pot.

Keep in mind, however, that these price savings depend largely on the prices that are practiced in your favorite stores back home. For example, in the U.S., stores offer so many different types of promotions that it is often possible to purchase Baccarat crystal on sale (Lalique prices are more consistent), which means that it is always smart to know the prices you normally pay in the States before you go on a wild shopping spree in Paris.

Nearly all of the boutiques on the rue de Paradis ship and accept phoned-in or faxed-in orders from overseas. (Some do up to 90% of their business in export.) You won't have any problems finding salespeople who speak English.

Spending a half day on the rue de Paradis is great fun. Plan to shop part of the time and save the rest for a visit to the Baccarat museum and showroom. I suggest you start at the beginning of the street and work your way down, stopping into every other boutique that catches your eye. The following descriptions highlight my favorite rue de Paradis boutiques, but don't feel limited to them. You will certainly discover others that deserve to be earmarked in your own little black book!

▪ Rue de Paradis ▪

The closest Métro stop is Château d'Eau.

Limoges-Unic

Owned and operated by the Madronet family since 1930, Limoges-Unic is one of the oldest and most-respected establishments on the street. In addition to a tremendous selection of porcelain from Limoges, Limoges-Unic also carries German and Hungarian big names, Meissen and Herrend. Monsieur Madronet is one of the only shop owners on the rue de Paradis to carry Lalique along with his handsome selection of Baccarat and Saint-Louis crystal. You may shop here for Christofle as well. The main floor features a lot of gift-type items including a colorful collection of small hand-painted boxes from Limoges; the table settings continue upstairs in a space twice as big as the ground floor. The boutique at no. 58 is equally well stocked with similar merchandise.
12 and 58 rue de Paradis, 10e; tel.: 47.70.54.49 and 47.70.61.49
open Monday–Saturday 10 A.M.–6:30 P.M.

Aurelia Paradis

Aurelia Paradis specializes in an eclectic assortment of sumptuous table arts from Europe's most prominent big names: Haviland, Raynaud, Manufacture Royale, Baccarat, Ercuis, Spode, Royal Worcester, and many more. Frosted hand-blown creations from Italian glassmaker Cenedese sell here for considerably less than at Macy's in New York. The boutique's rich collection of hand-painted *faïence* from Gien (not to be confused with Gien's manufactured pieces) is the best on the street, and, once

again, their prices, although high, are better than those
elsewhere.
21 bis rue de Paradis, 10e; tel.: 42.47.07.00
open Monday–Saturday 9:30 A.M.–7 P.M.

Lumicristal

Lumicristal is the most lavish boutique on the street. The
ceiling is covered with a maze of sparkling crystal chandeliers and a sweeping selection of glittering delights line
the boutique's mauve-colored walls. Renée Lebahr has
composed an exquisite selection of Baccarat, Daum, Limoges, and countless other table-arts frontrunners. Madame Lebahr is also the only one on the street to show
Puiforcat's elegant collection of porcelain and silver. The
boutique, which marks the sight where the first table-arts
retailer opened on the rue de Paradis 125 years ago, is
located in the building where the great 19th-century landscape painter Corot was born and died.
22 bis rue de Paradis, 10e; tel.: 47.70.27.97
open Monday–Saturday 9:30 A.M.–7 P.M.

Baccarat

The Cristalleries de Baccarat were founded in 1764 by
the Bishop of Metz under the reign of Louis XV. Baccarat
crystal has often been referred to as "the Crystal of the
Kings" and its degree of purity has granted it a place at
the world's most prominent tables.

Enter the Baccarat kingdom by passing through the
archway at 31 bis rue de Paradis; across the courtyard
and up the stairs you'll discover the vast Baccarat store
and museum which traces the legacy of this celebrated
luxury-goods company from its earliest beginnings. Ask
to see their videos which show the birth of a crystal goblet,
a diamond-cut vase, and a multicolored paperweight. All
of Baccarat's magnificent pieces are made by hand and
are subjected to rigorous quality-control inspections.
You'll learn more from the video than from the museum
itself. For more on Baccarat, see Right Bank description
p. 78.
30 bis rue de Paradis, 10e; tel.: 47.70.64.30
open Monday–Friday 9 A.M.–5:30 P.M.; Saturday 10
A.M.–noon and 2–5 P.M.

Porcelainor

In case you haven't already noticed, each boutique represents a wide range of famous French table-arts manufacturers as well as a handful of other big names that are less common on the street. Porcelainor is of course no exception. In addition to the standard offerings, this pleasant boutique features Cristal de Sèvres, Christofle, Ercuis, Gien, Wedgewood, and several German suppliers. Porcelainor also offers a stunning array of everyday tableware such as rainbow-colored cutlery by Scof and reasonably priced porcelain (about $17 a plate) by Philippe Deshoulières, whose designs are based on Pierre Frey's delightful garden print fabrics.
31 rue de Paradis, 10e; tel.: 48.24.49.30
open Tuesday–Friday 10 A.M.–6:30 P.M.; Monday and Saturday 10 A.M.–1 P.M. and 2:15–6:30 P.M.

· Coup De Foudre (Love at First Sight) ·

Coup de foudre literally means bolt of lighting, but the French use it to define love at first sight. Although all of the boutiques in this chapter are located outside of "the promenades," I find them so unique that I simply had to give them special mention. Each one is as different as the others, and if you feel the way I do, you'll think it's worth going off the beaten path to see them.

1st *arrondissement*

Anne Parée

Not far from the *Madeleine* is another one of my favorite haunts for buying perfume, cosmetics, and beauty creams at bargain-basement prices. The shop is owned and run by an American, Mr. Allan Grossman, who will gladly take care of mailing your purchases back home at an honest price. Be sure to ask for their mail order catalogue before you leave.
10 rue Duphot, 1er; tel.: 42.60.03.26;
Métro: Madeleine
open Monday–Saturday 9:30 A.M.–6:30 P.M.

Lionel Cros

At first it might just look like a sado-masochist's vision of women's fashions, but if you look a little closer you'll understand why every other fashion model, singer, and young starving actress is snatching up Lionel Cros's creations as fast as this rising-star designer can make them. Cros is into heavy metal, plastic, and industrial-strength twine, which he turns into slinky wire-mesh sheaths (not unlike those of Medieval knights), skintight waterproof *bustiers*, and macramé minis and vests. The look is sexy, humorous, and, needless to say, quite outrageous. His innovations have not yet arrived stateside and the best news is that they are cheap and chic.

21 rue du Roule, 1er; (See Place des Victoires and Les Halles map p. 165) tel.: 45.08.83.41;
Métro: Châtelet or Louvre
open Monday 2:30–7 P.M.; Tuesday–Saturday noon–7 P.M.

4th *arrondissement*

Maison Brocard

The earliest recorded trace of this well-appointed embroidery house dates back to an order that was passed for Marie-Antoinette's bed in 1775. Since then the Maison Brocard has decorated the walls and furniture of the world's greatest homes with their hand-woven fabrics and intricately designed needlepoints. From the newly restored bedroom of Louis XIV at Versailles (paid for by the American Friends of Versailles) to the recently refurbished Queens' Room at the Palace of Fontainebleau, la Maison Brocard continues to produce some of the finest handiwork this side of the Atlantic. In the tattered setting of this Bastille shop, Madame Brocard may be found overseeing the cautious tracing of an original 18th-century design or the meticulous restoration of a 17th-century tapestry from the provinces. (The Maison Brocard often restores works for museums including the Smithsonian in Washington, D.C.)

You don't have to be a king or a tycoon to afford a piece of tradition from the Maison Brocard; the house also sells custom-made needlepoint kits that may be used to cover furniture or pillows. It may take you a year to

finish the seat of your favorite armchair, but it will outlive you by more than 100 years!
1 rue Jacques-Coeur, 4e; tel.: 42.72.16.38;
Métro: Bastille
open Monday–Friday 9 A.M.–noon and 2–7 P.M.

5th *arrondissement*

Les Comptoirs de la Tour d'Argent

Not too far from *Notre Dame* is this delightful shop that specializes in handsome gift ideas from Paris's famous restaurant, La Tour d'Argent. Instead of snitching the ash trays from the restaurant's tables, here you may actually buy them along with their collection of blue and white china, mustard-yellow tablecloths, and glassware engraved with the establishment's centuries-old emblem: the silver tower. More affordable gift ideas include dish towels, aprons, and soap—also bearing the Medieval-like symbol of la Tour d'Argent. You may also bring home some of the restaurant's savory comestibles in the form of jam, coffee, cognac, or melt-in-your-mouth *foie gras de canard.*
2 rue du Cardinal-Lemoine, 5e; tel.: 46.33.45.58;
Métro: Cardinal-Lemoine or Maubert-Mutualité
open Tuesday–Saturday 10 A.M.–midnight!; Sunday noon–midnight!

Diptyque

One of my clients, tight fistedly clutching the precious address in her hand, asked me to bring her and her two friends to this Left Bank boutique. Word got around that Diane Sawyer religiously buys generous supplies of their honeysuckle-scented candles. (The same odiferous little wonders sell for nearly twice as much at Barney's in New York.) Say no more! We were off! After judiciously sniffing an almost endless variety of these glass-contained gems—our noses carefully discriminating between jasmine, almond, cedar, musk, leather, cinnamon, orange, rose, mimosa, and cut hay (to name a few)—we were all the more convinced that the *chèvrefeuille* (honeysuckle) was indeed the winner. We depleted their supply by about 30 and left without giving their divine soaps, unique-smell-

ing toilette waters, or homemade potpourris proper attention—they'll have to wait until the word catches on.
34 bd St.-Germain, 5e; tel.: 43.26.45.27;
Métro: Maubert-Mutualité
open Tuesday–Saturday 10 A.M.–7 P.M.

L'Objet Trouvé

Just across the Seine from *Notre Dame* is one of Paris's most exotic boutiques, L'Objet Trouvé, which means found object. Madame Nellie Lauer has traveled to the Orient for the past 20 years in search of unusual *objets*, pieces of art, and, most of all, trinkets that she uses in the creation of her one-of-a-kind pieces of jewelry. Half of one wall is covered with Madame Lauer's handsome necklaces which range in price from $200 to $500. Old beads, relics, and bits of gold and silver have been fashioned into stylish pieces that work well with both casual and high-style apparel. The look is bold, inventive, and one of ethnic sophistication!
5 rue Frédéric-Sauton, 5e; tel.: 43.54.76.82;
Métro: Maubert-Mutualité
open Monday 2–8 P.M.; Tuesday–Saturday 11 A.M.–8 P.M.

La Tuile à Loup

Crafts from nearly every province of France—including Brittany, Savoie, Burgundy, and Provence—fill every nook and cranny of this out-of-the-way boutique. Since the 1970s, sensitized shoppers from all corners of the earth have come to see Marie-France and Michel Joblin-Depalle's heartwarming collection of traditional handiwork. Folkloric dolls, baskets, clogs, pottery, *faïence*, glassware, and Roland Roure's circus-like metal sculptures provide an endless variety of gift-giving ideas that can't be found elsewhere.
35 rue Daubenton, 5e; tel.: 47.07.28.90;
Métro: Censier-Daubenton
open Tuesday–Saturday 10:30 A.M.–1 P.M. and 3–7:30 P.M.; sometimes on Sunday mornings

6th *arrondissement*

Rigodon

The pirate-cave decor of this small Left Bank shop adds to the enchantment of the magical assortment of marionettes, porcelain-faced dolls, and carnival-like masks presented inside. Marie-Paule and Gilbert Rigodon sell dreams and fantasies in the shape of their own hand-painted Limoges dolls dressed in glittery costumes of iridescent taffeta and billowy silk. Priced between $350 and $1400, all of these pieces are unique and difficult to find in the U.S. The boutique's hand-sculpted leather, ceramic, papier-maché, and wood marionettes ($115–$1150) have been crafted into soul singers, witches, Vikings, and even a Dickens-like photographer by many of France's finest artisans. Rigodon's miniature bean-baggish "fat ladies" also make beguiling—and considerably more affordable—gifts ($38–$58) for bewitching friends back home.

Once you leave the boutique, be sure to take a look next door at Schmock Broc's eccentric collection of *objets* from the Art Nouveau and Art Deco epochs.

13 rue Racine, 6e; tel.: 43.29.98.66;
Métro: Odéon
open Monday–Saturday 10:30 A.M.–7 P.M.

7th *arrondissement*

Marie-Pierre Boitard

Situated on the same resplendent *place* as the Vogue magazine headquarters, the Senate, and one of Paris's most luxurious florists, Moulie Savart, is this elegant boutique that features finely selected arts of the table by French product designer Marie-Pierre Boitard. Madame Boitard has applied her sense of color, composition, and form to the creation of colorful hand-engraved crystal goblets and vases, hand-embroidered table linens, and specially made patterns for Haviland china. These home accessories, as well as a choice selection of antique silver, *faïence*, and porcelain from Herend, are set off in the striking lapis lazuli decor that enrobes this exclusive boutique.

9 place du Palais-Bourbon, 7e; tel.: 47.05.13.30;
Métro: Invalides or Chambre des Députés
open Monday–Saturday 10 A.M.–7 P.M.

Guillet

The house of Guillet has been handcrafting exquisite silk
cotton, and leather flowers in their Paris workshops since
1896. Although the boutique carries a blooming array of
faux bouquet, to me the highlight of this shop is their
extensive selection of silk flowers that look stunning
pinned on lapels, evening bags or around the waist. The
choice of color and flower is magnificent in a price range
that starts at only $13!
99 av de la Bourdonnais, 7e; tel.: 45.51.32.98;
Métro: Ecole Militaire
open Monday–Saturday 9:30 A.M.–12:30 P.M. *and*
2–6:30 P.M.

Petrossian

The Petrossian brothers were the first to import Russian
caviar into France more than a half century ago and today
the Petrossian name stands for one of the world's finest
caviars. Different-sized blue metal boxes, painted with
Petrossian's famous seascape logo, may be filled with
fresh Beluga, Ossetra, or Sevruga caviar and meticulously
wrapped for long-distance travel. Aside from their handsome selection of various-priced gift packages, Petrossian
also sells many other top-quality products such as Russian
vodka, Sauternes, smoked salmon, and their own specialties from the Périgord region of France including *foie
gras* and *confit de canard.*
18 bd de Latour-Maubourg, 7e; tel.: 45.51.38.74;
Métro: Latour-Maubourg
open Monday 10 A.M.–1 P.M. *and 2:30–7* P.M.;
Tuesday–Saturday 9 A.M.–1 P.M. *and 2:30–7* P.M.

La Pharmacie Piquet

From herbal wraps to cellulite removal cream, some of
the world's most miraculous forms of healing and beauty
treatments have originated in Europe. Monsieur Patrick
Piquet's herbal preparations are no exception, and although they have not yet arrived in America, they have

received great acclaim from body-conscious folk both in and out of Paris.

If you are suffering from insomnia, poor digestion, or migraine headaches or if you just need to lose a few pounds, Monsieur Piquet will recommend the appropriate treatment to remedy these and countless other ailments that plague the body and soul. These 100% natural treatments, in the form of *tisane* (herbal tea) or capsules, are not unlike those developed by pharmacists many years ago, before big-name pharmaceutical companies came into power.

Monsieur Piquet, who studied dietary nutrition in the U.S. and homeopathic medicine in France, regularly supplies diplomats from the neighboring consulates not only with these special preparations, but also with the French equivalents of foreign medication. Monsieur Piquet also concocts tailor-made homeopathic treatments for those interested in practicing a *médecine douce* (soft medicine).

In addition to these personalized preparations, Monsieur Piquet also sells his own special mixtures of luxurious bath oils for relieving stress, fatigue, poor circulation, and respiratory problems. An equally well appointed selection of soaps, creams, and shampoos serves to keep you feeling as beautiful on the outside as on the inside.

If you're hankering for just one more pick-me-up before you start your specially designed treatment, stop next door at Poujauran, one of Paris's most talked-about bakeries, to taste Jean-Luc Poujauran's buttery specialties from the Basque region of France.

18 rue Jean-Nicot, 7e; tel.: 47.05.17.88;
Métro: Latour-Maubourg
open Monday–Friday 8:30 A.M.–8 P.M.; Saturday
8:30 A.M.–2 P.M. and 3:30–7 P.M.

Richart

Immaculately packaged and presented chocolates are the trademark of this high-quality chocolate maker from Lyon. The Richart chocolates, as well as their boxes, evoke a purity of line and form that is best appreciated by sophisticated chocolate lovers. Each of their geometrically shaped chocolates is arranged in a white glossy box, complete with pull-out drawers for easier and more aesthetically pleasing consumption. The shop offers other eccentric gift ideas in the shape of a chocolate humidor

($320–410), a lacquered wooden box, similar to those for cigars, used to monitor the humidity level of the chocolate gems stored inside!

Stop here on your way back from a visit to the nearby Musée d'Orsay. Richart also sells creamy chocolate ice cream cones during the warm months.

258 bd Saint-Germain, 7e; tel.: 45.55.66.00;
Métro: Solférino
open Monday and Saturday 11 A.M.–7 P.M.; Tuesday–
Friday 10 A.M.–7 P.M.

8th *arrondissement*

Gien

Started in the French town of Gien in 1821 by an Englishman who set out to duplicate the refined sort of earthenware found on the other side of the Channel, Gien has gained international acclaim within the past few years for its wide selection of *faïence* based on traditional designs. After the rise in popularity of inferior-quality earthenware from Italy and Portugal in the 70s, Gien almost folded in the early 80s. The company was later taken over by Pierre and Evelyne Jeufroy, who assumed a more aggressive sales approach and began exporting throughout all of Europe, the U.S., and Japan. This of course explains why most of you hadn't heard about this almost 200-year-old company until a few years ago. Now Gien *faïence* is distributed in the U.S. by Baccarat and may be found in all of the better stores at a price that is roughly 25% higher than in France.

One of the reasons for the new-found success of Gien is their ability to adapt their designs to today's tastes and decor. The majority of their designs are based on classical motifs of fruits and flowers, but more recent additions—such as luncheon plates painted with *trompe l'oeil* fruit, holly-covered Christmas dishes, and series reproduced from famous works by Gauguin and Antoine de Saint-Exupéry (*The Little Prince*)—have contributed to a wider appeal. Most of the pieces in their *Faïence d'Art* collection are based on early 19th-century designs and have been painted by hand; the others are not hand painted, which explains why Gien's prices are less than those at Malicorne and Ségriès.

If you happen to be in Paris toward the beginning of February, try to take in their annual sale when much of the *faïence* is marked down another 30%.

This boutique may be incorporated into the Promenade Saint-Honoré (See map p. 55) if you intend to visit the shops near the Madeleine Church.
18 rue de l'Arcade, 8e; tel.: 49.24.07.77;
Métro: Madeleine
open Monday noon–7 P.M.; Tuesday–Saturday 10
A.M.–7 P.M.

Hélion

Just down the street behind the *Madeleine* church is the boutique Hélion, one of Paris's oldest glove specialists. Started in 1925, during the height of Paris's *années folles* or roaring 20s, when women rarely went out without wearing a pair of gloves, Hélion is a family-owned business dedicated to perpetuating the elegant look of Parisian chic. Buttery soft ostrich, kid, cotton, lace, satin, and gold and silver lamé have been cut (often from one skin, thus necessitating only one seam) into classic and fantasy-like styles by top-quality manufacturers throughout France. The selection for both women and men is as diverse as the prices one has to pay. Before you leave, take a peek at Hélion's fairy-tale–like collection of hand-embroidered treasures from the *Belle Epoque*.
22 rue Tronchet, 8e; (See Promenade Saint-Honoré
map p. 55) tel.: 47.42.26.79;
Métro: Madeleine
open Monday 2–6:45 P.M.; Tuesday–Saturday 10
A.M.–6:45 P.M.

Peter

Up until only 100 years ago or so, French people's knives were always different from the rest of their place settings, partly because it was considered bad luck to offer knives as wedding gifts along with the rest of the silver. Although today this 200-year-old cutlery firm continues to craft superior-quality knives that are different from the rest of their silver and vermeil, people are no longer so superstitious about giving cutlery as gifts. At prices reaching $1000 a blade for lapis lazuli (the lower-end is $265 for ebony), these hand-forged beauties more closely resemble precious *objets* than ordinary steak knives. Carved out of tiger's eye, malachite, ebony, and buffalo horn, and crowned with either solid gold and sterling or gold and silverplate, Peter's knives have won their place at some of the most distinguished tables of the world.

In addition to every imaginable type of knife used for hunting, sailing, ranching, or cutting cheese and bread, this family-owned business also features a stupendous selection of personal accessories (many from Eloi Pernet) including razors, manicure sets, and scissors, as well as luxurious table arts from Raynaud, Baccarat, St. Louis, and Ercuis.

191 rue du Faubourg–St.-Honoré, 8e;
tel.: 45.63.88.00;
Métro: Ternes
open Monday 1:30–7 P.M.; Tuesday–Saturday 10
A.M.–1 P.M. and 2–7 P.M.

Trousselier

At first glance it might seem like an exceptionally beautiful florist, but once you notice the absence of heady fragrant smells, you realize that the flowers *chez* Trousselier are not even real. It would be inappropriate to use the word *artificial* for these exquisite works of art that have attracted Paris's *haute bourgeoisie* for more than 100 years.

Just a few steps away from the city's big department stores, you may discover Trousselier's handmade silk, crêpe, and cotton imitations of real-life flowers and buds. One perfectly shaped rose requires at least 90 individually placed petals, and a craftsperson can only make four of them in one day. (President Mitterand offered a bouquet of these same roses to Madame Gorbachev during a recent visit to France.) In addition to their own fashionable flower accessories for sale in the boutique's garden-like setting, Trousselier also works hand in hand with Paris's great couturiers.

Following a recent takeover by brothers Christophe and Stéphane Olivier, plans are being considered for an openings in Geneva, New York, and Tokyo, but for now, you have to come to Paris to see the artful creations that have made the Trousselier name famous throughout the world.

73 bd Haussmann, 8e; tel.: 42.66.97.95;
Métro: St.-Augustin or Havre-Caumartin
open Monday–Saturday 9:30 A.M.–6:30 P.M.

9th *arrondissement*

Archi-Noire

Located at Pigalle, an area known chiefly for its over-abundance of seedy sex shops and world-reknown music stores, is Archi-Noire, a boutique worth the detour—especially if you are an Art Deco fan. Madame Renault-Culty devotes most of her weekends to combing the antique shows outside of Paris in search of stream-lined *objets* from the 30s, and even sometimes a few rareties from the 50s.

The boutique's selection of costume jewelry is particularly rich and in addition to Bakelite geometrics from this century, Madame Renault-Culty has also handpicked a few vermeil, silver, and gold treasures from the 18th and 19th centuries. Prices on the older, more ornate pieces run as much as $800, whereas some of the more modest Art Deco creations start at $150. Other less expensive gift items include 30s cordial glasses ($32 for 5) or reproductions of Art Deco gems at $40.

19 rue Victor Massé, 9e tel.: 48.78.01.82
Métro: Pigalle
open Tuesday–Friday 12 A.M.–8 P.M., Saturday 1–8 P.M.

16th *arrondissement*

La Châtelaine

This is where the ladies from the 16th come to buy superior-quality babies' gifts that guarantee a distinctively BCBG look as early as the cradle. La Châtelaine (the mistress of the château) features layette, smock dresses, and little boys' trousers of heirloom quality that only the elite (or the most extravagant) can afford. The store's collection of house linens is equally luxurious and particularly exclusive, because (like the children's clothing), La Châtelaine's handsome goods are sold only in this boutique.

170 av Victor-Hugo, 16e; (See Promenade BCBG map p. 249) tel.: 47.27.44.07;
Métro: Pompe
open Tuesday–Friday 9:30 A.M.–6:30 P.M., Saturday 9:30 A.M.–12:30 P.M. and 2:30–6:30 P.M.

Christian Benais

If you have always longed for a trousseau fit for a princess or even just part of one, then you must visit this luxury boutique, reputed for its elegant selection of antique linens. Satin and velvet-trimmed pillows made from antique, oriental floral-print embroideries ($250), delicate, white lace pillow shams ($315 per pair), and crisp 100% cotton bedsheets ($700–2,400 per sheet) assure a more dreamy sleep, while antique tablecloths ($580–2,350), decorated with intricate cut-work designs, set the mood for romantic feasts. Italian linens, cashmere shawls ($1100), and blankets, as well as Monsieur Benais's own rich-hued brocade bedspreads, also contribute to the success of this boutique, so well known by the Paris elite.

18 rue Cortambert, 16e; (See Promenade BCBG map p. 249) tel.: 45.03.15.55;
Métro: Pompe
open Monday—Saturday 10 A.M.–1 P.M. and 2–7 P.M.

P. de Nicolaï

Since she grew up in the Guerlain family, developing a keen sense of smell became second nature to Patricia de Nicolaï, founder of this recently opened perfume emporium. All of the fragrances sold here have been created by this young woman in the laboratory behind the glass window to the back of the boutique. This in itself provides you with the rare opportunity of seeing the workplace of the *parfumeur*, made up of hundreds of meticulously arranged vials and one small scale. Here infinitesimal doses of extracts are measured in order to achieve a perfectly balanced mixture of scents. (Highly complex perfumes may be composed of some 100 extracts.)

You may either purchase one of P. de Nicolaï's fragrances in its own distinguished *flacon* or buy it separately and choose from the luxurious collection of hand-blown glass and crystal bottles sold in the boutique. If this is not exclusive enough, P. de Nicolaï will create your own personalized perfume especially for you to the tune of about $2,400!

69 av Raymond-Poincaré, 16e; (See Promenade Victor Hugo map p. 249) tel.: 47.55.90.44;
Métro: Victor-Hugo
open Monday–Saturday 10 A.M.–6:30 P.M.

17th *arrondissement*

L'Esprit et le Vin

You don't have to be a connoisseur to appreciate this interesting boutique, filled with every imaginable type of wine paraphernalia. Aside from a large selection of wine glasses and carafes, L'Esprit et le Vin features an extensive selection of accoutrements used to enhance the *dégustation* of fine wines: archaic-looking wine-bottle warmers; sophisticated thermometers for determining the best temperatures for consuming select wines; cork tags for displaying noteworthy vintages when using carafes, and more!

81 av des Ternes, 17e; tel.: 45.74.80.99;
Métro: Ternes
open Tuesday–Saturday 10 A.M.–7 P.M.

18th *arrondissement*

Coolman

My sister-in-law gave me this address when my husband and I decided to splurge and buy designer fabrics for our freshly painted apartment a few years ago. Coolman sells all of the big-name European upholstery fabrics at 20% off regular French retail prices. Canovas, Frey, Etamine, Lelievre, Rubelli, and many others are here in grand array. Either you can go first to the decorators' posh Paris showrooms (See Left Bank descriptions pp. 110, 160) to see the fabrics handsomely presented and ask for/buy samples, or you may go directly to Coolman to flick through the books. Coolman handles shipping; with *détaxe*, price savings can run up to 45% off of what you pay in the U.S. Another bonus is that you won't have to wait six to eight months to receive your merchandise (as in many New York showrooms), because with Coolman, the maximum wait is three weeks, plus another two to three months for shipping.

17 rue de la Chapelle, 18e; tel.: 42.09.00.33; or
42.09.30.09;
Métro: Marx-Dormoy
open Monday–Saturday 10:30 A.M.–12:30 P.M. and
2–6 P.M.

Neuilly-sur-Seine

Handpainted Silk Creations

French big names Carven, Léonard, Porthault, and Revillon have used Madame Maryvonne de Follin's (countess in private life) hand-painted silk designs to enhance their collections, and many top society ladies on both sides of the Atlantic have bought her silken creations to accessorize their wardrobes. Madame de Follin's hallmark accessory is a large square throw (about $350) that may be draped and tied, either as a light wrap or as an elegant *paréo*. These crêpe de chine creations are painted in colorful swirls of flowers, clouds, and Matisse-like arabesques; many are doubled with a figurative design on one side and an abstract one on the other. In addition to the shawls, the artist also creates tailor-made silk jackets (about $1,170), wall panels, and ceiling coverings to fit clients' personal tastes and dimensions. Madame de Follin receives in her atelier just on the outskirts of Paris in Neuilly. Call 47.22.38.51 for an appointment.

■   ## Discount Shopping   ■

Imagine spending your precious time in Paris rummaging through unattractive boutiques filled with poorly displayed merchandise, last year's fashions, and inadequate dressing rooms. A lot of Paris discount shopping does fill this scenario. However, don't despair. There are some real bargains out there and it doesn't necessarily mean you have to stress yourself out while locating them.

The key to happiness in the Parisian discount-shopping world is not to expect to discover the same type of fantastic markdowns or broad selection of sizes and styles for this season's merchandise that you are accustomed to finding at home in the U.S. Adjusting one's expectations is an important rule to follow, in general, in France and one of the techniques that I regularly use to help me through all types of situations. Expecting to find this year's fashions in a variety of sizes at stupendous savings is like having washcloths in your French hotel room. Hint: you have to bring your own washcloths when traveling in France.

I grew up in upstate New York, not too far from one of the greatest meccas for bargain-hunting shoppers, Cohoes Mfg. Co., where lip-smacking, credit-card–happy ladies were bussed in from all corners of the Northeast. Mom and I swore by Cohoes Mfg. Co., good ole Loehmann's, and factory-outlet stores that sold everything from bed linens to rubber boots! We rarely bought anything at full price and, if we weren't lucky enough to find our heart's delight at a reduced-price store, we were sure to strike it rich at one of Macy's famous three-day sales. After frequent visits to Filene's basement during my college years in Boston, I became even more convinced that buying full-price was only for those with unlimited cash flows. That was of course until I came to live in France.

To my own surprise, I've done a complete turnabout and now I often find myself paying right through the nose like the rest of the French shoppers. (Maybe this explains why the French have such long, aquiline noses.) I do feel, however, that succumbing to higher prices does have its payoffs; I tend to buy less, yet each purchase corresponds more with what I really wanted in the first place and the quality is generally much better. Like most other American women I know in Paris, I've learned not to rely too much on the discount shopping available here. The true bargain hunting is reserved for the January and July sales or *soldes*.

American visitors to the French capital stay on an average of less than three days (according to French Ministry of Tourism figures), so between the Louvre, the Eiffel Tower, and the Musée d'Orsay, how much time should be devoted to potentially disappointing shopping? No one likes to walk away empty-handed, especially if you are on a limited time frame. The point is that seeking out rock-bottom prices is not necessarily the best way to spend your vacation in the City of Lights. My advice to you is not to venture into the Paris discount scene *unless* you are a seasoned shopper or *unless* you like to work hard when you shop or *unless* you are going to be in Paris for a week or more. If you don't fall into any one of these three categories, Paris reduced-price shopping could easily turn into a fretful and frustrating experience. But if you do fall into any of those categories, then the following boutiques might just provide you with one of the most exhilarating jaunts in the world!

1st *arrondissement*

Courrèges

The last time I walked into this shop I was greeted by a sexy, little black and silver, geometrically designed, sequined dress—originally priced at $1,300, here marked down to a meager $330. Although the dress looked as though it just walked out of the 70s, it would have been perfect for a sizzling night out on the town.

Most of what Courrèges has to offer fits that description: terrific price reductions (between 30 and 75% off), a lot of small sizes, and that indefatigable Courrèges look that says bring out your go-go boots! The white-walled (the designer's favorite color) boutique is neatly arranged and the help is not at all bothersome. Most of the merchandise tends to be a year or two old and, of course, the older the garment, the better the markdown.

If you are an André Courrèges fan, don't miss this boutique. If you're not, then you still could flash for a shiny fuchsia trench coat at half price, a mint-green and black plaid wool coat at a quarter of the original price, or even a more classic-looking, silk moiré blouse for $35.

7 rue de Turbigo, 1er; (See Place des Victoires and Les Halles map p. 165) tel.: 42.33.03.57;
Métro: Etienne-Marcel
open Tuesday–Saturday 10:15 A.M.–6 P.M.

2nd *arrondissement*

Dépôt des Grandes Marques

Discretely located on the third floor of a building five minutes from the Paris stockmarket is this men's-clothing outlet. This year's fashions, bearing labels by Louis Féraud, Cerruti 1881, Jacques Fath, and Renoma, cost roughly 30–50% less than the boutique price. A Cerruti 1881 *smoking* (tuxedo), priced here at $375, sells for twice as much at their place de la Madeleine boutique. Exquisitely cut Jacques Fath wool sport jackets go for about $200, and an elegant, navy-blue wool Louis Féraud suit will set you back about $400. The bad news is that they don't give tax refunds and there are no dressing rooms.

15 rue de la Banque, 2e; (See Passages map p. 195)
tel.: 42.96.99.04;

Métro: Bourse
open Monday–Saturday 10 A.M.–7 P.M.

C. Mendès

None of the clients that I have brought here have ever had any luck, but if you are a true, dyed-in-the-wool Yves Saint Laurent fan, then you might just strike it rich! Pay attention when you look for this boutique because the entrance is not clearly marked and, as you enter, head up stairs.

Mendès has a licensing agreement with Saint Laurent Rive Gauche that enables them to sell the six-months–to–a-year-old womenswear at nearly 50% less than the boutique price. Yet even with those reductions, the buys are not always a steal. Unfortunately, the shopping conditions in this store are far from ideal: the merchandise is very shabbily arranged (with all of my 5′ 11″, I can barely reach the top rack), the store is often overcrowded, and there are no dressing rooms (reinforcing the fact that you should always wear nice lingerie when discount shopping in Paris).
65 rue Montmartre, 2e; (See Passages map p. 195) tel.: 42.36.83.32;
Métro: Sentier
open Monday–Thursday 9:30 A.M.;–6 P.M.; Friday and Saturday 9:30 A.M.—5 P.M.

3rd *arrondissement*

Biderman

Biderman is to Yves Saint Laurent, Kenzo, and Courrèges as Mendès is to Saint Laurent Rive Gauche. This warehouse-like store, specializing in menswear, is far bigger and better organized than Mendès yet the 20–30% markdowns are not nearly as exciting. They have a nice selection of YSL wool and cotton sweaters, most priced around $120; YSL casual and dressy suits galore are about $350; sporty Kenzo leather jackets run between $500 and $700; and Courrèges informal shirts go for about $60. It's a great address for early birds because they open at 8:30 A.M.!
114 rue de Turenne, 3e; (See Marais Map p. 214) tel.: 44.61.17.14;
Métro: Filles-du-Calvaire

open Monday–Friday 8:30 A.M.–noon and 2–6 P.M.;
Saturday 8:30 A.M.–6 P.M.

7th *arrondissement*

Azzedine Alaïa

The name Alaïa, unobtrusively written on a mailbox in the
entrance way to this *bourgeois* apartment building, is the
only indication that you are at the right address. It is not
until you pass through the doorway of the first-floor apartment that you realize that you have landed in the land of
Alaïa knockdowns. Racks of merchandise, arranged according to style and color, hold the remnants of this
triumphant designer's collections from two years past, all
at half price. Some of the styles haven't survived the test
of time whereas others look as though they could easily
be shown on this year's runways. A slithery red and grey,
wool stretch dress sells for about $270. A skintight, terra-
cotta–colored leather suit is still a bit steep at $1,000—
especially since it will probably be out of fashion by the
time you break it in. Spike-heeled pumps run for about
$165. There are no dressing rooms (which makes squeez-
ing into these little numbers a bit difficult), and be
careful—the people who work here can be downright
nasty.

   This Alaïa outpost is not far from the Musée d'Orsay.
60 rue de Bellechasse, 7e; tel.: 47.05.13.18;
Métro: Solférino
open Monday–Saturday 10 A.M.–6:30 P.M.

8th *arrondissement*

Anna Lowe

This is one of the best discount shops in Paris. The location is convenient; the store is elegant; the 25–50% markdowns are tempting; the merchandise is nicely presented;
and the saleswomen are lovely—what more could a girl
ask for! It's no surprise that the store is run and owned
by Suzy, an American woman who has lived in Paris for
over 15 years. Names such as Chanel, Ungaro, Valentino,

Jean-Louis Scherrer, and Louis Féraud prevail throughout the boutique in everything from elegant, *prêt-à-porter* suits to glamourous *haute couture* eveningwear. And the good news is that some of the clothing is this year's. Although limited, Suzy's selection of accessories is also a big success; pearl-embellished Chanel earrings sell for about $70—half their price *chez* Chanel. If you're lucky, you will hit upon a few gold-chain belts, cuff bracelets, and a smattering of used Chanel bags priced anywhere between $750 and $1,000!

35 av Matignon, 8e; (See Promenade Saint Honoré map p. 55) tel.: 43.59.96.61;
Métro: Miromesnil
open Monday–Saturday 10:30 A.M.*–7* P.M.

Nina Ricci

Walk down the winding, spiral staircase in the main Nina Ricci store to discover an elegant, cream-colored room overflowing with last year's spring and fall couture collections, on sale for more than half the price. All of the dresses, suits, and blouses were shown in Nina Ricci's haute couture *défilés* so if you don't have a model-size shape, this is not the place for you—it's mostly size 6.

Certainly the main attraction is their formal wear—netting and lace cocktail dresses, feather-trimmed ball gowns, and even silk taffeta wedding dresses engulf the space. Evening-dress prices start around $600 and go well into the thousands for some of the more elaborate, hand-embroidered gowns. Their wedding dresses sell quite well and with the *détaxe* you can pick one up for about $2,800. A few classics are also apt to catch your eye and may well be worth the investment, such as a navy-blue, wool dress for $720 or a white, daisy-patterned, cotton eyelet blouse for $230. Even if you don't have the slightest intention to buy, you may just want to stop here anyway because this boutique provides you with a rare opportunity to actually see and touch the exquisite clothes that have graced some of the world's most famous runways.

39 av Montaigne, 8e; (see Promenade Golden Triangle Map p. 55) tel.: 47.23.78.88;
Métro: Alma-Marceau or Franklin-Roosevelt
open Monday–Friday 10 A.M.*–6:30* P.M.

9th *arrondissement*

Rodier

Here's another discount shop that could very well leave you cold, but if you happen to be in the neighborhood (behind Fauchon) and if you have some extra time, then why not stop by. Last year's Rodier knits are sold at half price, but of course most of what is left has been picked over so much that the possibility of finding anything really special is nil. Basic items such as a plain, navy-blue cardigan are even harder to come by, but your chances are greater if you happen to stop in more toward the beginning of the season. To make matters worse, the women who run this boutique are more or less *désagréable*, no credit cards are accepted, and the lighting is poor—factors that hardly encourage a small purchase.

If you're interested in more modish fashions, check out the Annexe des Créateurs at no. 19 rue Godot-de-Mauroy—a considerably less organized discount shop that offers designer togs at terrifically reduced prices.
34 rue Godot-de-Mauroy, 9e; (See Promenade Saint-Honoré map p. 55) tel.: 47.42.62.04;
Métro: Madeleine or Havre-Caumartin
open Monday–Saturday 10 A.M.–7 P.M.

12th *arrondissement*

Jean-Louis Scherrer

Don't judge a book by its cover. One look at the attractive, black-lacquered facade and you think you're in for something really special, but unfortunately the limited supply of ready-to-wear (very little couture) that you find inside rarely lives up to your expectations. If you get lucky, though, you may very well find that long, lace and chiffon evening dress that you've always dreamed of owning, priced at $800, marked down from $1,700. Prices tend to run between 40 and 70% lower than the normal boutique prices. A good selection of fabrics from this big-name designer's recent collections is also for sale at reduced prices.
29 av Ledru-Rollin, 12e; tel.: 46.28.39.27;
Métro: Gare de Lyon or Quai de la Rapée

*open Monday–Saturday 10 A.M.–6 P.M. (closed
Wednesday in the winter, Saturday in the summer)*

14th *arrondissement*

The closest Métro stop for all of these stores is Alésia.

Cacharel Stock

The only place in Paris to have such a large "stock" of
Cacharel mens, womens, and childrenswear at such unbeatable prices: 40–50% off on last year's merchandise.
The store lacks charm and is dimly lit, but the countless
racks of clothing are all impeccably arranged, offering a
wide selection of sizes and styles. Cacharel's famous delicate, flower-print cotton blouses go for $35–$50. Men's
La Chemiserie shirts in everything from a rich cobalt blue
to a sporty wide red stripe cost $25–60.
*114 rue d'Alésia, 14e; tel.: 45.42.53.04
open Monday–Saturday 10 A.M.–6:45 P.M.*

Dorotennis Stock

As the name implies, Dorotennis manufactures a lot of
tenniswear but also skiwear and slick casualwear for men,
women, and children—perfect for doing sports or just
hanging around the house. Most of what is shown here is
priced at 40–50% off and is, once again, last year's merchandise, but with this sort of clothing it doesn't matter
too much—especially since fluorescent colors have been
the trend on the slopes for at least the past 10 years or
so. The store, like the clothes, is bright and the merchandise is well displayed in a fine variety of sizes and styles.
Adults' down jackets go for $120; fun, colorful cotton/
polyester blend sweatshirts will set you back about $30.

   As you leave the boutique, take a look at Dorothée Bis's
discounted knitwear next door.
*74 rue d'Alésia, 14e; tel.: 45.42.13.93
open Monday 2–7 P.M.; Tuesday–Friday 10:15 A.M.–
7 P.M.; Saturday 10 A.M.–7 P.M.*

Fabrice Karel

In the winter, wool knits, and in the summer, cotton knits
and cottons are the name of the game for this women's

apparel shop. You can count on 50% markdowns and last year's collection, *bien sûr*. The boutique is pleasant, the saleswomen are friendly, and the selection of sizes is fairly complete. The only drawback is that depending upon when you hit it, you might find 15 of the same knit skirts with no matching tops or vice versa.

105 rue d'Alésia, 14e; tel.: 45.42.42.61
open Monday 2–7 P.M.; Tuesday–Friday 10:15 A.M.–
7 P.M.; Saturday 10 A.M.–7 P.M.

Stock 2

Did you say Daniel Hechter? That is who this modern, megastore for men, women, and children is all about. Too bad the prices aren't better because a paltry 25–40% off doesn't seem like much for last year's merchandise. Nevertheless, you can choose from a wide selection of sportswear and, if you're lucky enough to be there in January, they mark their merchandise down another 30% (no *détaxe* at that time).

92 rue d'Alésia, 14e; tel.: 45.41.65.57
open Monday–Saturday 10 A.M.–7 P.M.

16th *arrondissement*

Bab's

Not far from the Golden Triangle, center of Paris big-name shopping, is this lovely store that sells many of the same designer womenswear for 30–50% less. This is one of Paris's best addresses for buying big names such as Guy Laroche, Ungaro, Louis Féraud and Saint Laurent. Unfortunately, most of the labels have been cut out (*degriffe*) and, alas, much of the clothing is from last year. Their collection of costume jewelry and belts is also very *parisienne*. Most of the saleswomen in the boutique are quite helpful and polite as is their seamstress, who once carried out a rush alteration for one of my clients in less than 24 hours!

29 av Marceau, 16e; (See Promenade Golden
Triangle map p. 55) tel.: 47.20.84.74;
Métro: Alma-Marceau
89 bis av des Ternes, 17e; tel.: 45.74.02.74;
Métro: Porte-Maillot
open Monday–Saturday 10:15 A.M.–7 P.M.

Réciproque

I'm not much on buying second-hand clothing, but if you love wearing creations by Paris's top designers—but can't afford to pay the prices—then this place is for you. The men's and women's clothing, accessories, and gift items for sale in these three large shops are in excellent condition, clean, and best of all, up-to-date.

The women's store is particularly rich in big-name merchandise because many of Paris's most fashionable women put their used clothing up for sale at Réciproque. Many of these women are slaves to fashion, which means that they change their wardrobes about every three months—that of course only makes Réciproque's stores all the more interesting! The display racks are clearly marked, mostly according to designer. If their merchandise wasn't so squashed together, I'd give this store star billing. Most of their goods are priced about 50% below their original cost.

A plentiful and neatly organized selection of women's bags and costume jewelry is located all the way to the back of the boutique at 123 rue de la Pompe. I'm often disappointed by their scarce supply of Chanel, Vuitton, and Hermés bags, but if you are lucky enough to spot one, snatch it up—you may not see those kinds of savings again for a long time!

95 rue de la Pompe, 16e (women's clothing);
tel.: 47.04.30.28;
Métro: Pompe
101 rue de la Pompe, 16e; (men's clothing and gifts); tel.: 47.27.93.52
123 rue de la Pompe, 16e (women's coats and accessories);
(See Promenade Golden Triangle of the Sixteenth map p. 249)
Open Tuesday–Saturday 10:15 A.M.–6:45 P.M.

Department Stores   .

I usually discourage people from department-store shopping in Paris for several reasons: the smaller, more charming boutiques provide a more attractive setting for shopping *à la parisienne*, the salespeople in these same

boutiques are friendlier and considerably more servic‹
able; and, most of all, the merchandise in French d‹
partment stores is not as attractively presented as in the
U.S. counterparts. The Paris department stores do, hov
ever, provide you with the opportunity to see a treme⌐
dous amount of French merchandise together under on
roof—a factor that is far from negligible, especially if yo‹
are in town only for a couple of days.

It was in fact a Frenchman, Aristide Bouçicaut, wh‹
started the world's first department store, Au Bon March›
(now called Le Bon Marché), in 1863. The rising capitali⌐
tide, brought on by the Industrial Revolution and the ne⌐
phenomenon of fixed prices (prior to that customers ha‹
to haggle in order to obtain fair prices), whetted shopper
appetites for a more abundant selection of goods. Mo⌐
sieur Bouçicaut emphasized the shopper's right to brows‹
freely, to return unwanted purchases, and to pay the sam
price as the next person for merchandise that was order‹
presented for all to see. Other retailers caught on fast ar‹
by the end of the 19th century, Paris witnessed the birt‹
of several major department stores including Au Pri⌐
temps, Galeries Lafayette, La Samaritaine, and Le Baz⌐
de l'Hôtel de Ville (BHV).

If you look beyond the shabby displays that have inf⌐
trated many of Paris's grandest department stores, you
discover handsome architectural elements from the e⌐
of the past century and the beginning of this one. Massi⌐
glass cupolas, flowery Art Nouveau paintings, and intrica
hand-forged framework give evidence of a time whe⌐
these commercial spaces were Paris's most comely sho‹
ping emporiums. Encircled in spindly gold-leaf metal ba⌐
isters and crowned by a cathedral-high stained-gla⌐
dome, the main floor of Galeries Lafayette merits a speci⌐
trip just to see one of the French capital's most perfe‹
examples of turn-of-the-century splendor.

If you do plan to go shopping in one of Paris's sprawli⌐
grands magasins and want to beat the crowds, I sugge⌐
you go early in the morning and never on Saturdays. T⌐
shopping system in Paris's larger stores differs from th‹
of the smaller boutiques. Here the salesperson only writ‹
up and packages your purchases—it is up to you to ⌐
to the cashier (or *caisse*) in a separate area to actual⌐
pay. Once this is taken care of, you go back to the sale‹
person to pick up your merchandise. Often the clerk ⌐

no longer at his or her post or is busy chatting with a neighbor; this of course creates confusion, frustration, and a great loss of time. In order to minimize this sort of hassle and to avoid long lines at several different cashiers, you may want to accumulate all of your purchase slips (or have all of the purchases put on one slip) and pay everything together at the end. Totaling your purchases will also help you to attain the minimum balance required for your tax reduction. Nearly all of the major stores ship, and if you plan to do some serious shopping, it is best to consult with the welcome desk in each store regarding its own particular policies and benefits for foreign shoppers.

Although the Christmas decorations inside the major department stores are disappointing, their mechanical-toy–filled windows depict whimsical storybook scenes that entertain young and old alike. Most of the stores are open on Sundays the two weeks prior to Christmas, and, like the smaller boutiques, they hold sales in January and July.

As one last hint before you go, keep in mind that many of Paris's department stores are actually divided up into several different buildings, so you may want to consult the store directory before you go charging through!

Galeries Lafayette

Family-owned Galeries Lafayette is best known for their up-to-date fashion "boutiques." However, their recently renovated arts-of-the-table department (in the basement) features a seductive selection of treasures from France's top tableware manufacturers. Fashion shows are conducted at 11 A.M. on Wednesdays year-round and on Fridays between April and October; additional shows are often added at 12:30 P.M. Call 48.74.02.30 to reserve ahead.
40 bd Haussmann, 9e; tel.: 42.82.34.56;
Métro: Chausée-d'Antin
open Monday–Saturday 9:30 A.M.–6:30 P.M.

Printemps

Just next door to Galeries Lafayette are Printemps' three distinctly different stores: Mode, Maison, and Brummel, or, in other words, fashion, home, and for men. Their table-arts department is so well known that it is one of

the bride-to-be's favorite places to register. Printemps' fashion show is a good way to begin the day because it starts at 10 A.M. (when the store opens) on Tuesdays year-round and on Fridays from the first of March to the end of October. Reservations are not always necessary, but you may want to call 42.82.47.79 to make sure they're not booked up. An elegant glass cupola may be viewed from their top-floor restaurant, Brasserie Flo.
64 bd Haussmann, 9e; tel.: 42.82.50.00;
Métro: Chausée-d'Antin
open Monday–Saturday 9:35 A.M.–7 P.M.

Le Bon Marché

Le Bon Marché is Paris's Left Bank department store. The store's most original attractions include reputable gourmet-food halls, a well-stocked oriental rug department, and 19th-century antiques! Le Bon Marché has lost much of its gutsy chic since its early beginnings, but if you're following the Left Bank promenade, it may be more convenient for you to stop in here rather than going to the *grands boulevards.*
corner of rue de Sèvres and rue du Bac, 7e; (See
Left Bank map p. 103) tel.: 45.49.21.22;
Métro: Sèvres-Babylone
open Monday–Saturday 9:30 A.M.–6:30 P.M.; the food
store is open 8:30 A.M.–9 P.M.

La Samaritaine

Don't go out of your way to shop at La Samaritaine because the interior of the store most closely resembles an upscale K-Mart rather than a sophisticated department store. La Samaritaine is made up of a maze of several different stores, which makes it even more difficult to know where you are or where you want to go. If you've finished your day at the Louvre and only have a short time to shop in a Parisian department store, La Samaritaine is about 10 minutes away. The café on the fifth floor of store 2 furnishes a glorious view of the Seine and its river banks.
75 rue de Rivoli, 1er; tel.: 40.41.20.20;
Métro: Pont-Neuf
open Monday–Saturday 9:30 A.M.–7 P.M. (Tuesday
and Friday until 8:30 P.M.)

BHV

The BHV is your typical French family-styled department store—no frills, no glamour, just a whole lot of utilitarian items to keep you and your home looking shipshape. The highlight of the BHV is its world-famous basement which looks like a handyman's dream; aside from an astronomical selection of screws, bolts, and nuts in every imaginable size, you will also find Louis XVI–styled door handles, French wine-bottle caddies, Belle Epoque bathroom fixtures, and weather vanes from the provinces.
52 rue de Rivoli, 4e; (See Marais map p. 214)
tel.: 42.74.90.00;
Métro: Hôtel de Ville
open Monday–Saturday 9 A.M.–7 P.M. (until 10 P.M. on Wednesday)

• More Big Stores •

FNAC

FNAC specializes in all types of electric equipment ranging from stereos to answering machines. Prices on these types of articles are much higher in France, however, the store's extensive selection of French records, tapes, CDs, and books does provide endless gift-giving possibilities at the best prices in town.
Forum des Halles, 1er; (See Place des Victoires and Les Halles map p. 165) tel.: 40.41.40.00;
Métro: Les Halles
26 av Wagram, 8e; tel.: 48.88.58.00;
Métro: Etoile
136 rue de Rennes, 6e; (See Left Bank map p. 103) tel.: 49.54.30.00; Métro: Rennes
open Monday 1–7 P.M.; Tuesday–Saturday 10 A.M.– 7 P.M.
1 rue de Charenton, 12e; tel.: 43.42.04.04;
Métro: Bastille
open Monday 1–8 P.M.; Tuesday, Thursday and Saturday 10 A.M.–8 P.M.; Wednesday and Friday 10 A.M.–10 P.M.

Go Sport

With over 63 stores in France, Go Sport ranks as one of the Gaul's leading sporting goods outlets. Le Coq Sportif,

Adidas, Repetto, Rossignol and Killy (as in Jean Claude) are just some of the French labels that have made their mark in the world of sports. They're all here in great force along with many other European brands.

1 rue Pierre-Lescot, 1er (Forum des Halles);
tel.: 45.08.92.96;
Métro: Les Halles
open Monday–Saturday 10:30 A.M.–7:30 P.M.
68 av du Maine, 16e; tel.: 43.27.50.50;
Métro: Gaité
open Monday–Friday 10 A.M.–7:30 P.M.; Saturday
9:30 A.M.–7:30 P.M.
Palais des Congrès, 2 pl Porte-Maillot;
tel.: 46.40.22.46;
Métro: Porte-Maillot
open Monday–Saturday 10 A.M.–7 P.M.

Prisunic

Just a few steps away from Virgin, also on the Champs-Elysées, is Prisunic—France's answer to Woolworth's. Amid much of the junk of this Printemps-owned five and dime, you may be able to unearth some typically French (and cheap) gift ideas that will make a hit back home. Other Prisunics, as well as the Galeries Lafayette–owned Monoprix, are located throughout the French capital. This is the only branch that stays open until midnight.

109 rue de La Boétie, 8e; (See Promenade Golden
Triangle map p. 32) tel.: 42.25.27.46;
Métro: Franklin-Roosevelt
open Monday–Saturday 9:45 A.M.–midnight

Virgin Megastore

This recently opened music and book store has turned out to be one of the star attractions on the Champs-Elysées. Open until late at night, Virgin Megastore offers an immense selection of music from the Virgin record label as well as from countless other music companies.

52 av des Champs-Elysées, 8e; (See Promenade
Golden Triangle map p. 32) tel.: 40.74.06.48;
Métro: Franklin-Roosevelt
open Monday–Thursday 10 A.M.–midnight; Friday
and Saturday 10 A.M.–1 A.M.; Sunday noon–
midnight

The Markets

Every visitor to Paris should experience at least one of the city's lively open-air food markets. Whether you are just strolling through or shopping for provisions for a picnic on the banks of the Seine, *les marchés de Paris* promise a colorful glimpse at how ordinary Parisians lead their lives.

Most Parisians still shop on a daily basis even if it's just to pick up a crispy *baguette*, a ripe red tomato, or a perfectly creamy piece of camembert. Here you encounter local housewives and young discriminating gourmets carefully selecting ingredients (you never touch anything yourself—you are always served) for their midday and evening repasts. Row after row of meticulously arranged sweet red peppers, green baby courgettes, and plump juicy grapes provide a feast for the eyes, as the animated and often exaggerated gestures of the market vendors entertain the heart and soul. As you walk down the cornucopia-like alleys and see the merchants selling everything from freshly killed pheasant to the Mediterranean's choicest stingray, you will certainly feel a long way from your local supermarket back home.

There are three different types of markets in Paris: roving markets, market streets, and covered markets. Each of these markets has its own personality, created largely by the neighborhood clientele. One of my favorite markets is the roving market on the avenue du President-Wilson (Métro: Iéna or Alma-Marceau, between place d'Iéna and place d'Alma). Open on Wednesdays and Saturdays between 8 A.M. and 1 P.M., this is where the chic ladies of the 16th shop in search of prime foods for their families and evening entertaining. The street markets at rue Mouffetard (Métro: Monge—begin at rue de l'Epée-du-Bois) and rue Poncelet (Métro: Ternes) reflect a more heterogeneous mix of devout *gastronomes* and local customers. Both of these markets are open Tuesday–Saturday 8 A.M.–1 P.M. and 4–8 P.M. The covered and outdoor markets at the place d'Aligre (Métro: Ledru-Rollin) provide one of the greatest spectacles of all of the markets. Here the flavor is derived from an ambiance not too unlike that of North African souks. Open Tuesday–Saturday 8 A.M.–1

P.M., the Marché Aligre also touts an interesting selection of *fripes* (antique clothing) and a few *brocanteurs*. In addition to food items, most of the Paris markets also sell typically French gift ideas including honey-smelling soaps from Provence, country French ceramic dishes, and porcelain *demitasses* and teapots.

The food markets are not the only markets that enable you to experience just one more aspect of French life, because the city also boasts an array of specialized markets within its different *quartiers*. The Marché aux Fleurs (flower market), open daily until 4 P.M. (Métro: Cité), at place Louis-l'Epine is one of the oldest and most famous; this pleasant market turns into an enchanting bird market on Sundays from 9 A.M. to 7 P.M. Another one of Paris's famous markets is the Marché St.-Pierre, the fabric market at the foot of Montmartre (Métro: Anvers). Here housewives and young struggling designers ferret out every imaginable type of material at the best prices in Paris. If you are a stamp collector, don't miss the Marché aux Timbres (stamp market) set up at the rond-point des Champs-Elysées (Métro: Champs-Elysées–Clémenceau; see Promenade Golden Triangle map p. 32) on Thursday, Friday, and Saturday from 10 A.M. to 7 P.M. The pickings are not always extraordinary, but if you know what you're buying, you're sure to walk away with a few finds.

These are just a few of my favorite markets. However, I'm sure that you will discover more on your own just by walking down the streets of Paris. Remember that many of the markets open early in the morning, around 8 A.M., and close by 1 P.M. Be sure to dress casually and bring a lot of change—sorry, no plastic. If you are interested in finding out about the markets closest to your hotel, your concierge will be able to indicate where and when you should go. Have fun!

• ## 55 Gift Ideas Less Than $100 •

Yes, it is possible to shop in Paris on a limited budget. In addition to the inexpensive gift suggestions throughout the book, I thought you might appreciate a more precise list of some of my favorite ideas. The following items are listed from least expensive to most expensive. The recommended gift idea is listed under the boutique name, page number, and price. All of the goods mentioned here should be available in their respective shops in years to come. Prices, however, may vary due to inflation and fluctuations of the dollar. In other words, this list should simply serve as a guideline—don't follow it to your last nickel! Remember that if you buy enough to benefit from the *détaxe* in any given boutique, you will save approximately 15% more off of the following prices. You will also notice that most shops do beautiful gift packages (in their own exquisitely designed bags) for free, so even the simplest bar of soap becomes an elegant remembrance of Paris.

Pain d'Epice, p. 197; **$1**
miniature plastic dish or straw basket for playing grown-up *à la française*

Destinations, p. 95; **$2**
packet of ten colorful olive sticks topped with views of the Eiffel Tower, Sacré Coeur, Notre Dame, and more.

Soleil de Provence, p. 139; **$3**
honey-scented olive oil soap

Les Comptoirs de la Tour d'Argent, p. 283; **$9**
souvenir ashtray from the famous La Tour d'Argent restaurant

A l'Image du Grenier sur l'Eau, p. 219; **$10**
turn-of-the-century postcard of voluptuous French nudes (perfect for framing and hanging in your bathroom)

La Tuile à Loup, p. 284; **$10**
traditional, handmade ceramic bowl from the Alps

L'Esprit et le Vin, p. 293; **$12**
handy wine thermometer in wooden case for determining the best temperature for consuming wines

Guillet, p. 286; **$13**
handmade silk flower to add to your fashion accessories collection

La Chaise Longue, p. 208; **$14**
chromed demi-tasse *café* cups

Fauchon, p. 80; **$15**
crate-like box filled with six different varieties of mustard

La Maison du Champagne, p. 254; **$17**
bottle of the house's special brand of François Daumale
champagne

A. Simon, p. 180; **$18**
condiment set just like the ones you find in Paris *cafés*

Bathroom Graffiti, p. 256; **$20**
over-sized Coup de Coeur slippers in whimsical motifs

Les Contes de Thé, p. 143; **$20**
violet-colored, laquered canister filled with mango tea

Dalloyau, p. 155; **$22**
230 grams of candied chestnuts packaged in an elegant
golden carton

Territoire, p. 70; **$22**
handmade wooden fire-blower stick from Auvergne

A La Bonne Renommée, p. 233; **$23**
patchwork change purse

Boutique Paris-Musées, p. 191; **$25**
T–shirt of France's favorite cartoon character, Tin Tin

Papier Plus, p. 231; **$27**
colorful, canvas-covered *livre d'or* (guest register)

Patrick Frey, p. 109; **$29**
spice-scented Okiasis candle

Pixie & Cie, p. 118; **$29**
mini-mannequins dressed in your favorite French designer fashions

Charvet, p. 90; **$30**
three braided-knot cuff links in a parade of colors

La Maison du Chocolat, p. 46; **$30**
assortment of 400 grams of chocolate wonders in a cocoa-
brown box

Si Tu Veux, p. 203; **$30**
fairy angel costume kit for playing make believe

Hédiard, p. 79; **$33**
two-foot-long transparent bar of these famous pure fruit
jellies

L'Usine, p. 238; **$34**
sporty, crescent-shaped bag in rubbery P.V.C. from Moon Line

Ryst-Dupeyron, p. 159; **$36**
personalized bottle (70cl) of 12-year-old Armagnac

Chantal Thomass, p. 128; **$37**
sultry black net stockings graced with a classic ribbon motif

Archi-Noire, p. 291; **$38**
half a dozen cherry-tinted cordial glasses from the 30s

Jean Patou, p. 85; **$41**
spray bottle of Amour, Amour (the first perfume Jean Patou created in 1925)

Rigodon, p. 285; **$40**
bean-baggish "fat ladies" for your home or office decor

Kalinger, p. 62; **$45**
pair of forward-moving resin ear baubles

Orient Express, p. 70; **$45**
six 100% cotton dish towels emblazoned with the name Venice-Simplon Orient Express

Parfums Caron, p. 37; **$48**
tassle-trimmed, jewel-like compact for concealing their special powders

Annick Goutal, p. 87; **$48**
scented pebbles and diffuser for perfuming your interior

Creed, p. 50; **$49**
spray bottle of *Zeste Mandarine,* fragrance for men and women

Furla, p. 145; **$52**
all-leather imitation crocodile belt

Claudie Pierlot, p. 128; **$55**
cute little jersey top

Ermenegildo Zegna, p. 92; **$43**
luxurious silk *pochette* for jazzing up suit coats

Saponifère, p. 121; **$56**
one of Comptoir Sud Pacifique's exotic-smelling *eau de*

toilette for men or women, packaged in a tinny, silver flask

Diapositive, p. 184; **$57**
trendy print leggings in cotton/Lycra blend

Dîners en Ville, p. 158; **$58**
antique mother-of-pearl cheese or pâté knife

Au Nain Bleu, p. 81; **$60**
medium-sized wooden sail boat

Princesse Tam-Tam, p. 153; **$60**
teeny-bopper cotton bra and panties

Nina Ricci, p. 37 or 299; **$60**
velvet headband serendipitously dotted with NR's trademark bows

Limoges-Unic, p. 279; **$64**
handpainted Limoges porcelain boxes in the shape of vegetables and fruit

Lalique, p. 72; **$68**
mini crystal fish in a choice of six different frosty colors

Christofle, p. 72; **$72**
four sterling-silver–topped mini salt and pepper shakers from Christofle

L'Arlequin, p. 225; **$74**
pair of 19th-century Baccarat or Saint-Louis crystal champagne glasses

Gas, p. 178; **$75**
pair of charm-laden dangly earrings

Jules des Près, p. 141; **$78**
sculptural lavender bouquet

Hermès, p. 65; **$88**
classically designed silk tie for an elegant man

Wolff & Descourtis, p. 206; **$93**
paisley-print wool-challis shawl

Emilia, p. 150; **$95**
braid-trimmed leather gloves

Jean-Pierre de Castro, p. 221; **$99**
antique silverplate teapot from one of Paris's great hotels

· Shopping Glossary ·

accessoires de cheveux —hair accessories

accessoires de cuisine —kitchen accessories

accessoires de maison —home accessories

accessoires de mode —fashion accessories

achats—purchases

acheter—to buy

antiquités—antiques

arts de la table—table arts

boutique—shop or store

boutique de luxe— luxury-goods store

boutique à réduction— reduced-price store

cadeau—gift

carte de crédit—credit card

chaussures—shoes

cher, pas cher— expensive, not expensive

chèque, travellers— check, traveller's check

cosmétiques—cosmetics

couleur—color

couture—sewing (as in by-hand)

couturier—couture designer

créateur/créatrice— male or female creator/ designer

dégriffé—unlabeled designer clothing

délai—time limit

détaxe—tax refund

directeur/directrice de la boutique—shop manager

directeur/directrice du magasin—store manager

échange—exchange

espèce—cash

faire du shopping—go shopping

grand—big

grand magasin— department store

griffe—label

heures d'ouverture— store hours

linge de maison— houselinens

linge de table— tablelinens

lingerie—lingerie, underwear

livraison—delivery

magasin—store

mannequin—fashion model

marché—market

meubles—furniture

la mode—fashion

modèle—model

paiement—payment

parfum—perfume

petit—small

prix—price

prix à réduction— reduced prices, discount

produits—goods or products

produits de beauté— beauty products

produits de luxe—
luxury goods
*propriétaire de la
boutique*—boutique
owner
*propriétaire du
magasin*—store owner
les puces—the flea
market
retouche, retouches—
alteration, alterations
retoucheur/retoucheuse
—men or women who do
alterations
soldes—sales
style—style
styliste—designer
T.V.A.—V.A.T. or value
added tax

taille—size
tissu—fabric
vendre—to sell
vendeur/vendeuse—
salesman/saleswoman
vente aux enchères—
auction
vêtements d'enfant—
children's clothing
vêtements de femme—
women's clothing
vêtements d'homme—
men's clothing
vitrine—store window

For more shopping-
oriented vocabulary,
consult a phrase book.

Categories:

Antiques and Collectibles
Art Deco
Art Nouveau
Arts and Crafts
Bath and Beauty Accessories
Books
Children's Clothing and Shoes
Costume Jewelry
Eveningwear and Wedding Dresses
Eyeglasses and Sunglasses
Fabrics, Yarns, and Trims
Food and Drink Establishments
Food Items, Fine Wines, and Spirits
Furniture
Furs
Hair Accessories
Hats

Home Accessories and Table Arts
House Linens
Interior Decoration
Jewelry and Watches
Kitchen Supplies
Large-Sized Women's Fashions
Leather Fashions
Leather Goods
Lingerie, Hosiery, Sleepwear, and Bathwear
Maternity Clothes
Men's Accessories
Men's Designer Fashions and Accessories
Men's Fashions
Men's Shoes
Miscellaneous Gift Ideas
Music
Perfumes, Beauty Products, and Cosmetics
Pharmacies
Silk Flowers
Smoking Articles and Accessories
Sports Equipment and Clothing
Stationery and Desk Accessories
Sweaters and Knits
Swimwear and Dancewear
Toys, Games, Dolls, and Stuffed Animals
Women's Accessories
Women's and Men's Luxury Boutique Fashions and Accessories
Women's and Men's Shirts
Women's Bags
Women's Designer Fashions and Accessories
Women's Fashions
Women's Shoes
Writing Instruments

Quick Reference
· According to Type of Item ·

Letter codes in parentheses show other districts where stores have branches. Boutique branches, discount shops and other stores from "More Shopping" are listed under the closest district or under the heading "Other District." Page numbers indicate where descriptions of stores appear.

Dollar signs signal the approximate costliness of the boutiques and establishments in comparison to each other. The frame of reference is Paris, not the U.S., which means that a boutique listed as expensive here could possibly be considered very expensive according to your standards.

Key:

RB—Right Bank (includes the 1er, 2e, 8e, 9e & 17e *arrondissements*)

LB—Left Bank (includes the 5e, 6e & 7e *arrondissements*)

V/H—Place des Victoires and Les Halles (includes the 1er & 2e *arrondissements*)

P—Passages (includes the 1er, 2e & 9e *arrondissements*)

M—Marais (includes the 3e & 4e *arrondissements*)

B—Bastille (includes the 11e *arrondissement*)

16th—The Sixteenth (includes the 16e *arrondissement*)

D—Discount Shopping
O—Other District

$$$$—very expensive
$$$—expensive
$$—moderate
$—inexpensive

Antiques and Collectibles

(See also Antiques and The Markets chapters.)

Right Bank

Au Bain Marie	pp. 70–71	$$$$
Rarissime	p. 98	$$$

Left Bank

Beauté Divine	p. 115	$$$
Brocante Store	p. 108	$$$
Dîners en Ville	p. 158	$$$
Boutique Go	p. 120	$$
Haga	p. 153	$$$$
La Mine d'Argent	p. 158	$$

Passages

Robert Capia	p. 209	$$
Galerie 34	p. 196	$$
La France Ancienne	p. 200	$
Librarie D.F. Jousseaume	p. 204	$
Didier Ludot	p. 212	$$
Photo Verdeau	p. 199	$$
La Vie de Château	p. 212	$$$

Marais

l'Arlequin	p. 225	$$
La Calinière	p. 230	$$
Jean-Pierre de Castro	p. 221	$
Carnavalette	p. 225	$$
A l'Image du Grenier sur l'Eau	p. 219	$
Meubles Peints	p. 229	$$
R.V. des Dames Curieuses	p. 272	$$
Térébenthine	(O, p. 272)	$$

Bastille

Dolce Vita	p. 244	$$
Verreglass	p. 244	$$

The Sixteenth

Christian Benais	(O, p. 292)	$$$$

Other District

Archi-Noire	p. 291	$$
Réciproque	p. 252	$$

Art Deco

(See also Antiques and Collectibles.)

Right Bank

L'Heure Bleue	p. 98	$$$

Left Bank

Beauté Divine	p. 115	$$$
Boutique Go	p. 120	$$

Marais

La Calinière	p. 230	$$

Bastille

En d'Autres Thermes	p. 243	$$$
Verreglass	p. 244	$$

Other District

Archi-Noire	p. 291	$$

Art Nouveau

Left Bank

Beauté Divine	p. 115	$$$
Boutique Go	p. 120	$$

Marais

La Calinière	p. 230	$$

Bastille

Verreglass	p. 244	$$

Arts and Crafts

(See also Antiques and Collectibles; Home Accessories and Table Arts.)

Right Bank

Artcurial	p. 58	$$$$
Gault	p. 99	$$

Left Bank
Galerie d'Amon	p. 115	$$$
La Tuile à Loup	(O, p. 284)	$$

Place des Victoires and Les Halles
Boutique Paris-Musées	p. 191	$

Passages
Lavrut	p. 212	$$

Marais
Artisflora	p. 230	$$$

Bath and Beauty Accessories

(See also Home Accessories and Table Arts.)

Left Bank
Beauté Divine	p. 115	$$$
Saponifère	p. 121 (V/H)	$$

Books

Right Bank
Artcurial	p. 58	$$$$
Au Bain Marie	p. 70	$$$
Brentano's	p. 95	$$
Le Drugstore	p. 57 (LB)	$$$
FNAC	(LB, V/H; O, p. 307)	$
Galignani	p. 99	$$$
William H. Smith	p. 98	$$
Virgin Megastore	(O, p. 308)	$

Left Bank
La Chambre Claire	p. 114	$$$$
Chantelivre	p. 144	$$
Le Drugstore	(RB, p. 57)	$$$
La Hune	p. 102	$$
FNAC	(RB, V/H; O, p. 307)	$

Place des Victoires and Les Halles

Boutique		
Paris-Musées	p. 191	$$
FNAC	(RB, LB; O, p. 307)	$

Passages

Cinédoc	p. 198	$
Le Grenier à Livres	p. 199	$
Librairie D.F.		
Jousseaume	p. 204	$

Marais

Casta Diva	p. 231	$$

Children's Clothing and Shoes

Right Bank

Bonpoint	p. 74 (LB)	$$$$
Catimini Babymini	(M, p. 224)	$$$
Christian Dior	p. 36	$$$$
Nina Ricci	p. 37	$$$$
D. Porthault	p. 35	$$$$
Elizabeth de	(LB; V/H, p.	
Senneville	189)	$$

Left Bank

Blanc Bleu	p. 136	$
Bonpoint	p. 74 (RB)	$$$$
Chipie	p. 124 (V/H, 16th)	$$
Kenzo	(V/H, p. 49)	$$$
Miki House	p. 124 (V/H)	$$$$
Naj-Oleari	p. 125 (16th)	$$
Petit Faune	p. 107	$$$
Pom d'Api	p. 135 (V/H, 16th)	$$
Elizabeth de	(RB; V/H, p.	
Senneville	189)	$$
Sonia Rykiel	p. 60	$$$
Tartine et Chocolat	p. 131	$$$

Place des Victoires and Les Halles

Absorba	p. 174	$
Agnès B.	p. 114	$$

Chatmotomatic	p. 168	$$$$
Chipie	(LB, p. 124; 16th)	$$
Kenzo	p. 170 (LB)	$$$
Miki House	(LB, p. 124)	$$$$
Naf Naf	p. 184 (16th)	$
Pom d'Api	(LB, p. 135; 16th)	$$
Elizabeth de Senneville	p. 189 (RB, LB)	$$

Marais

Catimini Babymini	p. 224 (RB)	$$$

The Sixteenth

Bonnichon	p. 248 (LB)	$$$$
La Châtelaine	(O, p. 291)	$$$$
Chipie	(LB, p. 124; V/H)	$$
Creeks	p. 252	$
Jacadi	p. 255	$
Naf Naf	(V/H, p. 184)	$
Naj-Oleari	(LB, p. 125)	$$
Petit Bateau	p. 251	$$$
Pom d'Api	(LB, p. 135; V/H)	$$

Discount

Cacharel Stock	p. 301	$
Dorotennis Stock	p. 301	$
Stock 2	p. 302	$

Costume Jewelry

(See also Women's Accessories; Women's Designer Fashions and Accessories.)

Right Bank

Kalinger	p. 62	$$$
Ken Lane	p. 72	$$
Maupiou Accessoires	p. 93	$$$

Left Bank

Fabrice	p. 117	$$$

Isadora	p. 107	$$$
Naj-Oleari	p. 125 (16th)	$
Néréides	p. 136	$$$
L'Objet Trouvé	(O, p. 284)	$$$
Utility-Bibi	p. 136	$$$

Place des Victoires and Les Halles

La Droguerie	p. 185	$
Gas	p. 178	$$$

Marais

Apparence	p. 216	$$
Fugit Amor	p. 222	$$
Zandoli	p. 231	$$

Bastille

Duelle	p. 241	$$
Nota Bene	p. 240	$$$

The Sixteenth

Franck et Fils	p. 260	$$
Naj-Oleari	(LB, p. 125)	$

Other District

Archi-Noire	p. 291	$$

Eveningwear and Wedding Dresses

(See also Women's Fashions; Women's Designer Fashions and Accessories.)

Right Bank

Loris Azzaro	p. 61	$$$$

Left Bank

Clémentine	p. 117	$$$
Vicky Tiel	p. 109	$$$

Marais

Fanny Liautard	p. 227	$$

Eyeglasses and Sunglasses

(See also Men's Designer Fashions and Accessories; Women's Designer Fashions and Accessories.)

Right Bank
| Le Drugstore | p. 57 (LB) | $$$ |
| Michel Swiss | p. 92 | $$ |

Left Bank
| Le Drugstore | (RB, p. 57) | $$$ |
| Et Vous | p. 130 (M) | $$ |

Place des Victoires and Les Halles
| Interface | p. 181 | $$$ |

Marais
| Alain Mikli | p. 215 | $$$$ |
| Et Vous | (LB, p. 130) | $$ |

Bastille
| Optic Bastille | p. 240 | $$$ |

Fabrics, Yarns, and Trims

(See also Interior Decoration.)

Place des Victoires and Les Halles
| La Droguerie | p. 185 | $ |

Passages
| Wolff & Descourtis | p. 206 | $ |

Discount Shopping
| Jean-Louis Scherrer | p. 300 | $$ |

Food and Drink Establishments

Right Bank
Angelina's	p. 99	$$$
Harry's Bar	p. 94	$$
Ladurée	p. 74	$$$
Le Peny	p. 77	$$
Relais du Plaza	p. 31	$$$
Hôtel Ritz	p. 32	$$$$
Le Rubis	p. 96	$

Left Bank
| Café de Flore | p. 101 | $$ |
| Le Cherche-Midi | p. 142 | $$$ |

Christian Constant	p. 161	$$
Concertea	p. 162	$
Les Deux Magots	p. 101	$$
Les Nuits des Thés	p. 112	$$$
San Francisco		
Muffin Co.	p. 146	$
Au Sauvignon	p. 148	$
La Villa	p. 108	$$$

Place des Victoires and Les Halles

Café Beaubourg	p. 166	$$
Café Costes	p. 165	$$
Joe Allen	p. 165	$$
Lina's Sandwich	p. 176	$
Au Pére Tranquille	p. 165	$$
Au Pied de		
Cochon	p. 165	$$$
Ventilo	p. 182	$$
Willi's Wine Bar	p. 168	$$$

Passages

Le Grand Colbert	p. 207	$$$
A Priori Thé	p. 205	$$
La Tour des		
Délices	p. 196	$

Marais

Les Bourgeoises	p. 222	$$
Ma Bourgogne	p. 226	$$
Les Enfants Gâtés	p. 220	$
Jo Goldenberg	p. 217	$$$
Le Loir dans la		
Théière	p. 215	$
Marais Plus	p. 220	$
Mariage Frères	p. 232	$$$

Bastille

Bofinger	p. 239	$$$
Chez Paul	p. 245	$$
Pause Café	p. 244	$
La Rotonde	p. 239	$

The Sixteenth

Brasserie Stella	p. 249	$$$
Café Mexico	p. 249	$$$$
L'Entrepôt	p. 261	$

Bastille
Brûlerie Daval   p. 242 $

The Sixteenth
Hédiard   (RB, p. 79;
                                  LB) $$$$
La Maison du
  Champagne   p. 254 $$$

Furniture

Right Bank
Jean-Charles de
  Castelbajac   p. 96 $$$$
L'Heure Bleue   p. 98 $$$

Left Bank
Ségriès   p. 116 $$

Place des Victoires and Les Halles
En Attendant les
  Barbares   p. 175 $$$$

Marais
Meubles Peints   p. 227 $$

Bastille
En d'Autres
  Thermes   p. 243 $$$
Dolce Vita   p. 244 $$

The Sixteenth
Bonnichon   p. 248 $$$$

Furs

(See also Women's Fashions; Women's Designer Fashions
and Accessories.)

Right Bank
Christian Dior   p. 36 $$$$
Revillon   (LB, p. 145) $$$$
Nina Ricci   p. 37 $$$$

Left Bank
Revillon   p. 145 (RB) $$$$

Hair Accessories

(See also Hats; Women's Designer Fashions and Accessories.)

Right Bank
Alexandre de Paris   p. 83 $$$$
Carita   p. 69 $$$$

Hats

(See also Women's Designer Fashions and Accessories.)

Right Bank
Philippe Model   p. 96 $$$$
Motsch   p. 48 $$$

Left Bank
A la Bonne
    Renommé   (M, p. 231) $$$

Place des Victoires and Les Halles
Marie Mercié   p. 183 $$$

Marais
A la Bonne
    Renommée   p. 231 (LB) $$$
Olivier Chanan   p. 216 $$$$

Home Accessories and Table Arts

(See also Miscellaneous Gift Ideas; Antiques and Collectibles; Paradise Street chapter.)

Right Bank
Baccarat   p. 78 $$$
Au Bain Marie   p. 70 $$$
Bernardaud   p. 73 $$$
Agnès Comar   p. 50 $$$
Boutique Crillon   p. 71 $$$
Cristalleries de
    Saint-Louis   p. 73 $$$
Daum   p. 91 $$$
Christian Dior   p. 36 $$$
L'Esprit et le Vin   (O, p. 293) $

Gien	(O, p. 288)	$$
Hermès	p. 65	$$$
Kalinger	p. 62	$$$
Kenzo	p. 170 (LB)	$$$
Lalique	p. 72	$$$
Odiot	p. 77	$$$$
Orient Express	p. 70	$$
Peter	(O, p. 289)	$$$$
Paloma Picasso	p. 91	$$$$
Puiforcat	p. 57	$$$$
Nina Ricci	p. 37	$$$
Emilio Robba	(P, p. 205)	$$
Rochas	p. 48	$$$
Territoire	p. 70	$
Villeroy & Boch	p. 75	$$

Left Bank

A la Bonne Renommée	(M, p. 231)	$$
Manuel Canovas	p. 110	$$$
Marie-Pierre Boitard	(O, p. 285)	$$$
Les Comptoirs de la Tour d'Argent	p. 283	$$$
Les Contes de Thé	p. 143	$
Dîners en Ville	p. 158	$$$
Patrick Frey	p. 109 (V/H)	$$$
Galerie d'Amon	p. 115	$$$
Boutique Go	p. 120	$$
Laure Japy	p. 161	$$$
Jule des Prés	p. 141 (M)	$$$
Geneviève Lethu	p. 131 (V/H, RB)	$
Kenzo	(V/H, p. 170: RB)	$$$
La Mine d'Argent	p. 158	$$
Naj-Oleari	p. 125 (16th)	$$
L'Objet Trouvé	(O, p. 284)	$$
La Tuile à Loup	(O, p. 284)	$$
Ségriès	p. 116	$$$
Souleiado	p. 118 (16th)	$$$
Venini	p. 158	$$$

Place des Victoires and Les Halles

En Attendant les Barbares	p. 175	$$$
Gérard Danton	p. 166	$$$
Malicorne	p. 167	$$$
Patrick Frey	p. 109 (LB)	$$$
A. Simon	p. 180	$

Passages

Le Bonheur des Dames	p. 199	$
Thomas Boog	p. 197	$$$$
Casa Lopez	p. 204 (LB, 16th)	$$
Pain d'Epice	p. 196	$
Emilio Robba	p. 205 (RB)	$$
La Vie de Château	p. 212	$$$

Marais

L'Arlequin	p. 225	$$
A la Bonne Renommée	p. 231 (LB)	$$
Jean-Pierre de Castro	p. 221	$
Chevignon Trading Post	p. 224	$$$
Jule des Prés	(LB, p. 141)	$$$
Mariage Frères	p. 232	$$

Bastille

En d'Autres Thermes	p. 243	$$$
Axis	p. 245 (LB)	$$
Dolce Vita	p. 244	$$
L'Usine	p. 238	$
Verreglass	p. 244	$$

The Sixteenth

Naj-Oleari	(LB, p. 125)	$$
Souleiado	(LB, p. 118)	$$$

House Linens

Right Bank

Au Bain Marie	p. 70	$$$

Agnès Comar	p. 50	$$$$
Christian Dior	p. 36	$$$$
Frette	p. 63	$$$$
Hermès	p. 65	$$$$
Noël	p. 39	$$$$
D. Porthault	p. 35	$$$$
Nina Ricci	p. 37	$$$$

Left Bank

Manuel Canovas	p. 110	$$$$
Les Comptoirs de la Tour d'Argent	(O, p. 283)	$$$
Descamps	p. 133 (16th)	$$
Dîners en Ville	p. 158	$$$
Patrick Frey	p. 109 (V/H)	$$$
Boutique Go	p. 120	$$
Laure Japy	p. 161	$$$
Saponifère	p. 121 (V/H)	$$
Souleiado	p. 118 (16th)	$$$

Place des Victoires and Les Halles

| Gérard Danton | p. 166 | $$$ |
| Patrick Frey | (LB, p. 109) | $$$ |

The Sixteenth

Christian Benais	(O, p. 292)	$$$$
Descamps	(LB, p. 133)	$$
Souleiado	(LB, p. 118)	$$$

Interior Decoration

Right Bank

| Manuel Canovas | (LB, p. 110) | $$$$ |
| Tassinari et Chatel | p. 94 | $$$$ |

Left Bank

Laura Ashley	(RB, p. 82)	$$$
Manuel Canovas	p. 110	$$$$
Etamine	p. 160	$$$$
Patrick Frey	p. 109	$$$$
Casa Lopez	(P, p. 204; 16th)	$$
Naj-Oleari	p. 125	$$
Souleiado	p. 118 (16th)	$$$

Marais
Maison Brocard   (O, p. 282) $$$$

The Sixteenth
Casa Lopez   (P, p. 204;
                              LB) $$
Christian Benais   (O, p. 292) $$$$
Naj-Oleari   (LB, p. 125) $$
Souleiado   (LB, p. 118) $$$

Passages
Casa Lopez   p. 204 (LB,
                              16th) $$

Discount Shopping
Coolman   p. 293 $$

Other District
Maryvonne de
  Follin   p. 296 $$$

Fine Jewelry and Watches

(Refer also to big-name jewelers mentioned in the Right
Bank promenade introduction.)

Right Bank
Chanel   p. 85 $$$$
Christofle   p. 72 (LB,
                              16th) $$$
Hermès   p. 65 $$$$
L'Heure Bleue   p. 98 $$$
Pascal Morabito   p. 34 $$$$

Left Bank
Christofle   (RB, p. 72;
                              16th) $$$
Fabrice   p. 123 $$$

The Sixteenth
Christofle   (RB, p. 72;
                              LB) $$$

Other District
Archi-Noire   p. 291 $$

Kitchen Supplies

(See also Home Accessories and Table Arts.)

Right Bank
Culinarion	(LB, p. 132)	$$
Geneviève Lethu	(LB, p. 131; V/H)	$$

Left Bank
Culinarion	p. 132 (RB)	$$
Geneviève Lethu	(p. 131 RB, V/H)	$$

Place des Victoires and Les Halles
Dehillerin	p. 187	$$
Geneviève Lethu	(LB, p. 131; RB)	$$
A. Simon	p. 180	$$

Large-Sized Women's Fashions

Left Bank
Marina Rinaldi	p. 133	$$$

Leather Fashions

(See also Men's Fashions; Women's Fashions; Men's Designer Fashions and Accessories; Women's Designer Fashions and Accessories.)

Right Bank
Revillon	(LB, p. 145)	$$$$

Left Bank
Chevignon	p. 224 (V/H, M 16th)	$$$
Michel Klein	p. 107	$$$
Mac Douglas	p. 144 (V/H, 16th)	$$$
Revillon	p. 145 (RB)	$$$$

Place des Victoires and Les Halles
Chevignon	(LB, p. 171; M 16th)	$$$

Mac Douglas	(LB, p. 144;	
	16th)	$$$
Marais Chevignon	(LB, p. 226;	
	V/H, 16th	$$$

The Sixteenth
Chevignon	(LB, p. 137;	
	V/H, M)	$$$
Mac Douglas	(LB, p. 144;	
	V/H)	$$$

Leather Goods

(Including canvas, rubber, nylon, and faux-leather bags, luggage, and personal accessories; See also Men's Designer Fashions and Accessories; Women's Designer Fashions and Accessories.)

Right Bank
La Bagagerie	p. 69 (LB,	
	16th)	$$
Boutique Crillon	p. 71	$$$
Delvaux	p. 75	$$$$
Goyard	p. 84	$$$$
Gucci	p. 69	$$$$
Hermès	p. 65	$$$$
Didier Lamarthe	p. 84 (LB)	$$$
Lancel	p. 56 (LB)	$$
Loewe	p. 38	$$$$
Mandarina Duck	(LB, p. 113)	$$
Pascal Morabito	p. 63	$$$$
Trussardi	p. 67	$$$$
Louis Vuitton	p. 40	$$$$

Left Bank
La Bagagerie	(RB, p. 69;	
	16th)	$$
Il Bisonte	p. 141 (P)	$$$
Lancel	(RB, p. 56)	$$
Mac Douglas	p. 144 (V/H,	
	16th)	$$$
Mandarina Duck	p. 113 (RB)	$$
Prada	p. 150	$$$$
Soco	p. 122 (V/H)	$$$
Upla	p. 152 (V/H,	
	16th)	$$$

Place des Victoires and Les Halles

Bold	p. 179	$$$
Mac Douglas	(LB, p. 144; 16th)	$$$
Jean-Louis Imbert	p. 178	$$$
Soco	p. 122 (LB)	$$$
Upla	(LB, p. 152; 16th)	$$$

Passages

Il Bisonte	(LB, p. 141)	$$$

Bastille

L'Usine	p. 238	$

The Sixteenth

La Bagagerie	(RB, p. 69; LB)	$$
Bottega Veneta	p. 250	$$$$
Hervé Chapelier	p. 255 (RB)	$$
Chapitre 3	p. 259	$$
Mac Douglas	(LB, p. 144; V/H)	$$$

Lingerie, Hosiery, Sleepwear, and Bathwear

(See also Men's Designer Fashions and Accessories; Women's Designer Fashions and Accessories)

Right Bank

Boutique Crillon	p. 71	$$$
Christian Dior	p. 37	$$$$
S.T. Dupont	p. 40	$$$$
Frette	p. 63	$$$$
Hermès	p. 65	$$$$
Noël	p. 39	$$$$
Anita Oggioni	p. 41 (LB)	$$$
Orient Express	p. 70	$$$
D. Porthault	p. 35	$$$$
Nina Ricci	p. 37	$$$$
Rochas	p. 48	$$$$
Chantal Thomass	(LB, p. 125)	$$$

Left Bank

Kashiyama	p. 104	$$$
Anita Oggioni	(RB, p. 41)	$$$

Princesse Tam-Tam	p. 153	$
Sabbia Rosa	p. 148	$$$$
Saponifère	p. 121	$$
Souleiado	p. 118 (16th)	$$$
Chantal Thomass	p. 126 (RB)	$$$

Marais

Fanny Liautard	p. 227	$$$

The Sixteenth

Franck et Fils	p. 260	$$
Souleiado	(LB, p. 118)	$$$

Maternity Clothes

Right Bank

Bonpoint	p. 74 (LB)	$$$$

Left Bank

Bonpoint	(RB, p. 74)	$$$$
Formes	p. 126 (V/H)	$
Tartine et Chocolat	p. 131	$$$

Place des Victoires and Les Halles

Formes	(LB, p. 126)	$

Men's Accessories

(See also Men's Designer Fashions and Accessories)

Right Bank

Chanel	p. 85	$$$$
Charvet	p. 90	$$$
Creed	p. 50	$$$
Dunhill	p. 92	$$$
S.T. Dupont	p. 40	$$$$
Il Pour l'Homme	p. 84 (LB, M)	$$
Marcel Lassance	(LB, p. 127)	$$$
Jean Patou	p. 85	$$$
Ermenegildo Zegna	p. 91	$$$$

Left Bank

Il Pour l'Homme	(RB, p. 84 M)	$$
Marcel Lassance	p. 127 (RB)	$$$
Naj-Oleari	p. 125 (16th)	$
Souleiado	p. 118 (16th)	$$

Marais

Il Pour l'Homme	(RB, p. 84;	
	LB)	$$

The Sixteenth

John Demersay	p. 253	$$
Franck et Fils	p. 260	$$
Lemaire	p. 251	$$$
Naj-Oleari	(LB, p. 125)	$
Souleiado	(LB, p. 118)	$$

Men's Designer Fashions and Accessories

Right Bank

Giorgio Armani	p. 89	$$$$
Balenciaga	p. 49	$$$$
Pierre Balmain	p. 44	$$$$
Pierre Cardin	p. 62	$$$$
Carven	p. 56	$$$
Jean-Charles de Castelbajac	p. 97 (V/H)	$$$
Cerruti 1881	p. 76	$$$$
Courrèges	p. 44 (LB, 16th)	$$$$
Christian Dior	p. 36	$$$$
Gianfranco Ferre Homme	p. 47	$$$$
Daniel Hechter	(LB, p. 103; 16th)	$$
Kenzo	(LB; V/H, p. 170)	$$$
Lanvin	p. 66	$$$$
Ted Lapidus	p. 43	$$$$
Thierry Mugler	p. 39–40	$$$$
Bernard Perris	p. 45	$$$$
Ricci Club	p. 41	$$$$
Rochas	p. 43, 48	$$$$
Francesco Smalto	p. 45	$$$$
Trussardi	p. 67	$$$$
Emanuel Ungaro	p. 34	$$$$
Valentino	p. 35	$$$$

Left Bank

Agnès B.	(V/H, p. 114)	$$

Courrèges	(RB, p. 44; 16th)	$$$$
Daniel Hechter	p. 103 (RB, 16th)	$$
Kenzo	(RB; V/H, p. 49)	$$$
Missoni	p. 162	$$$
Paco Rabanne	p. 142	$$$$
Sonia Rykiel Homme	p. 106	$$$
Yves Saint Laurent	p. 120 (RB)	$$$$
Junko Shimada	p. 105	$$
Olivier Strelli	p. 123 (V/H)	$$$
Yohji Yamamoto	(V/H, p. 149)	$$$$

Place des Victoires and Les Halles

Agnès B.	p. 114 (LB)	$$
Jean-Charles de Castelbajac	(RB, p. 96)	$$$
Comme des Garçons	p. 179	$$$
Adolfo Dominguez	p. 169	$$$
Junior Gaultier	p. 185	$$
Marithé & François Girbaud	p. 180	$$$
Kenzo	p. 171 (RB, LB)	$$$
Olivier Strelli	(LB, p. 123)	$$$
Yohji Yamamoto	p. 149 (LB)	$$$$

Passages

Dépôt des Grandes Marques	(D, p. 298)	$$
Jean-Paul Gaultier	p. 202	$$$

The Sixteenth

Courrèges	(RB, p. 44; LB)	$$$$
Daniel Hechter	(RB, p. 103; LB, 16th)	$$
Réciproque	p. 252	$$

Discount Shopping

Biderman	p. 297	$$
Dépôt des Grandes Marques	p. 298 (P)	$$

Réciproque	p. 252 (16th)	$$
Stock 2	p. 302	$

Men's Fashions

(See also Men's Designer Fashions and Accessories; Women's and Men's Luxury Boutique Fashions and Accessories.)

Right Bank

Cacharel	(V/H, p. 171)	$$
Charvet	p. 90	$$$$
Creed	p. 50	$$$$
S.T. Dupont	p. 40	$$$$
Façonnable	p. 76	$$$$
Marcel Lassance	(LB, p. 127)	$$$$
Rodier	p. 300	$$
Ermenegildo Zegna	p. 91	$$$$

Left Bank

Autour du Monde	(M, p. 111)	$$
Blanc Bleu	p. 137 (V/H, M)	$
Chevignon	p. 137 (V/H, M, 16th)	$$$
Chipie	p. 124 (V/H, 16th)	$$
Façonnable	(RB, p. 76)	$$$$
Le Garage	(M, p. 133)	$$$
Marcel Lassance	p. 127 (RB)	$$$$
Mac Douglas	p. 144 (16th)	$$$
Naf Naf	(V/H, p. 112; 16th)	$
Souleiado	p. 118 (16th)	$$$
Et Vous	p. 130 (M)	$$

Place des Victoires and Les Halles

Blanc Bleu	(LB, p. 137; M)	$
Cacharel	p. 171 (RB)	$$
Chevignon	(LB, p. 137; M, 16th)	$$$
Chipie	(LB, p. 124; 16th)	$$

Mac Douglas	(LB, p. 144; 16th)	$$$
Marlboro Classics	p. 173 (16th)	$$$
Naf Naf	p. 112 (LB, 16th)	$
Tous les Caleçons	p. 187	$
Ventilo	p. 182	$$

Passages

| Ixi : z | p. 203 | $$$ |

Marais

Autour du Monde	p. 222 (LB)	$$
Blanc Bleu	(LB, p. 136; V/H)	$
Chevignon	(LB, p. 137; V/H, 16th)	$$$
Le Garage	p. 133 (LB)	$$$
Et Vous	(LB, p. 130)	$$

Bastille

| Comptoir du Desert | p. 241 | $ |
| Pastille | p. 239 | $$ |

The Sixteenth

Chevignon	(LB, p. 137; V/H, M)	$$$
Chipie	(LB, p. 124; V/H)	$$
Creeks	p. 252	$
Curling	p. 255	$$
John Demersay	p. 253	$$
Mac Douglas	(LB, p. 144; M, V/H)	$$$
Hemisphères	p. 257	$$$
Marlboro Classics	(V/H, p. 173)	$$$
Naf Naf	(LB; V/H, p. 184)	$
Renoma	p. 253	$$$
Souleiado	(LB, p. 118)	$$$

Men's Shoes

(See also Men's Fashions; Men's Designer Fashions and Accessories.)

Right Bank
Charles Jourdan	p. 68 (LB)	$$$
Sidonie Larizzi	p. 52	$$$$
John Lobb	p. 46	$$$$
Walter Steiger	p. 59 (LB)	$$$$
J.M. Weston	(LB, p. 130; 16th)	$$$$

Left Bank
Aka	p. 146	$$$
Arche	(V/H, p. 192)	$$
Chipie	p. 124 (V/H, 16th)	$$
Church	p. 146 (V/H)	$$$
J. Fenestrier	p. 142	$$$
Free Lance	p. 135 (V/H)	$$
Charles Jourdan	(RB, p. 68)	$$$
Stéphane Kélian	p. 152 (V/H, M)	$$$
Tokio Kumagaï	p. 156 (V/H)	$$$
Walter Steiger	(RB, p. 59)	$$$$
J.M. Weston	p. 130 (RB, 16th)	$$$$

Place des Victoires and Les Halles
Arche	p. 194 (LB)	$$
Chipie	(LB, p. 124; 16th)	$$
Church	(LB, p. 148)	$$$$
Free Lance	(LB, p. 135)	$$$
Stéphane Kélian	(LB, p. 150; M)	$$$
Tokio Kumagaï	(LB, p. 154)	$$$

Marais
Casa Costanza	p. 223	$$
Stéphane Kélian	(LB, p. 150; V/H)	$$$

Bastille
Comptoir du Desert	p. 241	$

The Sixteenth
Chipie	(LB, p. 124; V/H)	$$

J.M. Weston	(LB, p. 130; RB)	$$$$

Miscellaneous Gift Ideas

Right Bank

L'Artisan Parfumeur	(LB, p. 157)	$$
Boutique Crillon	p. 71	$$$
Destinations	p. 95	$
L'Esprit et le Vin	(O, p. 293)	$
Il Pour l'Homme	p. 84 (LB, M)	$$
Orient Express	p. 70	$$
Territoire	p. 70	$$

Left Bank

L'Artisan Parfumeur	p. 157 (RB)	$$
Axis	(B, p. 245)	$$
Manuel Canovas	p. 110	$$$$
La Chaise Longue	(P, p. 209; M)	$
Au Chat Dormant	p. 140	$
Les Comptoirs de la Tour d'Argent	p. (O, p. 283)	$$$
Les Contes de Thé	p. 143	$$
Diptyque	(O, p. 283)	$$
Jeanne Do	p. 111	$$
Patrick Frey	p. 109 (V/H)	$$$
Il Pour l'Homme	(RB, p. 84; M)	$$
Jule des Prés	p. 141 (M)	$$$
Naj-Oleari	p. 125 (16th)	$$
L'Objet Trouvé	(O, p. 284)	$$
Pixi et Cie	p. 118	$$
Rigodon	(O, p. 285)	$$$
Soleil de Provence	p. 139	$
Souleiado	p. 118 (16th)	$$$
La Tuile à Loup	(O, p. 284)	$$

Place des Victoires and Les Halles

Boutiques Paris-Musées	p. 191	$
La Droguerie	p. 185	$
Duthilleul & Minart	p. 188	$
Patrick Frey	(LB, p. 109)	$$$
A. Simon	p. 180	$$

Passages

La Bôite à Joujoux	p. 198	$
Le Bonheur des Dames	p. 198	$
Robert Capia	p. 209	$$$
La Chaise Longue	p. 209 (LB, M)	$
Cinédoc	p. 198	$
La France Ancienne	p. 200	$
Alexis Lahellek	p. 210	$$$
Pain d'Epice	p. 198	$

Marais

Calligrane	p. 235	$$$
Carnavalette	p. 225	$$
La Chaise Longue	(P, p. 209; LB)	$
Il Pour l'Homme	(RB, p. 84 LB)	$$
A l'Image du Grenier sur l'Eau	p. 219	$
Melodies Graphiques	p. 235	$$$
A l'Olivier	p. 236	$
Papier Plus	p. 234	$$$
Jule des Prés	(LB, p. 141)	$$$

Bastille

Axis	p. 245 (LB)	$$
L'Usine	p. 238	$

The Sixteenth

Bathroom Graffiti	p. 256	$
l'Entrepôt	p. 261	$
Naj-Oleari	(LB, p. 125)	$$
Sephora	p. 262	$$
Souleiado	(LB, p. 118)	$$$

Music

Right Bank

Le Drugstore	p. 57 (LB)	$$$
FNAC	(LB, V/H, B; O, p. 307)	$$

Virgin Megastore	(O, p. 308)	$$

Left Bank

Chantelivre	p. 144	$$
Le Drugstore	(RB, p. 57)	$$$
FNAC	(RB, V/H, B; O, p. 307)	$$

Place des Victoires and Les Halles

FNAC	p. 307 (RB, LB, B)	$$

Marais

Casta Diva	p. 231	$$

Bastille

Bonus Beat	p. 243	$$$
FNAC	p. 307 (RB, V/H, LB)	$$

Perfumes, Beauty Products and Cosmetics

(All of the big names also sell their own fragrances and cosmetics in their boutiques.)

Right Bank

L'Artisan Parfumeur	(LB, p. 157)	$$$
Carita	p. 69	$$$$
Catherine	p. 88	$$
Creed	p. 50	$$$
Le Drugstore	p. 57 (LB)	$$$$
Annick Goutal	p. 87 (LB)	$$$
Guerlain	p. 89 (LB, 16th)	$$$$
Lancôme	p. 64	$$$$
Anne Parée	(O, p. 281)	$$
Jean Patou	p. 85	$$$$
Paloma Picasso	p. 91	$$$$
Michel Swiss	p. 92	$$$

Left Bank

L'Artisan Parfumeur	p. 157 (RB)	$$$
Diptyque	(O, p. 283)	$$
Le Drugstore	(RB, p. 57)	$$$$

Annick Goutal	(RB, p. 87)	$$$
Guerlain	(RB, p. 89, 16th)	$$$$
La Pharmacie Piquet	(O, p. 286)	$
Saponifère	p. 121 (V/H)	$$$
Soleil de Provence	p. 139	$

The Sixteenth

P. de Nicolaï	(O, p. 292)	$$$$
Guerlain	(RB, p. 89; LB)	$$$$
Sephora	p. 262	$$$

Passages

Le Bonheur des Dames	p. 198	$$
Pain d'Epice	p. 198	$$

Pharmacies

Right Bank

Le Drugstore	p. 57 (LB)	$$$

Left Bank

Le Drugstore	(RB, p. 57)	$$$
La Pharmacie Piquet	(O, p. 286)	$$

Silk Flowers

(see also Women's Designer Fashions and Accessories.)

Right Bank

Emilio Robba	p. 205	$$
Trousselier	(O, p. 290)	$$$$

Left Bank

Guillet	(O, p. 286)	$$$

Passages

Emilio Robba	p. 205	$$

Smoking Articles and Accessories

Right Bank
Le Drugstore   p. 57 (LB) $$$
Dunhill   p. 92 $$$$
S.T. Dupont   p. 40 $$$$

Left Bank
Le Drugstore   (RB, p. 57)

The Sixteenth
Lemaire   p. 251 $$$

Sports Equipment and Clothing

(See also Women's and Men's Fashions; Women's Designer Fashions and Accessories, Men's Designer Fashions and Accessories.)

Right Bank
Go Sport   p. 307 (LB,
                      V/H) $$$

Left Bank
Go Sport   p. 307 (RB,
                      V/H) $$$

Place des Victoires and Les Halles
Go Sport   p. 307 (RB,
                      LB) $$$

Discount Shopping
Dorotennis Stock   p. 301 $
Stock 2   p. 302 $

Stationery and Desk Accessories

Right Bank
Cassegrain   p. 81 (LB) $$$$

Left Bank
Cassegrain   (RB, p. 81) $$$$
Naj-Oleari   p. 125 (16th) $$
Souleiado   p. 118 (16th) $$$

Passages

Lavrut	p. 212	$$
Stern	p. 201	$$$$

Marais

Calligrane	p. 235	$$$
Mélodies Graphiques	p. 234	$$$
Papier Plus	p. 234	$$$

The Sixteenth

Naj-Oleari	(LB, p. 125)	$$
Souleiado	(LB, p. 118)	$$$

Sweaters and Knits

(See also Women's Fashions; Men's Fashions; Women's Designer Fashions and Accessories; Men's Designer Fashions and Accessories.)

Right Bank

Hervé Chapelier	(16th, p. 255)	$$$
Hobbs	p. 52	$$$$
Rodier	(D, p. 300)	$
Rodier Homme	p. 76	$$
Shirin Cashmere	p. 51	$$$$

Left Bank

Caroll	p. 134	$
Fabrice Karel	p. 117 (16th)	$$
Kookaï	p. 111 (16th)	$
Joseph Tricot	p. 120 (V/H)	$$

Place des Victoires and Les Halles

Joseph Tricot	(LB, p. 120)	$$

The Sixteenth

Hervé Chapelier	p. 255 (RB)	$$$
Hemisphères	p. 257	$$$
Fabrice Karel	(LB, p. 117)	$$
Kookai	(LB, p. 111)	$
Rodier Femme	p. 250	$$

Passages

Catherine Vernoux	p. 206	$$

Swimwear and Danceawear

(For Swimwear, see also Women's Designer Fashions and Accessories; Men's Designer Fashions and Accessories.)

Right Bank

Eres	p. 79 (LB)	$$
Léonard	p. 65	$$$$
Anita Oggioni	p. 41	$$$$
Repetto	p. 93	$$

Left Bank

Eres	(RB, p. 79)	$$
Souleiado	p. 118 (16th)	$$$

The Sixteenth

Souleiado	p. 118	$$$

Toys, Games, Dolls, and Stuffed Animals

Right Bank

Au Nain Bleu	p. 81	$$$
Territoire	p. 70	$$

Left Bank

Chantelivre	p. 144	$
Pixi & Cie	p. 118	$$
Rigodon	(O, p. 285)	$$$

Passages

La Boîte à Joujoux	p. 198	$
Robert Capia	p. 209	$$$
Pain d'Epice	p. 198	$
Si Tu Veux	p. 203	$

Women's Accessories

(See also Women's Designer Fashions and Accessories; including Women's Shoes; Women's Bags; Scarves; Gloves; and Costume Jewelry.)

Right Bank

Alexandre de Paris	p. 83	$$$$
Isabel Canovas	p. 35	$$$$
Hélion	(O, p. 289)	$$

Lesage/Schiaparelli	p. 90	$$$$
Anna Lowe	(O, p. 298)	$$
Philippe Model	p. 96	$$$
Jean Patou	p. 85	$$$
Paloma Picasso	p. 91	$$$$
Michel Swiss	p. 92	$$

Left Bank
A la Bonne		
Renommée	(M, p. 231)	$$
Jeanne Do	p. 111	$$
Emilia	p. 150	$$
Naj-Oleari	p. 125 (16th)	$$
Revillon	p. 145 (RB)	$$$
Souleiado	p. 118 (16th)	$$$

Place des Victoires and Les Halles
| Scooter | p. 189 | $ |

Passages
| Wolff & Descourtis | p. 206 | $ |

Marais
A la Bonne		
Renommée	p. 231 (LB)	$$
Zandoli	p. 229	$

The Sixteenth
Bottega Veneta	p. 250	$$$$
Franck et Fils	p. 260	$$
Naj-Oleari	(LB, p. 125)	$$
Souleiado	(LB, p. 118)	$$$

Discount Shopping
| Anna Lowe | p. 298 (RB) | $$ |

Other District
| Maryvonne de | | |
| Follin | p. 296 | $$$ |

Women's and Men's Luxury Boutique Fashions and Accessories

Right Bank
Burberry's	(LB, p. 130)	$$$
Hermès	p. 65	$$$$
Loewe	p. 38	$$$$

Left Bank
Burberry's   p. 130 (RB,
                              16th) $$$

The Sixteenth
Burberry's   (LB, p. 130) $$$

Women's and Men's Shirts

(See also Women's Fashions; Men's Fashions; Women's Designer Fashions and Accessories; Men's Designer Fashions and Accessories.)

Right Bank
Charvet   p. 90 $$$$
Alain Figaret   p. 92 (16th) $$$

Left Bank
Fil à Fil   p. 126 (V/H,
                              16th) $$
Le Garage   (M, p. 221) $$$

Place des Victoires and Les Halles
Equipment   p. 177 $$$
Fil à Fil   (LB, p. 126;
                              16th) $$$

Passages
Moholy-Nagy   p. 201 $$$

Marais
Le Garage   p. 221 (LB) $$$

The Sixteenth
Alain Figaret   (RB, p. 92) $$$
Fil à Fil   (LB, p. 126;
                              V/H) $$

Women's Bags

(See also Leather Goods; Women's Accessories; and Women's Designer Fashions and Accessories.)

Right Bank
Alexandre de Paris   p. 83 $$$
Harel   p. 34 $$$$

Charles Jourdan	p. 68 (LB)	$$$
Renaud Pellegrino	p. 97 (LB)	$$$$
Sepcoeur	p. 51	$$$

Left Bank

A la Bonne Renommée	(M, p. 231)	$$
Emilia	p. 150	$$
Maud Frizon	p. 147	$$$
Furla	p. 145	$$
Charles Jourdan	(RB, p. 68)	$$$
Renaud Pellegrino	(RB, p. 97)	$$$$
Prada	p. 150	$$$
Soco	p. 122 (V/H)	$$$

Place des Victoires and Les Halles

Jean-Louis Imbert	p. 178	$$$
Soco	(LB, p. 122)	$$$
Maria-Pia Varnier	p. 190	$$

Marais

Aïche A.	p. 218	$$
A la Bonne Renommée	p. 231 (LB)	$$

Women's Designer Fashions and Accessories

Right Bank

Annexe des Créateurs	(D, p. 302)	$$
Giorgio Armani	p. 89	$$$$
Laura Ashley	p. 82 (LB)	$$$
Bab's	(D, p. 302)	$$
Balenciaga	p. 49	$$$$
Pierre Balmain	p. 44	$$$$
Pierre Cardin	p. 62	$$$$
Carven	p. 56	$$$$
Jean-Charles de Castelbajac	p. 96 (V/H)	$$$
Céline	p. 37 (LB)	$$$$
Cerruti 1881	p. 76 (LB, 16th)	$$$$
Chanel	p. 85	$$$$
Chloé	p. 62	$$$$

Courrèges	p. 44 (LB; 16th)	$$$$
Christian Dior	p. 36	$$$$
Escada	p. 39	$$$
Sonia Farès	p. 51	$$$
Louis Féraud	p. 59 (LB)	$$$$
Gianfranco Ferre Homme	p. 86	$$$$
Givenchy	p. 47	$$$$
Grès	p. 80	$$$$
Gucci	p. 69	$$$$
Daniel Hechter	(LB, p. 103; 16th)	$$
Isabel Canovas	p. 35	$$$$
Kenzo	(LB, V/H, p. 170)	$$$
Krizia	p. 65 (LB)	$$$$
Christian Lacroix	p. 60	$$$$
Karl Lagerfeld	p. 67	$$$$
Lanvin	p. 66	$$$$
Ted Lapidus	p. 43	$$$
Guy Laroche	p. 36 (16th)	$$$$
Laurèl	p. 81	$$$
Léonard	p. 65	$$$
Hanae Mori	p. 61	$$$$
Thierry Mugler	p. 39	$$$$
Bernard Perris	p. 45	$$$$
Nina Ricci	p. 37	$$$$
Nina Ricci Discount	(D, p. 299)	$$$
Rochas	p. 43	$$$$
Sonia Rykiel	(LB, p. 104)	$$$
Yves Saint Laurent	(LB, p. 119)	$$$$
Jean-Louis Scherrer	p. 38 (LB, 16th)	$$$$
Angelo Tarlazzi	p. 60 (LB)	$$$
Torrente	p. 41	$$$$
Trussardi	p. 67	$$$
Emanuel Ungaro	p. 34	$$$$
Ungaro Parallèles	p. 63	$$$
Valentino	p. 35	$$$$
Gianni Versace	p. 68 (LB)	$$$$
Victoire	(LB; V/H, p. 172; 16th)	$$$

Left Bank

Azzedine Alaïa	(D, p. 298)	$$$
Anvers	p. 107	$$
Laura Ashley	(RB, p. 82)	$$$
Anne Marie Beretta	p. 114	$$$
Barbara Bui	(V/H, p. 181)	$$$
Céline	(RB, p. 37)	$$$$
Cerruti	p. 155 (RB, 16th)	$$$$
Courrèges	(RB, p. 44; 16th)	$$$$
Daniel Hechter	p. 103 (RB, 16th)	$$
Dorothée Bis	(V/H, p. 177)	$$$
Kashiyama	p. 104 (V/H)	$$$
Kenzo	(RB; V/H p. 170)	$$$
Emmanuelle Khanh	p. 115 (16th)	$$$
Michel Klein	p. 107	$$$
Krizia	(RB, p. 65)	$$$$
Odile Lançon	p. 153	$$$
Missoni	p. 160	$$$$
Claude Montana	(p. 154 V/H)	$$$$
L'Observatoire	p. 121	$$$
Paco Rabanne	p. 142	$$$$
River	p. 121	$$$
Inscriptions Rykiel	p. 149	$$
Sonia Rykiel	p. 104 (RB)	$$$
Jean-Louis Scherrer	(RB, p. 38; 16th)	$$$$
Yves Saint Laurent	p. 120 (RB)	$$$$
Yves Saint Laurent Diffusion	p. 116	$$$
Junko Shimada	p. 105 (V/H)	$$
Olivier Strelli	p. 123	$$
Angelo Tarlazzi	(RB, p. 60)	$$$
Chantal Thomass	p. 125 (RB)	$$$
Vicky Tiel	p. 109	$$$
Joseph Tricot	p. 120	$$
Gianni Versace	(RB, p. 68)	$$$$
Victoire	(RB; V/H, p. 172; 16th)	$$$
Yohji Yamamoto	(V/H, p. 176)	$$$$

Place des Victoires and Les Halles

Agnès B.	p. 185	$$
Claude Barthelemy	p. 181	$$$
Barbara Bui	p. 181 (LB)	$$$
Jean-Charles de Castelbajac	(RB, p. 96)	$$$
Comme des Garçons	p. 179	$$$
Courrèges Discount	(D, p. 296)	$$
Enrico Coveri	p. 173	$$$
Lionel Cros	(O, p. 282)	$$
Adolfo Dominguez	p. 169	$$$
Dorothée Bis	p. 177 (LB)	$$$
Junior Gaultier	p. 185	$$
Marithé & François Girbaud	p. 180	$$$
Kashiyama	(LB, p. 104)	$$$
Kenzo	p. 170 (RB, LB)	$$$
Claude Montana	(LB, p. 154)	$$$$
Elizabeth de Senneville	p. 189	$$
Junko Shimada	p. 175 (LB)	$$$
Victoire	p. 172 (RB, LB, 16th)	$$$
Yohji Yamamoto	p. 176 (LB)	$$$$

Passages

Jean-Paul Gaultier	p. 202	$$$
Didier Ludot	p. 212	$$
C. Mendès	(D. p. 297)	$$$
Yuki Torii	p. 204	$$$

Marais

Azzedine Alaïa	p. 233	$$$$
Romeo Gigli	p. 229	$$$$
Paule Ka	p. 220	$$$
Lolita Lempicka	p. 217	$$$
Issey Miyake	p. 227	$$$$
Popy Moreni	p. 226	$$$

Bastille

Franck Joseph Bastille	p. 241	$$

The Sixteenth

Cerruti	p. 155 (RB; LB)	$$$$
Courrèges	p. 44 (RB; LB)	$$$$
Daniel Hechter	(RB; LB, p. 103)	$$
Emmanuelle Khanh	p. 115 (LB)	$$$
Guy Laroche	p. 36 (RB)	$$$$
Réciproque	p. 303 (D)	$$
Francesco Smalto	(RB, p. 45)	$$$
Jean-Louis Scherrer	(RB, p. 38; LB)	$$$
Victoire	p. 172 (RB; LB; V/H)	$$$

Discount

Anna Lowe	p. 298 (RB)	$$$
Annexe des Créateurs	p. 302 (RB)	$$
Azzedine Alaïa	p. 298 (LB)	$$$
Bab's	p. 302 (RB)	$$
C. Mendès	p. 297 (P)	$$$
Courrèges	p. 296 (V/H)	$$
Réciproque	p. 303 (16th)	$$
Jean-Louis Scherrer	p. 38	$$$
Stock 2	p. 302	$

Women's Fashions

(See also Women's Designer Fashions and Accessories.)

Right Bank

Apostrophe	p. 86 (LB)	$$$
Cacharel	(V/H, p. 171)	$$
Chacok	(LB, p. 151)	$$$
Max Mara	(LB, p. 134)	$$$
Jacqueline Perès	p. 88	$$$
Georges Rech	p. 82 (LB, 16th)	$$

Left Bank

Apostrophe	(RB, p. 86)	$$$

Un Après-Midi de Chien	p. 138 (V/H)	$$
Autour du Monde	(M, p. 222)	$$
Blanc Bleu	p. 136 (V/H, M)	$
A la Bonne Renommée	(M, p. 231)	$$
Chacok	p. 151	$$$
Chevignon	p. 137 (V/H, M, 16th)	$$$
Chipie	p. 124 (V/H, 16th)	$$
Clémentine	p. 117	$$$
Creeks	(16th, p. 252)	$
Mac Douglas	p. 144 (V/H, 16th)	$$$
Le Garage	(M, p. 221)	$$$
Irié	p. 107	$$
Kookaï	p. 111 (16th)	$
Max Mara	p. 134 (RB)	$$$
Naf Naf	(V/H, p. 184; 16th)	$
Naj-Oleari	p. 125 (16th)	$$
Claudie Pierlot	p. 128 (V/H)	$$
Ursule Poney	p. 117	$$$
Georges Rech	(RB, p. 82; 16th)	$$
Souleiado	p. 118 (16th)	$$$
Tous les Caleçons	(V/H, p. 187)	$
Et Vous	p. 130 (M)	$$

Place des Victoires and Les Halles

Un Après-Midi de Chien	(LB, p. 138)	$$
Artic	p. 172	$$$
Blanc Bleu	(LB, p. 136; M)	$
Cacharel	p. 171 (RB)	$$
Chevignon	(LB, p. 137 M; 16th)	$$$
Chipie	(LB, p. 124; 16th)	$$
Mac Douglas	(LB, p. 144; 16th)	$$$

Diapositive	p. 184 (16th)	$
Naf Naf	p. 184 (LB, 16th)	$
Claudie Pierlot	(LB, p. 128)	$$
Scooter	p. 189	$
Tous les Caleçons	p. 187 (LB)	$
Ventilo	p. 182	$$

Marais

Apparence	p. 216	
Autour du Monde	p. 222 (LB)	$$
Blanc Bleu	(LB, p. 136; V/H)	$
A la Bonne Renommée	p. 231 (LB)	$$
Chevignon	(LB, p. 137; V/H, 16th)	$$$
Le Garage	p. 221 (LB)	$$$
Imex	p. 223	$$
Inna Kobja	p. 220	$$
Fanny Liautard	p. 227	$$$
Et Vous	(LB, p. 130)	$$

Bastille

Comptoir du Desert	p. 241	$
Pastille	p. 239	$$
Salambo	p. 240	$$

The Sixteenth

Chevignon	(LB, p. 137; M; V/H)	$$$
Chipie	(LB, p. 124; V/H)	$$
Creeks	p. 252 (LB)	$
Curling	p. 255	$$
Diapositive	(V/H, p. 184)	
John Demersay	p. 253	$$
Mac Douglas	(LB, p. 144; V/H)	$$$
Hemisphères	p. 257	$$$
Kookaï	(LB, p. 111)	$
Naf Naf	(V/H, p. 184)	$
Naj-Oleari	(LB, p. 125)	$$
Georges Rech	(RB, p. 82 LB)	$$

Renoma	p. 253	$$$
Rodier	(D, p. 300)	$$
Souleiado	(LB, p. 118)	$$$

Discount Shopping
Cacharel Stock	p. 301	$
Dorotennis Stock	p. 301	$
Fabrice Karel	p. 301	$
Rodier	p. 300 (RB)	$
Stock 2	p. 302	$

Women's Shoes

(See also Women's Designer Fashions and Accessories.)

Right Bank
Carel	(LB, p. 137; 16th)	$$$
Christian Dior	p. 36	$$$$
Harel	p. 34	$$$$
Charles Jourdan	p. 68 (LB)	$$$
Sidonie Larizzi	p. 52	$$$$
John Lobb	p. 46	$$$$
Sartore	(LB, p. 140)	$$$
Walter Steiger	p. 59 (LB)	$$$$
Miss Maud	(LB, p. 152)	$$$

Left Bank
Accessoire	p. 139 (V/H, M, 16th)	$$
Aka	p. 146	$$$
Arche	(V/H, p. 192)	$$
Carel	p. 137 (RB, 16th)	$$$
Chipie	p. 124 (V/H, 16th)	$$
Robert Clergerie	p. 169 (V/H)	$$$$
Xavier Danaud	p. 148	$$$
Emilia	p. 150	$$
Free Lance	p. 135 (V/H)	$$
Maud Frizon	p. 147	$$$$
Jet-Set	p. 143 (16th)	$$$
Charles Jourdan	(RB, p. 68)	$$$
Charles Kammer	p. 151 (V/H, M)	$$$

Stéphane Kélian	p. 150 (V/H, M)	$$$
Tokio Kumagaï	p. 154 (V/H)	$$$
Lario 1898	p. 132	$$$
Miss Maud	p. 152 (RB)	$$$
Prada	p. 150	$$$$
Sartore	p. 140 (RB)	$$$
Walter Steiger	(RB, p. 59)	$$$$
Camille Unglik	p. 149 (M)	$$$

Place des Victoires and Les Halles

Accessoire	(LB, p. 139; M; 16th)	$$$
Arche	p. 192 (LB)	$$
Chipie	(LB, p. 124; 16th)	$$
Robert Clergerie	(LB, p. 169)	$$$$
Free Lance	(LB, p. 135)	$$
Jean-Louis Imbert	p. 178	$$$
Charles Kammer	(LB, p. 151; M)	$$$
Stéphane Kélian	(LB, p. 150; M)	$$$
Tokio Kumugaï	(LB, p. 154)	$$$
Maria-Pia Varnier	p. 190	$$

Marais

Accessoire	(LB, p. 139; V/H; 16th)	$$
Casa Costanza	p. 223	$$
Charles Kammer	(LB, p. 151; V/H)	$$$
Stéphane Kélian	(LB, p. 150; V/H)	$$$
Camille Unglik	(LB, p. 149)	$$$

Bastille

Comptoir du Desert	p. 241	$

The Sixteenth

Accessoire	(LB, p. 139; V/H; M)	$$
Carel	(RB; LB, p. 137)	$$$

| Chipie | (LB, p. 124; V/H) | $$ |
| Jet-Set | (LB, p. 143) | $$ |

Writing Instruments

Right Bank
Cassegrain	p. 81 (LB)	$$$$
Le Drugstore	p. 57 (LB)	$$$
S.T. Dupont	p. 40	$$$$

Left Bank
| Cassegrain | (RB, p. 81) | $$$$ |
| Le Drugstore | (RB, p. 57) | $$$ |

Passages
| Lavrut | p. 212 | $$ |

The Sixteenth
| Lemaire | p. 251 | $$$ |

INDEX